JOURNAL FOR THE STUDY OF THE OLD TESTAMENT
SUPPLEMENT SERIES
117

Editors
David J.A. Clines
Philip R. Davies

JSOT Press
Sheffield

SECOND
TEMPLE
STUDIES

1. Persian Period

Edited by
Philip R. Davies

Journal for the Study of the Old Testament
Supplement Series 117

Copyright © 1991 Sheffield Academic Press

Published by JSOT Press
JSOT Press is an imprint of
Sheffield Academic Press Ltd
The University of Sheffield
343 Fulwood Road
Sheffield S10 3BP
England

Typeset by Sheffield Academic Press
and
Printed on acid-free paper in Great Britain
by Billing & Sons Ltd
Worcester

British Library Cataloguing in Publication Data

Second Temple Studies
    1: Persian period.—(Journal for the study of the
    Old Testament. Supplement series. ISSN 0309-0787;
    117)
    I. Davies, Philip R. II. Series
    221.6

ISBN 1-85075-315-6

CONTENTS

CRITIQUE

ABBREVIATIONS

AASOR	Annual of the American Schools of Oriental Research
AB	Anchor Bible
AGJU	Arbeiten zur Geschichte des antiken Judentums und des Urchristentums
AP	A. Cowley, *Aramaic Papyri of the Fifth Century B.C.*
Apion	Josephus, *Against Apion*
Ant.	Josephus, *Antiquities of the Jews*
AJA	*American Journal of Archaeology*
AJS	*American Journal of Sociology*
AJSL	*American Journal of Semitic Languages and Literatures*
ANET	J.B. Pritchard (ed.), *Ancient Near Eastern Texts*
ATANT	Abhandlungen zur Theologie des Alten und Neuen Testaments
BARev	*Biblical Archaeology Review*
BASOR	*Bulletin of the American Schools of Oriental Research*
BZAW	Beihefte zur ZAW
CAH	*Cambridge Ancient History*
CBC	*Cambridge Bible Commentary*
CBQ	*Catholic Biblical Quarterly*
CHJ	*Cambridge History of Judaism* (ed. W.D. Davies and L. Finkelstein)
FRLANT	Forschungen zur Religion und Literatur des Alten und Neuen Testaments
Geog.	Strabo, *Geographia*
HAR	Hebrew Annual Review
HAT	Handbuch zum Alten Testament
Hist.	Herodotus, *Historia*
HSM	Harvard Semitic Monographs
HUCA	*Hebrew Union College Annual*
ICC	International Critical Commentary
IEJ	*Israel Exploration Journal*
JAOS	*Journal of the American Oriental Society*
JBL	*Journal of Biblical Literature*
JCS	*Journal of Cuneiform Studies*
JNES	*Journal of Near Eastern Studies*
JSJ	*Journal for the Study of Judaism in the Persian, Hellenistic and Roman Period*
JSOT	*Journal for the Study of the Old Testament*
JSOTSup	Journal for the Study of the Old Testament Supplement Series

JTS	*Journal of Theological Studies*
KAT	Kommentar zum A.T.
OTS	*Oudtestamentische Studiën*
OTL	Old Testament Library
PEQ	*Palestine Exploration Quarterly*
PJ	*Palästina-Jahrbuch*
RB	*Revue biblique*
SBLDS	SBL Dissertation Series
SBLMS	SBL Monograph Series
SSN	Studia Semitica Nederlandica
SUNT	Studien zur Umwelt des Neuen Testaments
SWBAS	Studies in the World of Biblical Antiquity Series
TSAJ	Texte und Studien zum antiken Judentum
VT	*Vetus Testamentun*
VTSup	Vetus Testamentum, Supplements
War	Josephus, *The Jewish War*
WBC	Word Biblical Commentary
WMANT	Wissenschaftliche Monographien zum Alten und Neuen Testament
ZA	*Zeitschrift für Assyriologie*
ZAW	*Zeitschrift für die alttestamentliche Wissenschaft*

LIST OF CONTRIBUTORS

Peter Ross Bedford
Western Australian College of Advanced Education

Joseph Blenkinsopp
University of Notre Dame

Robert P. Carroll
University of Chicago

Philip R. Davies
University of Sheffield

Lester L. Grabbe
University of Hull

John M. Halligan
St John Fisher College

Kenneth Hoglund
Wake Forest University

Richard A. Horsley
Harvard University

David Jobling
University of Saskatchewan

David L. Petersen
Iliff School of Theology

David L. Smith
Loyola Marymount University

SOCIOLOGY AND THE SECOND TEMPLE

Philip R. Davies

I

The SBL *Sociology of the Second Temple Consultation*, for which all but one of the following papers were written, was proposed by me[1] initially from several motives, both public and personal. First, it was certainly inspired to some extent by the *Sociology of the Monarchy Seminar*, which has proved the value of a sociological approach to a period of ancient Israelite history, and generated a series of important monographs.[2] Several members of that seminar migrated to the new consultation. Another motive was an increasing shift of emphasis in the study of biblical history and literature away from the 'pre-exilic' towards the 'postexilic', evidence by, among other things, proposed new datings for Pentateuchal sources, a renewed interest in the prophetic books as literary products of a time well after that of their eponym, and burgeoning interest in the Pseudepigrapha, and, of course, a general hermeneutical shift towards final forms as against primitive origins in the study of the Bible as a literary text. Deserving of especial mention is the enormous amount of fairly recent interest in Chronicles, Ezra and Nehemiah, sustained and inspired to a great extent by the SBL Chronicles–Ezra–Nehemiah Group, whose membership also formed a vital core of the new consultation.

For myself, four important considerations underlay the proposal of a *Sociology of the Second Temple Consultation*. First was a desire to see the 'biblical period' properly defined as the period in which the

1. Lest I appear to be claiming total credit, let me record my thanks to Carol Meyers, Jim Flanagan and Joseph Blenkinsopp, who sponsored the proposal, the Executive Committee of the SBL who accepted it, and also John Halligan, who is currently co-chair and doing most of the work.

2. The *Social World of Biblical Antiquity* series, edited by J.W. Flanagan, and published by the Almond Press, Sheffield.

Bible was written—or, more correctly, when the literature in its 'biblical' form was composed, since by its very nature, the Bible, being a collection of scriptures, was not *written*, but *ratified* by consent or decree or both (and thus, of course, the term 'biblical authors' is also misleading). Second was a desire to replace 'history' with 'sociology'. I am not tempted here to define 'sociology', and I am completely aware of all the reasons why the term is inappropriate. But since the question surfaced more than once during our deliberations, some comments are in order. The premise of a sociological approach is the construction of the human subject as a *social* being, and a prescription to define and explain this being in terms of social consciousness and behaviour. This entails the study of a social system, in the broadest sense, including ecology, economics, politics, and ideology (which is where the biblical literature fits). It corresponds in fact very closely to what modern historians call what they do, and historical sociology, it might be argued, is the most productive way of conducting historical inquiry into ancient times, since the sources for the reconstruction of individuals (a form of history-writing inherited from antiquity, not yet dead in biblical studies) are inadequate and the nation-state, the object of historical inquiry inherited from the 18th and 19th centuries, is an anachronism for the biblical period (though, again, perpetuated in the unreflected use of the term 'Israel' in biblical historiography). The third reason for the establishment of a '*Second Temple* sociology' follows directly from this; the Second Temple period, running from the end of the 6th century BCE to nearly the end of the 1st century CE, covers a longer timespan than either the monarchic period, or the exilic period, and although not as long as the patriarchal period (some 1000 years), it is no figment of the imagination. It cuts across a number of traditional-defined eras (Israelite, Intertestamental, New Testament), thus violating the periodization prompted by literary-canonical criteria, replacing it by a different criterion, namely the presence of the Temple as a social, economic and ideological central factor. Admittedly, the weight of that factor has itself been questioned in our discussions; but that it played, whether acknowledged or not, a major role in the evolution of the society, and marked by its destruction what was recognized as a crucial point of transition in the development of Judaism seems probable. Moreover, the primary choice of a long period for scrutiny was the acceptance of the fact that there are long-term trends in the course of human events that remain undetected unless the *longue durée* is embraced.[1]

The fourth reason for the birth of this consultation was a desire to bring together 'historical' and 'literary' approaches to a phenomenon which could prove amenable to both. Whether literature and 'history' can in the end be accommodated to one another remains to be seen, but biblical studies in which the two remain entirely divorced can hardly be contemplated. A problematic tension is in any case preferable to reductionism. It is possible, at any rate, to extrapolate a world from a text, from archaeological data, and from social-scientific analysis, including modelling. Even so, as Carroll says, 'texts are not photographs of social reality, but complex social constructions generated by such reality in conjunction with various ideological factors controlling their production', yet the effort to bring together the ideological constructs of ancient texts and those of the modern scholar into a common focus of 'social reality', however philosophically vulnerable, is preferable to confusing the ideological construction of the text itself with that 'reality'.

Two objections may be quickly answered: is any attempt to read the biblical text as a function of a social and historical context reductionist? On some theories of language, yes. It is often argued that texts are not time-bound, neither by the constraints of authorial intention nor traditional exegesis. The reader reads from the reader's own stance and construes meaning. But every reader has an ego, a role. That being so, as long as there are modern readers who define themselves as historians or anthropologists or sociologists then a corresponding reading of the literature is authorized. The second objection is directed against the use of social-scientific theory, and even of archaeological data, as a starting point for the interpretation of biblical texts. It is argued that archaeological and sociological data cannot match in bulk, detail or clarity the evidence of the biblical literature itself, while the constructs used to interpret them are theoretical. To the extent that these criticisms are valid (and this is a considerable extent), they nevertheless cannot suffice to justify

---

1. The concept of the *longue durée* derives from the *Annales* school of historiography, particularly the work of F. Braudel. For a discussion and application of this perspective to Israelite history see R.B. Coote and K.W. Whitelam, *The Emergence of Early Israel in Historical Perspective* (Sheffield: Almond Press, 1987).

creating a history out of the biblical stories. No alternative is available
by means of an essentially midrashic historiography, in which
rationalistic glosses are introduced into a paraphrase of the biblical
story. For the pre-monarchic period such history is not only dead but
interred. For the period of the so-called 'United Monarchy' it is
moribund. There can be no refuge in the biblical stories of the so-
called 'postexilic' period, either. One cannot read from the texts a
historical Jeremiah, a historical Ezra or Nehemiah. One can, however,
read the texts as products of a *society*, in which its beliefs and ideas
and memories (whether sound or unsound or invented) are expressed.

Of course the idea of the Hebrew Bible/Old Testament as the
product of a real historical society has always been affirmed. Yet the
form of its affirmation is usually wrong on two important premises.
One is the idea of an entire society producing a body of literature
which most of it had not the leisure or resources to write nor the
ability or opportunity to read. The literature was not 'written' by
'Israel' and does not represent the 'faith' of 'Israel'. From a sociological point of view, the proper first question to be asked of a book
like Chronicles or Jeremiah or Amos is 'who *within the society*
produced it, *and why*?' These questions are hardly ever asked.
Obviously Jeremiah did not write the book of Jeremiah for his
contemporaries, nor Amos the book of Amos for his. Nor was the
book of Chronicles written to teach the people 'their history'. The real
problem with biblical history as previously practised is that it has
never asked most of the obvious or basic historical questions such as
these. As Hoglund insists,

> it is simply not possible to construct an accurate understanding of the
> social context of the post-exilic community solely on the basis of literary
> sources. Yet, this is precisely how most of the authors cited earlier have
> attempted to construct their various models of life in the post-exilic
> community under the Persians.

Let us formulate the problem thus: is 'Israel' the subject or the
author of the biblical literature? Most writing on the Bible in the last
two thousand years has taken for granted that 'Israel' is both. But it is
not, as I have just stated, the author, for the authors have to be more
precisely defined *within* a society. What, then, of the object of that
literature? Is the 'Israel' of the Bible a real, flesh-and-blood historical
phenomenon? No, in a word: it is a product of literature. A sociology

of the Second Temple period will, in the end, be searching for the authorship of the biblical literature, and equally for the biblical 'Israel' which the literate parts of that society created as an ideological construct. Only from *this* angle, and from *this* starting point is it worthwhile proceeding thereafter to relate that construct to the inhabitants of the land of Palestine in the Iron Age and the Persian and Graeco-Roman periods. That, at any rate, is my opinion, not necessarily shared even by all the contributors to this volume.

Finally, on this topic: a more modest, and perhaps more persuasive, defence of a 'sociological' perspective, at any rate, might be the reintegration of 'religion' into the totality of social life in the ancient Levantine world, as urged by Richard Horsley:

> biblical literature and history are not 'religious' and do not deal with
> 'religious' matters in a way separate or separable from other dimensions
> of life, such as the 'political' or the 'economic'. 'Religion' is embedded
> with kinship and/or local community life and/or 'the state' in virtually any
> traditional agrarian society, and hence is inseparable from political and
> economic matters. Our scholarly habit of pretending that we are dealing
> with primarily religious texts or institutions, which means basically
> imposing modern presuppositions and concepts on historical materials that
> had neither concepts nor terms for religion, blocks rather than enhances
> understanding. The temple in Jerusalem was a political-economic
> institution.

II

The papers in this volume are the outcome of an attempt to juxtapose literary, sociological and archaeological data, and seek some synthesis. What seems widely agreed is that the foundation of Second Temple society was a Persian initiative, serving Persian interests. What is disputed is (a) how far its institutions developed from those created by Jews deported to Babylonia; (b) how far the society was divided between Babylonian and indigenous Jews; and (c) how pervasive was the influence of the Temple in that society. Blenkinsopp has produced a detailed appraisal and critique of the *Bürger-Tempel-Gemeinde* theory of J. Weinberg, a view which supposes a society within a society, maintaining the ideology of ethnic separation and exilic pedigree against outsiders who were nevertheless admitted in large numbers over the course of time. This thesis is given a twist by Hoglund, who suggests that from the outset of the reconstitution of the province of Yehud, the Persians established agricultural collectivities drawn from both elements of the population, as evidenced by sites of villages repopulated or newly-populated in the Achaemenid period. He remarks that 'the presumption of a class struggle between exiles and "remainees" over land rights does not fit the evidence of the pattern of these Persian period villages'.

While implying much of what Blenkinsopp suggests, Smith places more emphasis on the mentality and the social structures of the 'exiles', and in so doing introduces a significant issue into the discussion, namely one of partiality. While some of the participants are neutral in their comparison of the 'returnees' and the 'people of the land', Smith conveys a sympathetic impression of those deprived of their land and exiled:

> to be troubled by what appears to be 'exclusivism' on the part of Haggai, or to feel a need to put an acceptable face on the separation of the marriages in Ezra–Nehemiah, is to profoundly misunderstand the nature of group solidarity and survival of minorities. . . We are invited to look at Ezra–Nehemiah, Haggai, and others from an 'exilic consciousness', from the perspective of their worries and experiences in order to fully understand the 'politics of Ezra'.

On the contrary, Carroll's analysis (on which more is to be said below) implicitly criticizes these deportees as having, on their return, both ideologically, and perhaps in reality, taken legitimacy and land from those who did *not* go to Babylon. Whatever sympathies are invoked, it is important to bear in mind that in the Bible, 'Israel' is defined mostly as that which went into exile, and the period between exile and 'return' is effaced. At all events, the modern historian is not entitled to adopt the same bias without reflection.

All sides agree, however, that the emergence of the *bêt āb* is a product of such collectivities—and the (here unspoken) suspicion must be whether the entire tribal and sub-tribal system presented in the Hebrew Bible is in fact to be dated from this period and no earlier. Indeed, Blenkinsopp is led to wonder how far the pre-exilic structures really were perpetuated into the exile at all. Was there perhaps more of a new beginning than usually countenanced? Here too, an important general issue is raised. How important for our understanding of Second Temple society is the pre-exilic period? Indeed, insofar as the biblical history of that period is written in Second Temple literature, how far is the picture accurate? Here again, a fundamental element of the ideology of the biblical literature, that pre-exilic Israel/Judah are direct predecessors of the postexilic society, needs to be tested. Where, indeed, do the real origins of 'Israel' (as defined in the Bible) lie? Is there much continuity between the religion and social structure of the seventh and fifth centuries? For instance, is Moses or Mazda the key to Jewish monotheism? A propos of the extent of influence of Persian (and Achaemenid–Mesopotamian) models on the institutions of Second Temple Judaism, Blenkinsopp remarks:

> in earlier times the kings governed Zela not as a city but as a sacred precinct of the Persian gods, and the priest was the master of the whole thing. . . This was no doubt an example of officially sponsored syncretism, comparable to the situation with respect to Yahweh 'the god of heaven'—a view which we may be sure the Jerusalem priesthood did nothing to discourage.

The discussion exposes the lack of certainty on some crucial basic data. For instance, what was the religion of the deportees and of those left behind? What was the source of wealth in Persian period Yehud— was it the returnees? When was the Temple *really* built, and was there a real 'return'—however small? If so, was it under Cyrus or Darius, or both? How big was the population of Judah before, during and after the Babylonian deportation? Who in fact did own land? In Grabbe's powerful critique, the authenticity of what are widely taken as basic data is severely challenged, namely the 'documents' embedded in Ezra and Nehemiah.

From the standpoint of the literature, Carroll, in a brilliant demonstration of the method and results of ideological reading, exposes within certain texts an ideology of the 'empty land' whereby those who remained in Yehud after the deportations were ideologically obliterated. Petersen shows from the prophetic texts of the period that a number of assumptions about that period do not properly account for the literary evidence, which exhibits diversity of attitudes to the Temple. The sociological focus of this literary treatment is provided by attention to the hierarchies of status and power and the notion of 'sacred place'. He concludes that 'one key issue for the polity of reformed Judah was the relative power of the civil and religious leaders', and revises his earlier opinion (still maintained by many scholars) that the postexilic prophets were tied to the cult.

The problems raised in this section broadly concern the extent to which literary and other evidences construct the same kinds of reality (a superb example of this crucial problem is the Dead Sea scrolls, from which practically no information relevant to the archaeological data from Khirbet Qumran has come. The worlds of the texts and the site simply do not overlap, whether or not the authors, or some of them, lived at Qumran)—an issue addressed lucidly by David Jobling in the closing section.

This closing section, the critique, offers a fundamental and rational questioning of the assumptions and methods (Bedford), and a test-case which equally raises certain doubts about the models being used (Halligan). Bedford wonders how central the Temple was, Halligan suggests that Nehemiah's economic measures make no sense, and Horsley, who adopts the most explicitly sociological approach of all, offers a number of very interesting and important matters. In particular, he exposes the political and social assumptions which control the perspective of the sociological analyst: is it correct to speak of 'capitalism', 'cash economy' or 'middle class' in the context of the Second Temple period?

The final contribution, from Jobling, engages with the problems of a literary critic confronting the relationship between text and social life. While he takes issue with Carroll's scepticism in this regard, he writes 'I believe we can use a period of extreme reticence in trying to relate models of societies to models of texts'. He also raises one further issue, namely that of the interest of sociological analysis. It is not value-free, and does itself no good by setting itself as such in opposition to a 'theologically biased' approach to the biblical literature, which seeks to identify in the scriptural text that which justifies it as Scripture, whether it be a sacred history, or a unique secular history, or a peculiar access to a transcendental world, or whatever. A sociological approach is dictated by its own ideology, as is any approach, and that ideology is implicitly in opposition to much of the presupposition of a 'theological' approach. It represents, or it can represent, a certain claim on this literature, namely the right to approach it as a product of human, i.e., social activity, class interest, power relations. As such it is as reductionist as any other method is, but hardly more so. Sociologists are not dispassionate observers. They may, as this volume demonstrates, sympathize with returning deportees (Smith) or the poorer population they displaced and colonized (Carroll); they may view the biblical theory that land belongs to YHWH as a cover for hierocratic plunder (Carroll) or as a guarantee of security for owners and tenants (Horsley). They have, at least, the freedom to choose sides, and are not compelled ultimately to vindicate the literature because it is Scripture. In a broad sense, then, a sociological approach may also be read as a metaphor for a secular approach. In a more technical sense, the application of sociological methods to the biblical literature can only establish itself by its results, and it lies with the reader of this volume to decide whether in this case enough has been achieved, or enough promised.

ARCHAEOLOGY, HISTORY AND SOCIETY

TEMPLE AND SOCIETY IN ACHAEMENID JUDAH

Joseph Blenkinsopp

I

Any study of the Judaism which was emerging during the two centuries of Iranian rule (539–332 BCE) calls for an acute sense of the fragile and provisional nature of our knowledge of the past in general and this segment of the past in particular. Our principal biblical source, Ezra–Nehemiah, covers only the first and last quarter of the first of these two centuries, and the information which it offers is refracted through several interpretative and ideological prisms. The task of creating something like a three-dimensional model of Judaean society is also complicated by the one-dimensionally religious interests which inform this and other relevant biblical texts, especially where they speak of the Temple. The very sparse archaeological data available allow for a somewhat broader perspective, but their interpretation is no less elusive and even more subject to revision and subversion by new discoveries or new interpretations. There remains recourse to comparative data, in this instance information on the sociopolitical and economic function of temples in other parts of the Achaemenid empire, especially Asia Minor and Mesopotamia. While use of such material obviously calls for careful handling, it may at least permit the setting up and testing of different models in the light of which the situation in the province of Judah can be reviewed.

In ancient Mesopotamia, Syria, Asia Minor and the Greek mainland, city-state and temple belonged together. The point may be made by referring to the apparently artless story in Gen. 11.1-9 about the building of a city and tower in the land of Shinar; for the tower is surely the ziggurat shrine, which raises the possibility that this short narrative may be a satire directed against neo-Babylonian imperial pretensions and their supportive cultic apparatus.[1] A great deal of information has been available for some time and is constantly being augmented on the social and economic impact of temples on the regions in which they functioned. Many of the larger temples throughout the Achaemenid empire were wealthy institutions with their own land holdings and work force, their own capital in specie and produce from which they advanced loans, serving more or less the same function as banks and credit unions today.[2] Stimulation of the regional economies by temples serving as storage and redistribution centers, to the evident advantage of the imperial exchequer, helps to explain why they were supported by successive Achaemenid rulers. The priesthoods servicing these temples were under the supervision of imperial officers (in Mesopotamia *paqdu* or *rēš šarri*) whose chief function was to ensure payment of tribute and, in some cases, the service of temple slaves;[3] and we note that Nehemiah as local representative of the imperial government also took measures to control the

1. None of the arguments for the great antiquity of Gen. 11.1-9 as a component of a putative J source withstands close scrutiny. Note, too, that outside of Genesis, 'Shinar' occurs only in texts from the time of the Babylonian exile or later (Isa. 11.11; Zech. 5.11; Dan. 1.2). The multiplicity of languages may be taken to reflect the many ethnic minorities in the city during the neo-Babylonian period.

2. M.A. Dandamaev has written extensively on the temple economy in ancient Mesopotamia. His studies include 'Achaemenid Babylonia', in I.M. Diakonoff (ed.), *Ancient Mesopotamia. Socio-Economic History: A Collection of Studies by Soviet Scholars* (Moscow: Nauka Pub. House, 1969), pp. 296-311; 'Politische und wirtschaftliche Geschichte', in *Histora. Einzelschriften, 18: Beiträge zur Achämenidengeschichte* (Wiesbaden, 1972), pp. 15-58; 'Babylonia in the Persian Age', in W.D. Davies and L. Finkelstein (eds.), *The Cambridge History of Judaism*, I (Cambridge: Cambridge University Press, 1984), pp. 326-42. Other fairly recent studies are: A. Falkenstein, 'La cité-temple sumerienne', *Cahiers d'histoire mondiale* 1 (1954), pp. 784-814; E.R. Kraus, 'Le rôle des temples depuis la troisième dynastie d'Ur à la première dynastie de Babylon', *Cahiers d'histoire mondiale* 1 (1954), pp. 518-45; Rivkah Harris, 'Old Babylonian Temple Loans', *JCS* 14 (1960), pp. 126-37; R. Bogaert, *Les Origines antiques de la Banque de Dépôt* (Leiden: Brill, 1966); J.N. Postgate, 'The Role of the Temple in the Mesopotamian Secular Community', in P.J. Ucko *et al.* (eds.), *Man, Settlement and Urbanism* (London: Duckworth, 1972), pp. 811-25; E. Lipiński (ed.), *State and Temple Economy in the Ancient Near East. I. Proceedings of the International Conference Organized by the Katholieke Universiteit Leuven* (Leuven: Department Orientalistiek, 1979); Brigitte Menzel, *Assyrische Tempel* (2 vols.; Rome: Biblical Institute Press, 1981).

3. Dandamaev, 'Achaemenid Babylonia', pp. 309-10

economic resources of the Jerusalem temple (Neh. 13.13). In addition these priesthoods served as custodians of the legal traditions in the various regions; and it is well attested that the central government promoted the codification and implementation of local traditional law as an instrument of the *pax Persica* throughout the empire.[1] In the absence of an imperial cult of the type of the Assyrian Ashur, the Achaemenids tolerated and even cultivated local deities as imperial patrons, a situation reflected, with understandable exaggeration, in the biblical sources.[2]

The significance of regional cult centers within the Achaemenid imperial system may best be illustrated by examples. The tone was set by the propagandistic declaration of goodwill made by Cyrus on his famous cylinder. Despite justifiable reservations, his claims have received some support from excavated Babylonian sites.[3] In spite of his bad reputation in the Greek historiographical tradition (e.g. Herodotus 3.1-38), Cambyses seems to have followed the same policy in Egypt, exemplified by his restoration of the Saitic national sanctuary of the goddess Neith.[4] The great Eanna temple at Uruk

1. See my *Ezra-Nehemiah. A Commentary* (Philadelphia, 1988), p. 157 and 'The Mission of Udjahorresnet and Those of Ezra and Nehemiah', *JBL* 106 (1987), pp. 409-21.

2. The only exception may have been Xerxes, one of whose inscriptions speaks of the eradication of the daevas, perhaps referring to the destruction of Babylonian temples, including the great *esagila* shrine, after the revolt in that city. For the text see R.G. Kent, *Old Persian* (New Haven: American Oriental Society, 1953), pp. 150-52.

3. *ANET*, pp. 315-16. The Enunmakh temple enclosure was rebuilt during the reign of Cyrus, according to L. Woolley and M.E.L. Mallowan, *Ur Excavations. IX. The Neo-Babylonian and Persian Periods* (London & Philadelphia, 1962), pp. 2, 25. The Eanna temple in Uruk was restored at the same time, and similar restoration work is attested for Babylon on a fragment of the cylinder inscription identified in 1970; see C.B.F. Walker, 'A Recently Identified Fragment of the Cyrus Cylinder', *Iran* 10 (1972), pp. 158-59 and P.-R. Berger, 'Der Kyros-Zylinder mit dem Zusatzfragment BIN II Nr. 32 und die akkadischen Personennamen im Danielbuch', *ZA* 64 (1975), pp. 192-234; also the more general study of Amélie Kuhrt, 'The Cyrus Cylinder and Achaemenid Imperial Policy', *JSOT* 25 (1983), pp. 83-97.

4. See most recently M.A. Dandamaev and V.G. Lukonin, *The Culture and Social Institutions of Ancient Iran* (Cambridge: Cambridge University Press, 1989), pp. 360-66.

(Warka) seems to have regained some of its past glory under Darius I. He is also credited with restoring and building temples in Egypt, which munificence, Diodorus informs us (1.95.4-5), led to his posthumous deification.[1] His brief rescript addressed to Gadatas, imperial representative in Lydia, in favor of an Apollo sanctuary in Magnesia, points in the same direction.[2] Another inscription, copied from a rescript of the thirty-ninth year of either Artaxerxes I or Artaxerxes II, therefore either 426 or 365, refers to the Persian hyparch (satrap) of Lydia promoting the cult of a local Zeus and discouraging aberrant religious practices.[3] Also from Asia Minor is the trilingual (Lydian, Greek, Aramaic) Xanthos inscription authorizing the establishment of a sanctuary to the goddess Leto and granting land and tax exemption to its clergy in the name of the Carian satrap Pixodarus, probably under Artaxerxes III.[4] Also to be mentioned in this connection is the letter of Hananiah to Jedoniah, a leader of the Jewish military colony on the island of Elephantine, referring to a firman of Darius II mandating the observance of a festival according to accepted Jewish norms.[5]

1.   E.M. Yamauchi, 'The Archaeological Background of Ezra', *Bibliotheca Sacra* 137 (1960), pp. 195-211. On Achaemenid policy vis-à-vis local cults in general see R. de Vaux, 'Les décrets de Cyrus et de Darius sur la reconstruction du temple', *RB* 46 (1937), pp. 29-57 (reprinted in *The Bible and the Ancient Near East* [Garden City, NY: Doubleday 1971], pp. 63-96); E.J. Bickerman, 'The Edict of Cyrus in Ezra 1', *JBL* 65 (1946), pp. 249-75.

2.   R. Meiggs and D.M. Lewis, *A Selection of Greek Historical Inscriptions to the End of the Fifth Century BC* (Oxford: Oxford University Press, 1969), pp. 20-22.

3.   Discussed by P. Frei in P. Frei and K. Koch, *Reichsidee und Reichsorganisation im Perserreich* (Freiburg and Göttingen: Universitätsverlag/ Vandenhoeck & Ruprecht, 1984), pp. 19-21.

4.   H. Metzger, 'La Stèle trilingue récemment découvere au Létoon de Xanthos', *Comptes Rendus de l'Academie des Inscriptions et Belles Lettres* 1974, pp. 82-93, 115-25, 132-49; T. R. Bryce, 'A Recently Discovered Cult in Lydia', *Journal of Religious History* 10 (1978), pp. 115-27; J. Teixidor, 'The Aramaic Text in the Trilingual Stele from Xanthos', *JNES* 37 (1978), pp. 181-5; A. Dupont-Sommer, 'L'inscription araméenne', in H. Metzger *et al.*, *Fouilles de Xanthos* (Paris: Librarie C. Klincksieck, 1979), pp. 129-78.

5.   A. Cowley, *Aramaic Papyri of The Fifth Century B.C.* (Oxford: Clarendon Press, 1923), no. 21; on which see P. Grelot, 'Etudes sur le "Papyrus Pascal" d'Eléphantine', *VT* 4 (1954), pp. 349-84; *idem*, 'Le Papyrus Pascal d'Eléphantine:

These examples point to a standard Achaemenid policy vis-à-vis local cults, one which was followed, with few exceptions, by Alexander and the Diadochoi.[1] They at least confer a degree of plausibility on the measures recorded in Ezra–Nehemiah in favor of the Jerusalem temple, though the imperial documents reproduced in the book (Ezra 1.2-4; 6.2-12; 7.11-26) are at some remove from the factuality of the inscriptions just referred to. The interest of the imperial authorities was not, needless to say, motivated exclusively by sentiments of religious piety, though that may have played a part. One important reason for the considerable measure of success achieved by Achaemenid imperial policy was tolerance for, indeed active exploitation of, diverse local systems within an overarching imperial framework.[2] This policy involved granting a fair measure of local autonomy, once the central government had identified, or put in place, a dominant elite whose loyalty could be counted on. One such local system, particularly in evidence in Asia Minor and Mesopotamia, was centered on the temple. Temples served as catalysts of economic exchange and promoters of social cohesion. The temple may also have been seen as a point of convergence for the symbolic structures of the region, an 'emblem of collective identity',[3] thereby mitigating to some extent the inevitable resentment generated by subjection to a foreign power.

II

According to a theory first proposed by Soviet social historians, temples became the focus of a new type of sociopolitical organization

---

essai de restauration', *VT* 17 (1967), pp. 201-7; B. Porten, *Archives from Elephantine: The Life of an Ancient Jewish Military Colony* (Berkeley & Los Angeles: University of California Press, 1968), pp. 128-33, 280-82, 311-14.

1.　Both Alexander and Antiochus I ordered the rebuilding or restoration of Babylonian temples. Antiochus IV's addiction to plundering temples, occasioned by dire financial straits, was a notable exception.

2.　J.L. Myers, 'Persia, Greece and Israel', *PEQ* 85 (1953), pp. 15-18; J. Weinberg, 'Zentral- und Partikolar-gewalt im achämenidischen Reich', *Klio* 59 (1977), pp. 25-43.

3.　The phrase is Walter Burkert's ('The Meaning and Function of the Temple in Classical Greece,' in M.V. Fox (ed.), *Temple in Society* [Winona Lake, IN: Eisenbrauns, 1988], p. 44).

towards the beginning of the first millennium BCE, one which came into its own during the two centuries of Achaemenid rule and persisted into the Seleucid period and beyond.[1] This 'civic-temple community' (*graždansko-chramovaya obšina*; *Bürger-Tempel-Gemeinde*) resulted from the merger of temple personnel with the free, property-owning citizenry of a particular settlement. Out of this merger arose an autonomous and privileged social entity which provided its members with the means for self-management and mutual economic assistance. It is claimed that several of these sociopolitical units existed and flourished within the Persian imperial apparatus. According to the Latvian scholar Joel Weinberg, Achaemenid Judah provides a well-documented case history of such a temple community, though one with its own peculiar features. We shall evaluate his theory in due course, but in the meantime it will be useful to survey briefly some of the case histories on the basis of which the hypothesis is constructed.

In Asia Minor instances can be cited where the city appears to have been more or less an appendage of the temple. Comana in Cappadocia, center of the cult of the goddess Ma-Enyo, was governed by the high priest who, as Strabo informs us (*Geog.* 12.2.3) was next in status to the monarch. The temple possessed extensive domains, the usufruct of which was controlled by the priesthood. It was also the principal catalyst for the circulation of wealth in the city and its agrarian hinterland. Citizenship appears to have been contingent on participation in and support of the cult, and temple personnel made up a good percentage of the citizenry.[2] Much the same situation obtained

---

1. The earliest formulators of the theory, it seems. were I.D Amusin and G.Kh. Sarkisian. Earlier studies were in Russian, but Sarkisian has also dealt with it in 'City Land in Seleucid Babylonia', in I.M. Diakonoff (ed.), *Ancient Mesopotamia*, pp. 312-31, and 'Greek Personal Names in Uruk and the *Graeco-Babyloniaca* Problem,' in J. Harmatta and G. Komoróczy (eds.), *Wirtschaft und Gesellschaft im alten Vorderasien*, pp. 495-503. The theory has only recently begun to attract attention in the West; see W. Schottroff, 'Zur Sozialgeschichte Israels in der Perserzeit,' *Verkündigung und Forschung* 27 (1982), pp. 61-62 and H. Kreissig, 'Eine beachtenswerte Theorie zur Organisation altvorderorientalischer Tempelgemeinden im Achämenidenreich', *Klio* 66 (1984), pp. 35-39.
2. Pauly-Wissowa, *Realencyklopädie der klassischen Altertumswissenschaft*, XI.1.1127.

in the other Comana in Pontus, also dedicated to the goddess.[1] The royal sanctuary of Zela in the same province, seat of the Persian goddess Anahita (whose cult appears to have been introduced by Artaxerxes II), also disposed of extensive domains administered by temple officials under a high priest.[2] Strabo (12.3.27) reports that 'in earlier times the kings governed Zela not as a city but as a sacred precinct of the Persian gods. and the priest was the master of the whole thing'. This was no doubt an example of officially sponsored syncretism, comparable to the situation with respect to Yahweh 'the god of heaven'—a view which we may be sure the Jerusalem priesthood did nothing to discourage.[3]

Somewhat similar was the set-up in the city of Venasa dedicated to a local Zeus and home to almost 3,000 temple servants. It also possessed a sacred territory (*chora hiera*) bringing in an annual revenue of fifteen talents.[4] In these instances, and others from Mesopotamia to be considered shortly, the proponents of the 'civic-temple community' theory invite us to see a specific type of social organization with its own domains and operating its own economic system.[5] A somewhat different type is exemplified by the sanctuary of Mylasa-Olymos in Caria. The large corpus of inscriptions dealing with this sanctuary

1. Strabo 12.3.32: P-W XI.1.1126-7.
2. P-W Supp. XIV.984-6; A. Archi ('Città sacre d'Asia Minore', *La Parola del Passato* 20 [1975], pp. 329-44) fills in some of the history of these ancient cult centers.
3. On the title 'The God of Heaven' used for both Ahura Mazda and Yahweh, see D.K. Andrews, 'Yahweh the God of the Heavens,' in W.S. McCullough (ed.), *The Seed of Wisdom. Essays in Honor of T.J. Meek* (Toronto: University of Toronto Press, 1964), pp. 45-57.
4. 'In Morimene, at Venas, is the temple of the Venasian Zeus, which has a settlement of almost 3,000 temple servants (*hierodouloi*) and also a sacred territory that is very productive, affording the priest a yearly revenue of fifteen talents' (Strabo 12.2.6).
5. J. Weinberg, 'Die Agrarverhältnisse in der Bürger-Tempel-Gemeinde der Achämenidenzeit', in Harmatta and Komoroczy, *Wirtschaft und Gesellschaft*, p. 485. T. Zawadski ('Quelques remarques sur l'étendue et l'acroissement des domaines des grands temples en Asie Mineure', *Eos* 46 [1953-4], pp. 83-96) argues against W.M. Ramsay's theory of vast temple estates or 'theocratic principalities' in Achaemenid Asia Minor which were confiscated by the Seleucids. He warns against assigning villages and agricultural land to temples unless this is explicitly stated in the sources.

covers such matters as prebends, support of the clergy and who may participate in which rites.[1] Here, too, the priesthood of the local Zeus under an *archiereus* administered extensive temple holdings and played a leading role in deliberations of the city assembly (*boulē*). But since the citizens owned land in their own right and worked it themselves, this type of organization, with temple domains but no specific temple economy, is classified separately. Weinberg suggests that it was this type that came to prevail in the Hellenistic period.[2]

While much of the evidence adduced here comes from a time later than the Persian period, it may be taken to illustrate a type of temple economy which flourished during those two centuries, at least in Asia Minor. To what extent this represents a distinct type of *Gemeinde* is, however, rather less certain. As far as we can tell there had always existed a close symbiotic relationship between temple and *polis*.[3] Temple lands, theoretically property of the resident deity, had from the earliest times been administered by city officials (called *tamiai*, *hieropoioi* or *epitimētai*) answerable to the *boulē*. Priests were civic officials appointed by the city and they could also serve in municipal offices, especially as magistrates. The city treasury was often deposited in the temple, which also advanced credit and leased land holdings.[4] Temple privileges were automatically extended to free, propertied citizens who jealously guarded their status and controlled admission to their ranks. Given the generally negative verdict on Ezra's marriage policy, it is intriguing to compare it with the practically contemporary Periclean law of citizenship requiring Athenian ancestry on both paternal and maternal sides. Exclusion from the Judaean assembly (*qāhāl*, e.g., Ezra 10.8) is also paralleled by the Athenian decree of *atimia* involving loss of civic privileges.[5] The question arises, then, whether we are dealing with a quite distinct

---

1. P-W XVI.1.1046-64; E. Sokolowski, *Lois sacrés d'Asie Mineure* (Paris, 1955), pp. 146-8, 152-9.
2. Weinberg, 'Agrarverhältnisse', p. 485.
3. Burkert, 'Meaning and Function', pp. 27-47.
4. For examples see J.H. Kent, 'The Temple Estates of Delos, Rheneia and Mykonos', *Hesperia* 17 (1948), pp. 243-338.
5. H. Bengtson, *The Greeks and the Persians from the Sixth to the Fourth Centuries* (New York: Delacorte Press, 1968), pp. 89-93; G.J. Blidstein, 'Atimia: A Greek Parallel to Ezra X 8 and to Post-biblical Exclusion from the Community', *VT* 24 (1974), pp. 357-60.

form of sociopolitical organization, as the theory requires, or simply variations of a common pattern.

This last question may be posed more pointedly after a survey of the sociopolitical and economic role of temples in Achaemenid Mesopotamia. Here, fortunately, there is no dearth of documentation. Thousands of tablets from Babylonia of the neo-Babylonian, Achaemenid and Seleucid periods have been published, and many more await publication.[1] We therefore know much more about the social and economic situation there than we do about contemporary Judah at the other extremity of the Babili-Ebirnari satrapy. Here, too, as in the Greek-speaking regions, there are lines of continuity stretching back many centuries from the period of Iranian rule.[2] While a comprehensive study of temple economy in the later period still remains to be written, we know enough to draw at least some provisional conclusions relative to the issue under discussion.

One of the best documented case histories is the ancient temple-city of Uruk (*Tell el-Warka*) and its Eanna shrine dedicated to the cult of Inanna. About 1,500 legal and economic texts from the neo-Babylonian and Persian periods have been published which provide information on various aspects of the administration of this temple, and this information may be supplemented by the material dating to the Seleucid epoch.[3] The temple precinct covered about 60,000 square

1. For the source material see R. Borger, *Handbuch der Keilschriftliteratur*, III (Berlin: de Gruyter, 1975) and D.B. Weisberg, *Texts from the Time of Nebuchadnezzar* (New Haven & London: Yale University Press, 1980); and for a brief survey W. Hinz in G. Walser (ed.), *Beiträge zur Achämenidengeschichte*, pp. 5-14. The later Achaemenid period is covered by J. Oelsner, 'Zwischen Xerxes und Alexander: Babylonische Rechtsurkunden und Wirtschaftstexte aus der späten Achämenidenzeit', *Die Welt des Orients* 8 (1976), pp. 310-18, especially p. 312 n. 10. The Murašu archive, covering the years 454–404, is of prime importance but provides little information on temple economy. The most recent study is M.W. Stolper, *Entrepreneurs and Empire. The Murašû Archive, the Murašû Firm and Persian Rule in Babylon* (Istanbul: Nederlands Historisch-Archaeologisch Instituute te Istanbul, 1985).

2. C.J. Gadd, 'The Cities of Babylonia', in *CAH*, I (Cambridge: Cambridge University Press, 1962), ch. xiii; I.J. Gelb, 'Household and Family in Early Mesopotamia', in E. Lipiński (ed.), *State and Temple Economy*, pp. 1-97.

3. A.T. Clay, *Neo-Babylonian Letters from Erech* (New Haven:Yale University Press, 1919); A. Falkenstein, *Archäische Texte aus Uruk. Ausgrabungen der deutschen Forschungsgemeinschaft in Uruk-Warka*, II (Berlin: Deutsche

meters and included some 150 storage facilities. It owned substantial
holdings including arable and grazing land and farms for the
cultivation of the date palm. These domains of 'the Lady of Uruk'
were sublet to dependent farmers with specific provisions for the
amount of produce owed to the temple, the entire operation being
controlled by assessors answerable to the governing board of the
temple and the city administration. Day-to-day operation of the temple
was financed by tithes,[1] contributions (not all voluntary), and *ex voto*
offerings of the faithful, in addition to rents. The economic tablets
published to date reveal the remarkable variety of professions
required to operate this system. In addition to different classes of
priests—under the general rubric of 'temple enterer' (*ēreb bīti*)—we
hear of transactions involving temple musicians, exorcists, porters,
scribes, bakers, carpenters, etc.[2] Also attested is a class of temple slave
or oblate, given to the temple as a child by indigent or insolvent

Forschungs-gemeinschaft 1936); 'Zu den Inschriften der Grabung in Uruk-Warka
1960-1961', *Baghdader Mitteilungen* 2 (1963), pp. 1-82; M. San Nicolò,
'Neubabylonische Urkunden aus Uruk', *Orientalia* 19 (1950), pp 217-32;
D. Cocquerillat, *Palmeraies et cultures de l' Eanna d' Uruk (559–520) Ausgrabungen
der deutschen Forschungsgemeinschaft in Uruk-Warka*, VIII (Berlin: Deutsche
Forschungs gemeinschaft, 1968) (bibliography on p. 13 n. 13); H. Hunger,
Spätbabylonische Texte aus Uruk. I. *Ausgrabungen der deutschen Forschungs-
gemeinschaft in Uruk-Warka* (Berlin, 1974); J. Van Dijk and W.R. Mayer, *Texte aus
dem Rēš-Heiligtum in Uruk-Warka* (Baghdader Mitteilungen, 2; Berlin, 1980); L.T.
Doty, *Cuneiform Archives from Hellenistic Uruk* (Yale dissertation, 1977; Ann
Arbor: University Microfilms, 1981). Much information on Hellenistic Uruk is
available in G.J.P. McEwan, *Priest and Temple in Hellenistic Babylonia*
(Wiesbaden: Franz Steiner Verlag, 1981) and J. Oelsner, *Materialen zur
babylonischen Gesellschaft und Kultur in hellenistischer Zeit* (Budapest: Eötrös
University, 1986), pp. 77-97, 139-91, 250-52.
1. M.A. Dandamaev, 'Der Tempelzehnte in Babylonien während des 6.-4. Jh.
v.u.Z.', in Ruth Stiehl (ed.), *Festschrift für E. Altheim*, I (Berlin: de Gruyter,
1969), pp. 82-89.
2. On these and other categories see M. San Nicolò, 'Beiträge zu einer
Prosopographie neubabylonischer Beamten der Zivil- und Tempelverwaltung', in
Bayerische Akademie der Wissenschaften: Phil.-hist. Abt. (Munich, 1941);
D.B. Weisberg, *Guild Structure and Political Allegiance in Early Achaemenid
Mesopotamia* (New Haven: Yale University Press, 1967); H.M. Kümmel, *Familie,
Beruf und Amt in spätbabylonischen Uruk: Prosopographische Untersuchungen zu
Berufsgruppen des 6. Jahrhunderts v. Chr. in Uruk* (Berlin, 1979); McEwan, *Priest
and Temple*, pp. 1-66.

parents, known as 'child of the god' (*māru ša anu*). Throughout Mesopotamia in general, temples were among the leading employers of slave labor.[1]

Responsibility for the operation of the temple cult and the many economic activities dependent on it was in the hands of an assembly (*puḫru, puḫur uruk*) comparable to the *boulē*, which administered civic and cultic affairs in the Greek-speaking areas. As was the case with the latter, membership was restricted by ethnic and property qualifications and the members were grouped according to their ancestral 'house' (*bīt abim*) comparable to the *bêt 'ābôt* of which we hear often in Ezra–Nehemiah.[2] Not all inhabitants of the city, therefore, qualified for membership in the *puḫru*. So, for example, in the Hellenistic period we hear of Greek residents of Uruk who were not members of the assembly, though many would have become members by intermarriage in the course of time.[3] It is safe to assume that a comparable situation obtained under Achaemenid rule. It is also attested that ethnic minorities had their own distinct assemblies; we hear, for example, of an 'assembly of the elders of the Egyptians'.[4] The city-temple *puḫru*, presided over by a dean (*šatammu, paqdu*), dealt with a wide range of secular and religious matters. It decided issues relating to marriage and property, imposed penalties, and heard petitions and grievances. One of the Murašu tablets, for example,

1. On temple slaves, see R. P. Dougherty, *The Shirkûtu of Babylonian Deities* (New Haven: Yale University Press, 1923) and, more recently, McEwan, *Priest and Temple*, pp. 58-59. These have been compared with the postexilic *nᵉtînîm*, the lowest class (with descendants of Solomon's slaves) in the lists of temple personnel in Ezra–Nehemiah; see E.A. Speiser, 'Unrecognized Dedication', *IEJ* 13 (1963), pp. 69-73; B.A. Levine, 'The Netînîm', *JBL* 82 (1963), pp. 207-12. M.A. Dandamaev has written extensively on slavery, including temple slavery, in ancient Mesopotamia, most recently *Slavery in Babylon from Nabopolassar to Alexander the Great* (De Kalb, IL: N. Illinois University Press, 1984) and 'Slavery and the Structure of Society', in M.A. Dandamaev and V.G. Lukonin, *The Culture and Social Institutions of Ancient Iran* (Cambridge: Cambridge University Press, 1989), pp. 152-77.

2. Dandamaev in *CHJ*, I, pp. 330-31; McEwan, *Priest and Temple*, pp. 189-90.

3. Sarkisian, 'City Land', pp. 313-14, 330; 'Greek Personal Names', pp. 495-503.

4. Dandamaev, *CHJ*, I, pp. 338-39. See also D.J. Wiseman, 'Some Egyptians in Babylonia', *Iraq* 28 (1966), pp. 154-58.

records the case of a Jew heard before the *puḫru* of Nippur.[1]

It is reasonable to assume that a similar situation obtained in other less amply documented temple-cities in Babylonia—Ur, Nippur and Sippar, for example.[2] The citizens of Babylon itself belonged to the assembly of one or other of the temples in the city, and lived apart from the dependent farmers who had their own subdivision.[3] We hear of Babylonian members of the *esagila* assembly (*puḫur ša é-sag-gil*) under the supervision of a royal representative (*rēš šarri*).[4] Like the Eanna sanctuary, the *esagila* owned lands and irrigation canals—water being a particularly valuable commodity. It also leased out plots to dependent farmers (*ikkarātu*), for the most part reserving the less cost-productive labor of slaves for the temple itself. While no aspect of this situation is peculiar to the Achaemenid period, or a product of Achaemenid imperial initiative, the fact remains that this distinctive form of sociopolitical and economic organization centered on temples was allowed to continue, and indeed flourish, within the context of the Achaemenid imperial system.

Needless to say, we have no assurance that a similar situation obtained in the province of Judah (Yehud) under Persian rule. No archives have come down to us from the Jerusalem temple comparable to those recovered from the Eanna temple in Uruk, and there are no economic texts comparable to the extant files of the Murašu and Egibi commercial houses. The texts that we do possess are not designed to provide us with the information we need, so that the basis for a straightforward comparison simply does not exist. We can, notwithstanding, elicit some relevant information from the biblical texts, however uncertain its interpretation may be. It would also be surprising if the situation in Judah were entirely unique in this respect,

1. E.J. Bickerman, *CHJ*, I, p. 349.
2. On Ur, see H.H. Figulla, *Ur Excavation Texts*. IV. *Business Documents of the New-Babylonian Period* (London, 1949); on Sippar see G.G. Cameron in *AJSL* 58 (1941), pp. 320-21.
3. A.L. Oppenheim (*Ancient Mesopotamia* [Chicago: University of Chicago Press, 1964], pp. 115-56) notes the distinction between the inner and outer quarters of the city, the latter constituting the agrarian hinterland. There was also the 'harbor' (*kāru*) for foreign residents. One is reminded of the layout of the visionary city in Ezekiel 40–48 which is provided with a belt of agrarian land on each side (Ezek. 45.6; 48.15-20).
4. McEwan, *Priest and Temple*, pp. 17-18.

and our survey of the function of temples elsewhere in the empire at least establishes the range of possibilities. There also exist important connections between Babylonia and Judah. They belonged to the same satrapy down to the reign of Xerxes, and the dominant elite in Judah which came to control the temple originated in Babylonia. The implications of this association should emerge more clearly after a closer look at the political situation in Judah, and to this we now turn.

III

After the fall of Babylon in 539 BCE Judah, as a part of the neo-Babylonian empire, passed automatically under Persian rule. Effective control of the outlying western provinces must, however, have taken some time to establish; and in fact the Cyrus cylinder speaks only of the submission of 'all the kings of the west lands living in tents' (*ANET*, p. 136). The administrative situation of the region in the two decades preceding the reorganization of the empire by Darius is far from clear.[1] The territory of the former neo-Babylonian empire was governed by the satrap Gubaru (Gobryas), and the biblical sources tell of the appointment of a certain Sheshbazzar, described in Tattenai's report as 'governor' (*peḥâ*, Ezra 5.14), and in the Hebrew source as 'prince for Judah' (*nāsî' lîhûdâ*, Ezra 1.8). We do not know what the writer wished to suggest by this term *nāsî'*. It need not imply that he was a member of the Judaean ruling class, and there are no grounds for identifying him with Shenazzar, son of the exiled Jehoiachin.[2] The name suggests that he was a Babylonian, perhaps a Babylonian Jew, and his jurisdiction may have had a quite limited scope. The term *peḥâ* can mean different things, and its occurrence at Ezra 5.14 need not presuppose the division of the region into provinces, always assuming that the elders were filing a truthful report. Some administrative measures may have been taken in preparation for the conquest of

1. On which see K. Galling, 'Denkmäler zur Geschichte Syriens und Palästinas unter der Herrschaft der Perser', *PJ* 34 (1938), pp. 59-79; *idem, Studien zur Geschichte Israels im persischen Zeitalter* (Tübingen: Mohr, 1964), pp. 47-48; Dandamaev, 'Politische und wirtschaftliche Geschichte', pp. 15-58; *idem, CHJ*, I, pp. 328-29.
2. P.-R. Berger ('Zu den Namen ššbṣr und šn'ṣr', *ZAW* 83 [1971], pp. 98-100) has shown that the identification is highly improbable, but it continues to be accepted uncritically.

Egypt—perhaps already during the reign of Cyrus (as Herodotus 1.153)—but it is unlikely that they would have been completed before the reign of Darius I. And if this is so, it is unlikely that Babylonian Jews returned to the homeland in significant numbers before that time. Some may have accompanied Cambyses on his Egyptian campaign of 525 BCE and the resettlement may have been furthered by the revolts of Nidintu-Bel and Arakha, pretenders to the Babylonian throne, and the consequent disruption in Babylon during the two years following the death of Cambyses. It was at this time that Zechariah urged Babylonian Jews to seek safety by fleeing to Judah (Zech 2.10-16). At any rate, no significant progress was made towards rebuilding the temple before the reign of Darius, as Haggai explicitly attests (Hag. 1.4, 9; 2.15; cf. Zech. 1.16; 6.12, 15; 8.9).

During this early period, therefore, Judah was part of a vast satrapy coextensive with the former Babylonian empire, including therefore Babylonia itself and the Trans-Euphrates region. According to the tribute list of Herodotus (3.89-97), Phoenicia, Syria-Palestine and Cyprus formed the fifth of twenty satrapies (*archai* or *nomoi*), distinct from Babylon which was the ninth, but it is clear from the Behistun inscription and other inscriptions from the reign of Darius that this list corresponds to the situation following on the suppression of the Babylonian revolts by Xerxes, at which time Babylon was made into a separate satrapy.[1] The administrative center of the Trans-Euphrates region may have been Damascus, though other candidates have been suggested.[2] A certain Ushtani was satrap during the early years of Darius's reign, followed by another, a part of whose name appears on a recently published inscription dated to 486 BCE.[3] During part of this

1. The Behistun inscription and other inscriptions from Persepolis, Naqs-i-Rustam and Susa list Babylon (Babirush) but not Abar-nahara; see J.M. Cook, *The Persian Empire* (London: J.M. Dent & Sons, 1983), pp. 77-79 and E. Stern in *CHJ*, I, p. 78. For the texts see R.G. Kent, *Old Persian*, pp. 119, 123, 126, 136, 138, 145.
2. Tripoli on the Phoenician coast, according to Galling, *Studien*, p. 48 and Bengtson, *The Greeks and the Persians*, p. 404. At the end of the 5th century the palace of the satrap Belesys was in northern Syria near Aleppo; see Cook, *The Persian Empire*, p. 174.
3. O. Leuze, *Die Satrapieneinteilung in Syrien und im Zweistromlande von 520 bis 320* (Halle: Max Niemeyer Verlag, 1935), pp. 36-42. A Babylonian tablet published by W. Stolper (*JNES* 48 [1985], pp. 283-305) records instructions given

time Tattenai held a subordinate position as governor of 'Abar-nahara. The territory under the latter's jurisdiction included different kinds of polities, among them vassal kingdoms, tribal sheikhdoms and provinces of which Judah was one. It is therefore referred to in the biblical sources as *mᵉdînâ, yᵉhûd mᵉdîntā'*, though the term *mᵉdînâ* could also be used of larger administrative units.[1]

The hypothesis, first proposed by Albrecht Alt, that Judah became an administrative adjunct of Samaria after the assassination of the Babylonian-appointed governor Gedaliah (582 BCE?), and remained so until Nehemiah secured its independence of Samarian control in the mid-fifth century, has been widely accepted but is almost certainly wrong.[2] Nehemiah himself refers to governors who preceded him, the context strongly suggesting reference to Judah, and their existence is confirmed by other allusions in our sources, and perhaps also by archaeological findings.[3] That a governor is not mentioned on the occasion of Tattenai's tour of inspection (Ezra 5.3-5), or following the arrival in the province of both Ezra and Nehemiah (Ezra 8.32-34; Neh. 2.9), may mean that the office was temporarily vacant during these and possibly other times of political crisis.[4] Judah may have been

by a satrap, the first part of whose name is *Hu - a -*. One of the recipients is Gadalama (Gedalyahu?) and another Siha (cf. Ezra 2.43).

1. E.g. Ezra 2.1 = Neh. 7.6; Ezra 5.8; 6.20; 7.16; Neh. 1.3; 11.3. The term is also used of Media (Ezra 6.2) and Babylon itself (Ezra 7.16). See S.E. McEvenue, 'The Political Structure of Judah from Cyrus to Nehemiah', *CBQ* 43 (1981), pp. 359-61. F.C. Fensham ('Mĕdînâ in Ezra and Nehemiah', *VT* 25 [1975], pp. 795-97) thinks that in Ezra 2.1 *mᵉdînâ* refers to Babylon.

2. A. Alt, 'Die Rolle Samarias bei der Entstehung des Judentums', *Kleine Schriften zur Geschichte des Volkes Israel,* II (Munich: Beck, 1953), pp. 316-37, followed by M. Noth, *The History of Israel* (London: A. & C. Black, 1960), pp. 288-89; Galling, *Studien*, p. 92 n. 3, and many others.

3. Neh. 5.15; other references to an unnamed governor in Ezra 5.14; Hag. 1.1; Mal. 1.18. The dating of the bullae and seals bearing the names of governors remains uncertain at this date; see N. Avigad, *Bullae and Seals from a Post-exilic Judaean Archive* (Qedem, 4; Jerusalem: Hebrew University of Jerusalem, 1976). His reconstructed series of governors (Sheshbazzar, Zerubbabel, Elnathan, Yehoezer, Aḥzai, Nehemiah, Begohi, Yeḥezqiyah) should therefore be treated with some reserve.

4. The governor of the Jews' (*paḥat yᵉhûdāyē'*) at Ezra 6.7 is absent from LXX and may have been added (cf. 5.2). See Morton Smith, *Palestinian Parties and Politics that Shaped the Old Testament* (New York: Columbia University

placed under Samarian control after whatever event precipitated the complaints recorded in Ezra 4.7-16, but that is quite a different matter.

Judah, then, was a distinct administrative and fiscal unit from at least the time of Darius, one of the smallest in the Trans-Euphrates region, with its own governor and provincial administration, comparable in this respect to other provinces such as Samaria, Dor and Ashdod.[1] The further division of the province into districts (*pelākîm*), each again divided in two, under administrative officials (*sārîm*) may also date from this time (Neh. 3.9, 12, 14-18). There is no reason to believe that the system was subsequently altered, though there may have been interruptions at times of political crisis. One of these may have occurred towards the middle of the fifth century, following on which the vigorous measures of Nehemiah re-established the autonomy of the province against the encroachment of its neighbors.[2]

The decisive *political* event in the establishment of a viable Jewish community in the homeland was the rebuilding of the temple and organization of its cult. Unfortunately, however, the biblical sources do not leave us with a clear picture of how, when, and by whom this was accomplished. Following Ezra 1–6, it was mandated rather than permitted by Cyrus in a decree issued to the Jewish ethnic minority in Babylonia (Ezra 1.2-4), and we are told that his initiative met with an immediate and enthusiastic response with the return of some 50,000 led by Sheshbazzar, Zerubbabel, Jeshua the priest and other notables (Ezra 1.5–2.69). On arriving in Jerusalem, they at once set up an altar (3.1-3) and shortly thereafter laid the foundations of the temple (3.8-13). Further progress was impeded by the native population, with the result that work could be resumed only in the second year of Darius—therefore in 520 BCE—at which time the original work permit was confirmed, leading to the completion of the project in the sixth year of the same reign (4.1–6.15).

Press, 1971), pp. 195-98.

1.   These divisions go back to Assyrian imperial administration, on which see Alt, *Kleine Schriften*, II, pp. 188-205, 226-41.

2.   Yehud seal impressions and small silver coins dated to about this time have been taken to indicate the regaining of autonomy by the province under Nehemiah; see E. Stern, *Material Culture of the Land of the Bible in the Persian Period 538-332 BC* (Warminster: Aris & Phillips, 1982), pp. 202-14, 224-27; further bibliography on pp. 419-20.

The sources cited by the author in Aramaic, the official diplomatic language of the Persian chancellory (Ezra 4.7-22; 5.6-17; 6.2-12), are meant to confirm the historical accuracy of this version of events. In some respects they do so, but they create additional problems where they diverge from the author's own narrative. So, for example, the Hebrew narrator attributes the laying of the foundations to Zerubbabel and Jeshua (3.8), while the reply of the elders, cited in Tattenai's report, states that it was the work of Sheshbazzar (5.16). There are also discrepancies between the wording and substance of the Cyrus decree in its Hebrew and Aramaic versions (1.1-4; 6.1-5).[1] The problems multiply when we turn to the prophecies of Haggai and Zechariah, dated firmly in the early years of the reign of Darius I, for here there is no mention of royal decrees or of Sheshbazzar. Zerubbabel, and he alone, laid the foundations and supervised the building with the assistance of the high priest Jeshua (Zech. 4.9; 6.12-13). The role of diaspora Jews is mentioned only obliquely and incidentally,[2] and the clear impression is given that nothing much was accomplished prior to the reign of Darius. The unconscionable delay is explained not as the result of external opposition, as in Ezra, but of indifference, if not outright opposition, within the province itself.

It hardly needs saying that any reconstruction based on these sources will be quite speculative. That Cyrus should have taken the initiative attributed to him is at least consonant with Achaemenid policy, as we have seen. That he issued such a firman is therefore quite plausible, though neither version has escaped editing. If so much is accepted, the delay of some two decades may have been due to unfavorable social and economic conditions to which the sources attest. Contemporary prophetic texts associate the project, when it finally got underway, with messianic and nationalistic expectations comparable to what was happening in Babylon during the first two

1. E.J. Bickerman ('The Edict of Cyrus in Ezra 1', *JBL* 65 [1946], pp. 249-75) argued that Cyrus issued two decrees, the first (Ezra 1) an oral proclamation addressed to Babylonian Jews permitting the return and rebuilding, the second (Ezra 6) the official firman, a copy of which was deposited in the state archives. But this does not explain the major discrepancy between the versions, that the project is to be financed from the private sector in the former, and from government funds in the latter.

2. Zech. 6.9-14 speaks of the arrival of three wealthy Jews from Babylon, and it is implied that they and others like them will *assist* in the project.

years of the reign of Darius. But with the removal of Zerubbabel from the scene, however that happened, the rebuilt temple could function as a stabilizing and integrating factor within the overall administrative measures carried through by Darius during the late sixth and early fifth century.

About the temple itself the biblical sources provide little information. That it was constructed of stone and timber (Ezra 5.8; 6.4), and built on the site of its predecessor (Ezra 5.15), is no more than we would expect. The dimensions given in the Cyrus decree after it was recovered from the Ecbatana archives—sixty cubits broad and sixty high—are quite implausible, and remain no less so if we add sixty cubits for the length from the measurements given for the First Temple (Ezra 6.3; 1 Kgs 6.2). Though it is never said so explicitly, there is some suggestion that it was smaller and less impressive than its predecessor (Ezra 3.12; Hag. 2.3), and that too is hardly surprising. It should be noted that its status differed from that of Solomon's temple in one important respect. The latter was, like Bethel, 'a royal sanctuary, a temple of the kingdom' (Amos 7.13) in other words, a royal and state institution. The land on which it was built was purchased by David himself (2 Sam. 24.18-25), its construction was funded out of the royal treasury (1 Kgs 5.15-32; 7.51; 9.10-14), and the necessary endowments continued to be provided from the same source (2 Kgs 12.18). This did not, of course, exclude private gifts and *ex voto* offerings, but it is of interest to note that the public collection for the repair of the temple during the reign of Jehoash (Joash) is transformed by the author of Chronicles into a temple tax imposed on the entire population (2 Kgs 12.4-16; 2 Chron. 24.6, 9-10; cf. Neh. 10.33). With the rebuilt temple, however, the situation was quite different. Both the cost of the rebuilding and the endowment came from the central government and the satrapal exchequer (Ezra 6.4, 8-10; 7.15, 20-23; 8.25, 33). The requirement that sacrifices and prayers for the royal family be incorporated into the liturgy (Ezra 6.10) reinforced the point that the temple and all that it stood for was understood to be part of the apparatus of imperial control. But we are also told that substantial contributions were made by the Babylonian Jewish community represented by the heads of its 'houses' (Ezra 1.4, 6; 2.68-69; 7.16). Babylonian Jewry, therefore, shared with the imperial government the expenses of construction and maintenance. By means of this partial underwriting, and by reserving to themselves responsibility for the actual rebuilding to the exclusion of the natives (Ezra 4.1-5), the golah-community in effect claimed control of the Jerusalem cult under the supervision and protection of the imperial authorities. It is this circumstance of a *limited* participation in temple governance that gives some at least initial plausibility to the thesis of a civic-temple community in Judah during the Achaemenid period. It is now time to look more closely at this hypothesis.

IV

As stated by Weinberg, the thesis rests on the supposition that there existed in Achaemenid Judah a collectivity attached to the temple which was not identical with the province either demographically or territorially.[1] Given the nature of the evidence, whether literary or archaeological, demographic studies of ancient societies are notoriously hit-or-miss, and the situation is no different with ancient Israel. Starting out from 2 Kgs 15.19-20, which details the tribute paid by Menahem of the Northern Kingdom to Tiglath-pileser III and the means he took to pay it, Weinberg estimated the population of the kingdom of Samaria in the eighth century BCE at about 500,000 to 700,000 and, on the basis of comparative size, that of Judah at about 220,000 to 250,000.[2] He then turned to the biblical figures for Judaeans deported by the Babylonians between 598-582, where the major problem is the discrepancy between the Deuteronomistic History (2 Kgs 24.14-16; 25.11-12, 26) and Jeremiah (52.28-30).

1. I have had access to Weinberg's earlier studies written in Latvian and Russian only where a summary was available in a language familiar to me. My assessment is based on the following papers: 'Demographische Notizen zur Geschichte der nachexilischen Gemeinde in Juda', *Klio* 34 (1972), pp. 45-59; 'Probleme der sozial-ökonomischen Struktur Judäas vom 6. Jahrhundert v.u.Z. bis zum 1. Jahrhundert u.Z.', *Jahrbuch für Wirtschaftsgeschichte* 1 (1973), pp. 237-51 (a critique of the work of Heinz Kreissig); 'Das BÊIT ĀBÔT im 6.-4. Jh. v.u.Z.', *VT* 23 (1973), pp. 400-14; 'Der *'am hā'āreṣ* des 6.-4. Jh. v.u.Z.', *Klio* 56 (1974), pp. 235-335; 'Nᵉtînîm und "Söhne der Sklaven Salomos" im 6.-4. Jh. v.u.Z.', *ZAW* 87 (1975), pp. 355-71; 'Die Agrarverhältnisse in der Bürger-Tempel-Gemeinde der Achämenidenzeit', in Harmatta and Komoróczy (eds.), *Wirtschaft und Gesellschaft im Alten Vorderasien*, pp. 473-86; 'Bemerkungen zum Problem "Der Vorhellenismus im Vorderer Orient"', *Klio* 58 (1976), pp. 5-20; 'Zentral- und Partikulargewalt im achämenidischen Reich', *Klio* 59 (1977), pp. 25-43.
2. 'Demographische Notizen', p. 45.

Basing himself on the higher estimates in the History, Weinberg came up with a total of about 20,000 deportees or some 10 per cent of the total population.[1] This allowed him to assume that the population of the province in the early Persian period, before the repatriations, continued to stand at about 200,000.

A crucial point in Weinberg's thesis is the contention that the list of repatriates in Nehemiah 7—which he takes to be the original version reproduced in Ezra 2—is a census of the civic-temple community about the middle of the fifth century prior to the activity of Ezra and Nehemiah. The list gives a total of 42,360 exclusive of 7,337 slaves and 200 male and female singers, which he takes to represent only about 20 per cent of the population of the province at that time. By appealing to later lists, especially the census in Neh. 11.4-22, he goes on to claim that in the period subsequent to Nehemiah the membership increased to about 150,000 or about 70 per cent of the total population, a trend which would eventually lead to the total assimilation of the province to the temple community.

Weinberg goes on to argue that these conclusions are supported by the lists of settlements occupied by the repatriates. Following a common pattern, each of these settlements had its own agrarian holdings, referred to in Ezra–Nehemiah by such terms as *śādôt*, *migrāšîm* and *ḥāṣᵉrîm*. We are told that the Babylonian *'ôlîm* returned to their former settlements, each to his own *naḥᵃlâ* (Neh. 11.20; cf. Ezra 2.1 = Neh. 7.6; Ezra 2.70 = Neh. 7.73). The settlements listed in the community census (Ezra 2.20-35 = Neh. 7.25-38) are located in three distinct regions: the neighborhood of Jerusalem, the coastal plain, and the Jordan valley. They, therefore, by no means account for the total area of the province, and even within these regions there were settlements not occupied by the immigrants.[2] But when we turn to the settlement list in Neh. 11.25-36, corresponding to

---

1. 'Demographische Notizen', pp. 46-50; 'Agrarverhältnisse', p. 479, with which cf. H. Kreissig, *Die Sozialökonomische Situation im Juda zur Achämenidenzeit* (Berlin: Akademie Verlag, 1973), pp. 22-23: 15,600 deportees or one in eighth of the total population, leaving some 60,000 behind after 582 BCE.
2. 'Agrarverhältnisse', p. 54. However, in another article in *Archiv Orientálni* 42 (1974), pp. 341-53 (in Russian; summary in *ZAW* 87 [1975], p. 227 and *JSJ* 6 [1975], p. 242) he argues that this part of the census list refers to collectives which had never left the province but which merged with the temple community in the latter part of the fifth century.

places occupied by adherents of the temple community after the mid-fifth century, we note an increase from nineteen to about fifty occupation sites, the greatest concentration being in southern Judah which had suffered more severely from the effects of the Babylonian conquest.[1] Archaeological evidence for new settlements in the second half of the fifth century (e.g. Arad, Engedi, Lachish, Beersheba) provide additional support for this position.[2] Topographical data thus agree with the demographic analysis, and confirm the existence and gradual expansion of a social entity centered on the temple distinguishable from the province as a whole.

In assessing Weinberg's conclusions, it will be well to bear in mind a point already made about the difficulty of obtaining reliable demographic data on ancient societies. Weinberg compounds the problem by taking the biblical figures at face value, and some of his inferences from these figures are also questionable. If, for example, some researcher in the distant future were to calculate the population of the United Kingdom on the basis of its size relative to the United States, as Weinberg does for Judah relative to Israel, he or she would be wrong by a factor of about ten. But let us assume for the moment that his figures for the two kingdoms from the eighth to the sixth century BCE are roughly correct; they are at least within the range proposed by some other scholars and more or less consonant with data in Assyrian records.[3] The issue then is to determine the number of

1.	To the total of 48 post-458 BCE settlements Weinberg adds Arad and Engeddi, on archaeological grounds ('Demographische Notizen', p. 57; 'Agrar-verhältnisse', p. 481). He holds that southern Judah suffered more severely because, unlike the former territory of Benjamin to the north, it was strongly anti-Babylonian ('Demographische Notizen', pp. 47-50).

2.	'Demographische Notizen', pp. 55-57. For the relevant archaeological data see Stern's synthesis, by now necessarily somewhat out of date, in *The Material Culture*, pp. 38-39, 41-45.

3.	See, for example, E. Meyer, *Die Entstehung des Judentums* (Halle: Max Niemeyer, 1896), pp. 108-10; W. Rudolph, 'Sanherib in Palästina', *PJB* 25 (1929), p. 67; E. Janssen, *Juda in der Exilzeit* (Göttingen: Vandenhoeck & Ruprecht, 1956), p. 28. W.F. Albright (*The Biblical Period from Abraham to Ezra* [New York: Harper & Row, 1965 (1950)], pp. 84, 105 n. 118) estimates the population of Judah at the end of the eighth century at 250,000. Sargon claims to have taken 27,290 captive after the conquest of Samaria (*ANET*, pp. 284-85), and about two decades later Sennacherib boasts of having taken 46 towns and their surrounding villages in Judah, driving out of them 200,150 people (*ANET*, p. 288). It goes without saying deportees between 598 and 592, i.e., between the first Babylonian occupation and the exodus following the failed coup of Ishmael. The Deuteronomistic Historian conveys the impression that only the poorest stratum of the population—the *dallat hā'āreṣ*—was left behind, and adds that after the assassination of Gedaliah all the (remaining) people, great and small, fled to Egypt (2 Kgs 25.26). He provides statistics only for the first deportation in 598 (2 Kgs 24.14-16), at which point two parallel versions are conflated. The first (v. 14) lists the population of Jerusalem, the princes (*śārîm*), 10,000 'men of substance', and all the craftsmen and smiths. The second (vv. 15-16) itemizes the royal family, court officials (*sārîsîm*), the chief men of the land, 7000 'men of substance' and 1,000 craftsmen and smiths. The numbers for all three deportations in Jer. 52.28-30, totalling 4,600, convey a much clearer impression both of dependence on an archival source and of reality.[1] In defiance of what the text in question (Jer. 52.29) actually says, Weinberg, in agreement with Mowinckel,[2] maintains that the data in 2 Kings refer to Jerusalem and in Jeremiah to Judaeans exclusive of Jerusalemites. His total of 20,000 deportees, therefore, includes Jerusalemites (2 Kings), other Judaeans (Jeremiah) and those who left to avoid Babylonian reprisals or on account of the disastrous economic conditions.

However this may be, Weinberg's conclusion that the province still had a population of some 200,000 (a density of about 230 to the square mile) after the successive deportations and emigrations, not to mention the loss of life and destruction of property during the conquest and occupation, is considerably wide of the mark.[3] His calculation of the size of the temple community relative to the population also rests on doubtful assumptions: first, that the census list

that these figures cannot be taken at their face value either.

1.   As noted by Albright (*The Biblical Period*, p. 85), it would be natural to assume that this figure includes only adult males, though the text uses the terms *'am* and *nepeš* (twice) rather than *'ᵃnāšîm*.

2.   S. Mowinckel, *Studien zu dem Buche Esra–Nehemia*, I (Oslo: Universitetsforlaget, 1964), pp. 93-98. He estimated between 12,600 and 14,600 by adding together the 8,000 or 10,000 of 2 Kings (Jerusalemites) with the 4,600 of Jeremiah (other Judaeans).

3.   Compare, for example, Albright's estimate of 20,000 (*The Biblical Period*, p. 87 and n. 180). About all we can safely say is that the correct total is somewhere between these extremes, but closer to Albright than to Weinberg.

in Neh. 7 = Ezra 2 was drawn up prior to 458, the date he assigns to Ezra's mission; second, that the grand total of 42,360, which does not match even approximately the sum of the sub-totals in the list, is accurate.[1] Also problematic is his explanation of the settlement list in Neh. 11.25-36. Comparison with the boundary and city lists in Joshua 15–18 suggests that what we have here is a description of the *ideal* boundaries of Judah. The statement that the Judaeans 'encamped' (*yaḥᵃnû*, v. 30) from Beersheba to the Valley of Hinnom harks back to Israel in the wilderness, in keeping with the exodus-occupation typology in evidence elsewhere in Ezra–Nehemiah. That several of the places mentioned are known to have been under Edomite control in the fifth century, and that some even remained outside the Jewish sphere until the Maccabean conquests (cf. 1 Macc. 5.65; 11.34), also calls into question the use of the list to plot the territorial expansion of the temple community during the second century of Iranian rule. The hypothesis as applied to Judah remains highly suggestive, therefore, but if it is to be sustained it would need to be supported by a somewhat different line of argument. In the following sections I would like to suggest an alternative interpretation of the social situation which, though no less hypothetical, is, I believe, based more firmly on the few sources at our disposal.

V

In the summary of the census list which is central to Weinberg's hypothesis, those listed are described as an assembly or *qāhāl* (Ezra 2.64 = Neh. 7.66). While this word can have the general meaning of a company or crowd, it is also the traditional designation for Israel as a cultic collectivity.[2] Since the individuals and groups listed are

1. The aggregate of the subtotals is 29,818 in Ezra, slightly higher in Nehemiah and 1 Esdras. The reason for this discrepancy has not yet been explained. It may, of course, be due to a simple error in addition, especially in view of the system of horizontal and vertical slashes used for numbers, on which see H.L. Allrik, 'The Lists of Zerubbabel (Neh 7 and Ezr 2) and the Hebrew Numerical Notation', *BASOR* 136 (1954), pp. 21-27.
2. The cultic meaning is in evidence in the P legislation (e.g. Lev. 4.13-14, 21; 16.17, 33; Num. 10.7) and in Deuteronomy where the prototypal *qāhāl* is the assembly at Horeb (Deut. 5.22; cf. Josh. 8.35). The prototype is actualized in the 'day of assembly' (Deut. 9.11; 10.4; 18.16), a concrete sense also expressed by the

Babylonian immigrants, this *qāhāl* is identical with the golah-assembly (*qᵉhal haggôlâ*) convoked at the time of Ezra's marriage reform, an entity which defines itself over against the 'people(s) of the land' and from which one could be 'separated' (*yibbādēl*), in other words, excommunicated, with forfeiture of property (Ezra 10.8). A notable feature of Ezra–Nehemiah, not prominent in pre-exilic texts, is the convening of plenary assemblies to address issues as they arise; and in every case the assembly so convened is designated a *qāhāl*, generally with a qualifier—the assembly of the golah, the assembly of those who returned from captivity, the assembly of God.[1] In all cases we are dealing with a collectivity which defines itself over against others in the region, membership in which is regulated by incorporation in lists and genealogies, and which has its own procedures governing inclusion and exclusion.[2]

The preferred designation for the members of this *qāhāl* is 'those of the golah' (*bᵉn⁻ê haggôlâ*; in the Aramaic section *bᵉnê gālûtā'*), or simply 'the golah'.[3] By assuming responsibility for the actual rebuilding of the temple, with the backing of the imperial authorities and to the exclusion of the native population (Ezra 4.1-3), they reserved to themselves control of the temple operations, which translated into a large measure of social control. Those failing to attend the plenary

related verbal form *qhl* (Hiphil) at Deut. 4.10; 31.12, 28. Of particular interest for our present theme are the disqualifications from the *qᵉhāl yhwh* listed in Deut. 23.2-9.

1. The assembly convened to resolve the marriage crisis is described as *qāhāl rab mᵉ'ōd* (Ezra 10.1), reminiscent of the *qāhāl rab* mentioned in several Psalms (22.26; 35.18; 40.10-11); also as *qᵉhal haggôlâ* (Ezra 10.8). The gathering for the public reading of the law and celebration of Sukkoth is *kolhaqqāhāl haššābîm min haššᵉbî* ('the entire assembly of those who had returned from the captivity', Neh. 8.17), and a later assembly, also for reading the law, identified itself with the *qᵉhāl yhwh* of Deut. 23.2 (Neh. 13.1). That the agenda of these plenary assemblies was not confined to religious matters is indicated by the *qāhāl* or *qᵉhillâ* convened by Nehemiah to deal with social unrest (Neh. 5.7, 13).

2. Ezra 2.62 = Neh. 7.64. Separation from outsiders, and the exclusion from the community of recalcitrant insiders (e.g. Ezra 10.8; Neh. 13.3), are much more in evidence than the incorporation of new members (but see Ezra 6.21 and cf. Isa. 56.1-8). But we cannot explain the remarkable demographic expansion of the Jewish people between the Persian and Roman periods without large-scale recruitment in addition to marriage.

3. Ezra 1.11; 2.1 = Neh. 7.6; Ezra 3.8; 4.1; 6.16, 19-21; 8.35; 10.7, 8, 16.

session convoked to deal with the marriage crisis are threatened with expulsion from the assembly and confiscation of their property (Ezra 10.8), a threat reminiscent of the 'excommunication formula' of frequent occurrence in the Priestly matter in the Pentateuch (e.g. Lev. 7.21; 17.4; 18.29; Num. 15.30; 19.13). While such measures applied only to members of the golah group, it is clear that membership is not on principle confined to Babylonian repatriates. We hear of native-born Judaeans participating in cultic acts subject to conditions laid down by the leadership of the elite diaspora Jews (Ezra 6.21). Here, too, the distinction between 'Israelites who had returned from the diaspora' and 'those who had separated themselves from the impurity of the peoples of the land' may correspond to the distinction in P between 'Israelites' and 'strangers (tôšābîm) who sojourn with you... who were born in your land' (Lev. 25.45). If, moreover, Weinberg is correct (though inconsistent) in claiming that the groups designated by locality in the census list (Ezra 2.20-35 = Neh. 7.25-38) represent native recruits to the temple community, we would have another indication of a broader concept of membership, on which a great deal depended, including social and economic status in the province.

Another suggestion, proposed by Talmon,[1] is that the golah group referred to itself as a *yaḥad*, a term familiar from the Qumran texts but of extremely rare occurrence, as a substantive, in the Hebrew Bible (1 Chron. 12.17 and perhaps Deut. 33.5). He refers us to the passage in which the *bᵉnê haggôlâ* reject the offer to help in rebuilding the temple, extended by 'the people of the land': 'It is not for you and us to build the house of our God, כי נחנו יחד נבנה' (Ezra 4.1-3). He proposes to translate not 'we alone will build' (as in 1 Esd. 5.68: ἡμεῖς γὰρ μόνοι οἰκοδομήσομεν), which requires a different adverb, but 'we the community will build'. The troubling absence of the article might then be explained either by translating 'we as a community' or by assuming that the term is an abbreviated form of יחד בני ישראל. If Talmon is right this usage may have drawn on Deut. 33.5, יחד שבטי ישראל ('the community of the tribes of Israel'), and may therefore display another aspect of this group's self-understanding as the legitimate heirs of the old Israel.

1.   S. Talmon, 'The Sectarian YHḌ—a Biblical Noun', *VT* 3 (1953), pp. 133-40.

It is also worth noting in this connection how the gentilic *yehûdîm* (Aramaic *yehûdîn*) is used in Ezra–Nehemiah. Most commonly the term refers simply to inhabitants of the province of Yehud (e.g. Ezra 6.7; Neh. 1.2; 13.23) or to those of Judaean descent living outside the province (e.g. Neh. 4.6; 5.8). But the shift from the purely territorial to the broader ethnic-religious connotation—as in Esther—is already underway; for the members of the Jewish settlement in Elephantine, not descended from Judaeans, also refer to themselves routinely as *yehûdîm* (e.g. *AP* 6.3-10; 8.2; 10.3). But there seems to be a more specialized connotation where the Nehemiah memoir speaks of 'Jews' as a privileged class distinct from the common folk, and the most likely explanation is that he is referring to the socially and economically superior stratum of Babylonian immigrants. After his night ride round the city wall he says that he had not revealed his plans to the Jews, priests, nobles, officials and the rest of those who were to do the work (Neh. 2.16). Since 'nobles, officials and the rest of the people' is a routine listing in the memoir (Neh. 4.8, 13; 7.5), 'the Jews' cannot in this case be equated with the common people. Even clearer is the complaint of the common people and their wives against 'their brethren the Jews' (Neh. 5.1) who, as the context suggests, constitute a social and economic elite in the province. Special status is also suggested by the allusion to the one hundred and fifty *yehûdîm* and *seǧānîm* entertained by the governor on a regular basis (Neh. 5.17).[1] Taken together, these different designations support the thesis that there existed in the province a politically and economically dominant elite composed primarily of resettled Babylonian Jews.

According to Weinberg, the principal unit of which the Judaean temple community was composed was the *bêt 'ābôt* (ancestral house).[2] He points out that this term, as distinct from the pre-exilic *bêt 'āb*, is characteristic of the social organization of the province during the Persian period; it occurs sixty-five times in Chronicles–Ezra–Nehemiah and only six times in the Deuteronomistic History. According to the census list there were seventeen of these large agnatic units or phratries in the pre-Ezra temple community, the average size being in the order of 800 to 1000 adult males, somewhat larger

1.   See further Smith, *Palestinian Parties*, pp. 145-46; 'Jewish Religious Life in the Persian Period', in *CHJ*, I, pp. 219-20.

2.   'Das BÊIT ĀB̲Ō̲T', pp. 400-14.

than the average Iranian phratry, which numbered about 600.[1] This
basic unit, which could be applied to both laity and clergy (e.g. Neh.
11.13; 12.12, 22), was governed by leaders or elders (*râšîm, zᵉqēnîm*)
who played an important role in the affairs of the province, as they
had previously in the Babylonian diaspora.[2] Claiming descent from a
real or fictive eponym, the individual member (known as 'son' or
'brother') assured his good standing by inclusion in the official
genealogy of the agnatic group. Each ancestral house had its own land
(*ᵃḥuzzâ, naḥᵃlâ*) divided into plots worked by the individual families.
We shall see that this form of social organization, like so much else in
Achaemenid Judah, was essentially a Mesopotamian import.

Information on the different classes and functions within the
Judaean temple community is incomplete, to say the least. We can only
speculate on what the situation would look like if we had had the good
fortune to recover the archives of Zerubbabel's temple, as archae-
ologists have recovered those of the temple of Eanna in Uruk. Having
to make a virtue of necessity, we note that according to the census list
in Ezra 2 temple personnel made up rather more than a sixth of the
total number, a percentage similar to some of the case histories
considered earlier. Priests, levites, liturgical musicians, porters,
temple servants (*nᵉtînîm*) and 'descendants of Solomon's slaves' are
routinely listed together (Ezra 2.36-58, 70; 7.7; Neh. 10.29 omits the
last category). Beyond this we have little to go on, though we may
assume the need for other specializations, e.g., masons and carpenters
(Ezra 3.7), organized in guilds as in Mesopotamia.[3] Temple treasurers
in charge of the storerooms are also mentioned (Neh. 12.44; 13.13),
and the Eliashib of Neh. 13.4-9, one of several clerics to incur

1. 'Das BĒIT ĀBŌT', p. 405. Weinberg's figures are based on a calculation of
the average size of the seventeen phratries in the census list. Note, however, that the
Delaiah, Tobiah and Nekoda groups, which failed to come up with genealogical
support for the membership, averaged only 217 members (Ezra 2.59 = Neh. 7.61).

2. The *zᵉqēnîm* or *râ'šîm* feature often in the narrative, and at politically
important junctures (Ezra 5.5, 9; 6.7-8, 14; 10.8, 16; Neh. 10.15; 11.13). They
played an equally important role in the Babylonian diaspora (e.g. Jer. 29.1; Ezek.
8.1; 20.1).

3. I. Mendelsohn, 'Guilds in Ancient Palestine', *BASOR* 80 (1940), pp. 17-21
and, on the situation in Mesopotamia, his 'Guilds in Babylon and Assyria', *JAOS* 60
(1940), pp. 68-72 and D.B. Weisberg, *Guild Structure and Political Allegiance in
Early Achaemenid Mesopotamia* (New Haven: Yale University Press, 1967).

Nehemiah's wrath, was probably in charge of the temple maintenance crew and responsible for the temple fabric.[1] The Pethahiah of Neh. 11.24 seems to have functioned as overseer, an imperial appointee. Weinberg calculates the number of slaves at about 18 per cent of the total, though he bases this on the grand total (i.e. 7,337 out of 442,360) rather than on the sum of the sub-totals.[2] As in Mesopotamia, slaves would have been employed principally in the temple, the governor's residence and those of the nobility rather than on the land.

By the time of the Hasmonaeans, at the latest, the temple served as a kind of bank in which private funds could be deposited, and as a central storage area (2 Macc. 3.5-6, 10-12; Josephus, *War* 6.282; *Ant.* 14.110-13). That this was the case much earlier is suggested by the careful measures taken by Nehemiah to assure control of collections and disbursements through a panel, the composition of which reflected his own interests.[3] Our principal source alludes at several points to temple stores and treasury officials, and the facility provided for Tobiah the Ammonite in the temple precincts may well point to a commercial concession of some kind, since the room (*liškâ*) in question had previously been used for temple stores and it is difficult to see why Tobiah would otherwise be looking for accommodation in the temple (Neh. 13.4-9).

In this connection the question may be asked whether the Jerusalem temple also had its own domains, as was the case with other temples throughout the Achaemenid empire. Weinberg concluded that the Judaean temple community was *sui generis* in that the temple had no

1. This Eliashib was not the high priest. The name is common, and his function is given precisely to distinguish him from his namesake the high priest mentioned shortly afterwards (Neh. 13.28).

2. Weinberg's article on slaves and other categories of dependent producers in the Palestinian temple community appeared in *Palestinskij Sbornik* 25 (1974), pp. 63-66 and is summarized in *ZAW* 88 (1976), p. 129.

3. Neh. 13.13. This panel consisted of one priest, two members of the lower clergy and a fourth, Zadok, probably the governor's own representative. Nehemiah seems to have solicited and enjoyed the support of Levites as a counter to the priestly aristocracy. Levites were appointed to key positions as city guardians (Neh. 13.22), district administrators (3.17-19), and one, perhaps two, served on the temple treasury board (13.13). Special care was taken to see that they were adequately provided for (10.39; 11.23; 13.10-12), and these measures were even backed by an imperial edict (11.23).

land of its own and no temple-based economy.[1] Since Ezra–Nehemiah, our principal source, nowhere speaks of temple lands, the simplest solution would seem to be to agree with this judgment. The temple blueprint in Ezekiel 40–44, perhaps expanded during the Persian period,[2] does indeed emphasize the connection between temple and land by means of a quadratic spatial symbolism, and designates land reserved for Yahweh (i.e. for the temple personnel) as inalienable (Ezek. 48.14), but there is no guarantee that this corresponds with reality. The confiscated property ($r^e k\hat{u}\check{s}$, Ezra 10.8) of those expelled from the *qāhāl* presumably became property of the temple, as the verb *ḥrm* suggests and as 1 Esd. 9.4 and Josephus *Ant.* 11.148 explicitly note, but the substantive would more normally refer to personal belongings, especially livestock, rather than immovable property.

Perhaps the most interesting possibility, with regard to this question of temple land, is that the stipulation in Lev. 27.14-29 concerning the dedication of house or land to Yahweh reflects actual practice during this period. The law mandates assessment of the dedicated property by a priest and states the conditions—the assessed value plus 20 per cent—under which it might be redeemed if the donor had second thoughts. It also describes a situation in which a parcel of land becomes a *ś^edēh haḥerem*, a dedicated plot, and thus the inalienable property of the priesthood. Unless this is purely theoretical, it may be taken to reflect a situation in which the temple and its personnel drew part of their revenue from real estate as was the case elsewhere in the Persian empire.

VI

Putting all of this together, I suggest that the situation was something like the following. In keeping with a policy pursued in other parts of the empire, the imperial government encouraged the establishment of a dominant elite of proven loyalty in the province of Judah, a

1. 'Agrarverhältnisse', p. 485.
2. See H. Gese, *Der Verfassungsentwurf des Ezechiel (Kap. 40–48) traditionsgeschichtlich untersucht* (Tübingen: Mohr, 1957), especially pp. 108-23; W. Zimmerli, *Ezekiel 2. A Commentary on the Book of the Prophet Ezekiel Chapters 25–48* (Philadelphia: Fortress Press, 1983 [1969]), especially pp. 552-53; J.D. Levenson, *The Theology of the Program of Restoration of Ezekiel 40–48* (Missoula, MT: Scholars Press, 1976).

politically sensitive region in view of its proximity to Egypt. This new entity was recruited from the Jewish ethnic minority in Babylonia, settled there some two generations previously, and in the nature of the case only those of some social and economic standing, who had also resisted assimilation, would have had the ability and the motivation to answer the call. As an essential element of the establishment of a viable polity in the province, and again in keeping with well-attested Achaemenid practice, the imperial government mandated, rather than permitted, the rebuilding of the temple and financed the project out of the imperial and satrapal treasury. The result was the emergence, in the early decades of Achaemenid rule, of a semi-autonomous temple-community controlled by the dominant stratum of Babylonian immigrants, the *bᵉnê haggôlâ* of Ezra–Nehemiah.

It also appears that some of the most prominent features of this sociopolitical situation replicated that in which the Judaeans deported by Nebuchadrezzar found themselves after their resettlement in the alluvial plain of Lower Mesopotamia. And if this is so, the break in continuity at the exile was, at the level of social and political organization, more complete than we have been accustomed to think.

Little, unfortunately, is known about the social and economic situation of the Jewish ethnic minority in the Babylonian diaspora. The deportees were settled in the Nippur region of the alluvial plain. Ezekiel's vision took place near the Chebar canal (Ezek. 1, 3, etc.), the *nār kabari*, or 'Grand Canal' which looped through the city of Nippur on its way back to the Euphrates. Other sites mentioned in the biblical sources—Tel-abib, Ahava, Tel-melah, Tel-harsha, Cherub, Addan, Immer (Ezek. 3.15; Ezra 2.59; 8.15, 17, 21)—have not been identified but were doubtless in the same region. About 8 per cent of the personal names in the Murašu archive are of Judaean origin, and there were Jews living in twenty-eight out of some two hundred settlements in that area.[1] That they were not enslaved was due to

1. The percentage of Jewish names given here is based on G. Cardascia, *Les archives des Murašû* (Paris: Imprimerie nationale, 1951), p. 2 n. 2 and accepted by Bickerman, *CHJ*, I, p. 344. However, R. Zadok (*The Jews in Babylonia during the Chaldean and Achaemenid Periods* [Haifa: The University Press, 1979], p. 78) finds only about three per cent. Names, even with known theophoric elements, do not infallibly indicate the nationality of their bearers, so some uncertainty is inevitable. The bearing of the Murašu tablets on this issue is discussed, with up-to-date bibliography, in E.M. Yamauchi, *Persia and the Bible* (Grand Rapids: Baker

pragmatic economic reasons rather than to the magnanimity of the Babylonians. It appears that the Nippur region, recently taken over by the crown, was due for redevelopment—digging and dredging canals, working the land—for which slave labor, requiring constant supervision was not the most cost-effective instrument.[1] Prevalence of place-names formed with *tel*, meaning the ruins of a former settlement, points in the same direction since it suggests a deliberate policy of resettling abandoned sites. This policy of internal colonization, in which the establishment of ethnic minorities played a significant role, contributed to the great demographic and economic expansion of Lower Mesopotamia during the neo-Babylonian and Achaemenid periods.[2] We have good reason to believe that many of the Jewish settlers shared in the ensuing economic boom.

It is also attested that these ethnic minorities were encouraged to maintain their distinct identities, obviously more for administrative and fiscal than for humanitarian reasons. Elamites, Egyptians, Lydians, Jews and others formed self-governing collectivities under imperial supervision, internal affairs being regulated by an assembly (*puḫru*), organized according to the large kinship group (*bīt abim*) and composed of property owners (*mār banē*) together with cult personnel where the foreign cult persisted. Whether the Jewish ethnic minority had its own temple we do not know. It has been argued that the elders came to Ezekiel to seek his support for building their own temple (Ezek. 20.1, 32) and that a temple was actually built has been proposed on the basis of Ezra 8.15-20, which refers to 'the place Casiphia' under the regency of a certain Iddo, presumably a priest, where Ezra was able to recruit additional cult personnel.[3] In the

Book House, 1990), pp. 243-44.

1. M.A. Dandamaev, 'Social Stratification in Babylonia (7th–4th Centuries BC)', p. 437; E. Eph'al, 'The Western Minorities in Babylonia in the 6th–5th Centuries B.C.: Maintenance and Cohesion', *Orientalia* 47 (1978), pp. 74-90; Bickerman, *CHJ*, I, pp. 342-58.

2. Dandamaev, 'Achaemenid Babylonia', pp. 297, 309; R.McC. Adams, *The Uruk Countryside* (Chicago: University of Chicago Press, 1972), pp. 55-57; *idem, Heartland of Cities* (Chicago: University of Chicago Press, 1981), p. xiv.

3. That a Jewish temple was built in Babylonia was argued by L.E. Browne, 'A Jewish Sanctuary in Babylonia', *JTS* 17 (1916), pp. 400-401; A. Causse, *Les dispersés d'Israël* (Paris, 1929), pp. 76-77; A. Menes, 'Tempel und Synagoge', *ZAW* 50 (1932), pp. 268-76. Smith (*Palestinian Parties*, pp. 90-91) thinks it more

absence of a temple, there must at any rate have been some form of organized cult and some institutional framework for the preservation, implementation and development of the legal traditions, especially those known to modern scholarship as the Priestly Code (P).

The proposal is, then, that the Babylonian immigrants imported, and succeeded in imposing, the social arrangements with which they had become familiar in the diaspora. They reconstituted their own assembly (*puḥru*, *q āhāl*), organized according to ancestral houses including free, property-owning citizens and temple personnel, under the leadership of tribal elders and the supervision of an imperial representative, in a cohesive social entity which, while allowing for additional adherents, was jealously protective of its status and privileges. To this extent, at least, Weinberg's civic-temple community hypothesis appears to be acceptable. For this new form of social organization to be viable two goals had to be attained. The immigrants had to win back the land redistributed to the peasantry (*dallat hā'āreṣ*) after the deportations (2 Kgs 25.12; Jer. 39.10; 52.16; cf. Ezek. 11.14-21), and they had to rebuild and secure control of the temple as the sociopolitical and religious center of gravity of their existence. The achievement of both these goals, recorded in the biblical sources, laid the foundations for the distinctive social form assumed by the emergent Judaism of the Persian period.

likely that one was built there at the time of the rebuilding of the temple in Judah. Zech. 5.5-11 alludes to a shrine (to Asherah?) to be built in the land of Shinar, but whether anything came of this, or of any other plans that may have been thought up, we simply do not know.

THE ACHAEMENID CONTEXT

Kenneth Hoglund

From 539 BCE when Babylon fell to Cyrus until 332 BCE when Alexander the Great marched triumphantly through the Levant, the Judaean community was under Achaemenid imperial rule. For over two centuries, the over-arching requirements of the empire became the pervasive external influence on Judaean society, both on its institutions and on its very fabric. This fact is tacitly recognized in the Hebrew Bible by the preservation of accounts of the epochal reforms of Ezra and Nehemiah, both ostensibly acting as imperial functionaries (Ezra 7.21-26; Neh. 2.9). However, the attention one might anticipate would consequently be given to the social mechanisms employed by the Achaemenid empire in governing the postexilic community has proven to be highly limited, both in terms of the number of such studies and the methods employed in reconstructing the social forces at work within the Judaean community (Kippenberg 1978; Kreissig 1973; Weinberg 1973a, 1973b, 1976; Schottroff 1974). We still lack a clear, thorough assessment of Achaemenid imperial rule in Judah and the extent to which such rule shaped and oriented the basic social constitution of the postexilic community (for example, see the comments of Petersen 1984: 29-31).

Two factors in particular seem to contribute to this dilemma, namely the problematic nature of the relevant ancient sources and the ephemeral nature of the theoretical understanding of imperial systems and their social manipulation.

Regarding the problematic character of the literary sources, one may begin with their linguistic diversity. Texts relating to Achaemenid imperial functions are available in Demotic, Late Babylonian, Greek, Elamite, Old Persian, Phoenician and Aramaic, creating an interminable maze of potential semantic equivalences for a bewildering variety of political and social referents. For the Judaean community itself, the primary documents in the Hebrew Bible (notably Ezra–Nehemiah) have been the subject of decades of critical study over the authenticity of the imperial dispatches and memoranda contained in them, the possibility of first-person memoirs underlying the narratives, and the number of potential redactors of varying dates who have influenced the extant shape and slant of the narratives. While real progress has been made in the understanding of these works, there remain some particularly difficult issues.

From outside the Achaemenid world we do have descriptions of the empire and some of its peculiar dynamics, thanks to the ever-curious Greeks. Despite the helpfulness of the *Histories* of Herodotus or the *Anabasis* of Xenophon, it is essential to keep in mind Arnaldo Momigliano's cautionary note regarding this literary evidence:

> there was no effort to see what kept the empire together behind the administrative facade; and—most significantly—there was no attempt to understand how people lived under Persian rule (1979:150).

Many contemporary histories of the Achaemenid empire, following the example of such writers, still organize their presentation on the basis of individual monarchs as though the empire was simply the extension of the Great King's personality. In sum, it is simply not possible to construct an accurate understanding of the social context of the postexilic community solely on the basis of literary sources. Yet, this is precisely how most of the authors cited earlier have attempted to construct their various models of life in the postexilic community under the Persians.

Perhaps more central to the reconstruction of the aims of the Achaemenid empire is the near-absence of a body of social theory relating to imperial functions and the social mechanisms employed to facilitate those functions. In a recent effort to develop such a theory, Karl Kautzky could locate only five other authors who touched on this theoretical area (1982: 19). More symptomatic is the discussion by Duverger (1980) of the inability to formulate a comprehensive definition for this entity we call 'empire'. Without such a body of social theory on imperial efforts to shape the territories under imperial control, the evidence of particular aspects of Achaemenid practice remains just that, *particular* aspects of imperial practice. Drawing from an ecological analogy, without a clear definition of what is meant by the term 'forest' as an interrelated community of plants, we are equipped only to analyse and describe particular members of the community and not the community itself. In other words, it is not a failure to see the forest for the trees; we are not even aware that there is supposed to be anything beyond the particular trees we see.

In sum, the task with which I am concerned, describing the Achaemenid imperial context within which the Judaean community had its being, is permeated with pitfalls and traps. By necessity, any general assessment must be provisional until further analysis can be undertaken. Nonetheless, I wish to describe my own method for approaching this general subject, and to highlight four basic mechanisms that appear to be major influences on, and within, the Judaean community as a function of its being part of the Achaemenid empire.

With regard to the problem of a social theory for imperial systems, a few basic points need to be articulated at the outset. While an empire may begin as the extension of power over a territory, few empires continue to maintain themselves with such simple coercive relationships, owing to their inherent instability. Rather, once the coercive dominance of a foreign governmental entity is established, the empire seeks to put into effect a series of interrelated mechanisms designed to integrate a particular territory and its population into a mutually beneficial series of relationships with the imperial center (Eisenstadt 1963: 16; 1986: 3-4). These mechanisms insure the reproducibility of imperial possession of, and control over, the conquered territory. Moreover, such mechanisms, while they could take advantage of fixed forms of social relationships and/or groups, had to be constructed in such a manner as to be independent of such forms (Eisenstadt 1963: 24-25). In sum, an empire is more than coercive military and political structures, but coheres in the systematic employment of interrelated mechanisms independent of existing forms of social organization.

Coupled with the need for an effective social theory regarding imperial systems is the need for a check on such concepts. No empire was totally successful in creating an homogeneous rule over all its territories, and in the specific case of the Achaemenid empire, one of its strengths was its willingness to entertain a diversity of local governmental structures in a larger satrapal region (Frye 1984: 110). If a theorized mechanism possibly was employed in administering the postexilic community, in the absence of pertinent documentation, what assurance is there that such a mechanism was actually utilized? Also,

given the inherent bias of the Greek historiographic tradition toward
the Achaemenid empire, and the theological focus of the biblical
narratives, it is absolutely essential that any investigation of the
Achaemenid imperial context of the Judaean community actively
utilizes the evidence of the material culture of the Levant under
Achaemenid rule as an independent data source with a different
orientation. Indeed, as will hopefully become obvious in the following
analysis, it is the patterning of the postexilic community's material
remains when combined with a consciousness of the social dimensions
of imperial rule that provides the surest evidence of social
transformations under the Achaemenids.

Regrettably, the knowledge of the ceramic chronology for the
Persian period has not arrived at the level of refinement available for
other archaeological periods (Lapp 1970: 186-87; Stern 1982: 93-142
often uses unstratified materials to arrive at chronological conclusions,
thus raising serious questions over the dates he assigns to various
types). Consequently, it is currently impossible to reconstruct the
developmental stages of any social transformation. Thus in what
follows, it is necessary to speak in static terms, though doubtless there
were periods in which these conditions were in a formative stage.

Ruralization
The first imperial mechanism for consideration is a process of
ruralization, a deliberate decentralization of the population in the
former Judaean territories following the return of the exilic groups to
the district of Yehud. The primary, indeed, perhaps the only evidence
comes from archaeological survey data. In Fig. 1, the number of
settlements yielding ceramic materials of the Iron II and Persian (the
latter defined as post-587 to the conquest of Alexander) periods are
shown for the traditional territories of Benjamin, Ephraim and
Manasseh, and the Judaean desert as compared to the same data for
Judah. As can readily be seen, in all the surrounding regions there was
a pervasive and dramatic drop in the number of settlements from the
Iron II period to the Persian period, reflective of a process of
urbanization or depopulation. The Judaean territory is the only
exception to this pattern, showing a 25 per cent increase in the
number of settlements, the vast majority of which are small unwalled
villages (Kochavi 1972: 23).

Despite the striking nature of this unique trend in the Judaean territory, it is not *necessary* to conclude that this rural settlement pattern was the result of intentional imperial policy. However, two factors would lead one to conclude that this is a reasonable inference. First, there is the degree of discontinuity in these settlements when compared with the immediately prior period. If these rural settlements simply represented the rehabitation of traditional familial or tribal villages by a returning population, one would anticipate that approximately the same settlements would be inhabited as prior to the dispersal of the population. In addition, one would expect that even with an increase in population, few new settlements would be founded, as most of the population would orient toward the traditional settlements. However, of these settlements, 65 per cent had no occupation in the Iron II period (and thus are presumably not traditional 'hometowns' for any of the exiles), and 24 per cent represent new communities with no prior settlement at any period.

Region	Iron II	Persian
Benjamin and hill country of Ephraim	51	15
Ephraim and Manasseh	119	81
Judaean desert	27	2
Judah	27	34

(This data is a summary of the reports in Kochavi 1972)

Figure 1: Comparative Numbers of Settlements in Traditional Regions of Eretz-Israel

Secondly, there is the date of the foundation of these communities. While the uncertainties of the ceramic chronology for this period must be kept in mind, most of these settlements appear to have been founded by the end of sixth century BCE, that is, in the course of the return from Babylon of the first groups of exiles. In other words, the settlement pattern is fixed within the first generation of returned exiles and does not represent a chronological dispersal over the entire period of Persian rule. The fact that this pattern is set basically at one time and at the very point when, if the empire were to specify a particular form of settlement of Judaean territory, it would be as the first exiles are returning to the region, strongly suggests that the ruralization of Yehud was deliberate policy.

Several conditions regarding the specific relationship of Achaemenid imperial rule and the management of land tenure and settlement patterns are pertinent to this data. Most Near Eastern imperial systems worked on the premise of 'imperial domain' over conquered territories, and Dandamaev (1974) has demonstrated the existence of such concepts within Achaemenid policies. In general terms, imperial domain meant that land was alienable by the conquered population unless the empire chose to put it to other uses. Ultimately, the land was the empire's, and could be possessed or dispossessed at imperial whim. A classic example of this practice is the Eshmunezer inscription where the Achaemenid monarch gave the king of Sidon the city of Dor and portions of the Sharon Plain.

Also, the rural countryside possessed considerable significance for Achaemenid rule. Working from the somewhat better-documented Hellenistic period, Briant has argued that for both the Achaemenid and Hellenistic empires, the economics of the imperial systems were rooted in a tributary mode of production. In this economic structure, the rural countryside was instrumental in supplying a continual flow of tribute to the imperial centers in order to fuel the bureaucracy necessary for the administration of the imperial program (Briant 1975). Under this structure, the encouragement of ruralization in territories being newly settled would be perfectly comprehensible.

The existence of this form of settlement in Yehud raises a number of implications for the reconstruction of the social setting facing the postexilic community. The most apparent is the oft-repeated assumption that the returning exiles encountered considerable opposition from those who had moved onto the arable lands of Judah following the destruction of the kingdom (for example, Bright 1981: 366; Kippenberg 1978: 47; Petersen 1984: 29). If the empire was mandating the ruralization of the Judaean territory by the returning exiles, then a process of imperial domain was in effect, and those who had moved onto arable lands or by default had taken over former estates would have found themselves being reorganized along with the exiles. There would be no land claims by any group rooted in the notion of familial or tribal possession. *The presumption of a class*

*struggle between exiles and 'remainees' over land rights does not fit
the evidence of the pattern of these Persian period villages.*

Commercialization

A second imperial mechanism at work in the Judaean community in
the postexilic period was an increasingly commercialized economic
environment; that is, exchange relationships were established involving long-distance transport of goods. While the presence of foreign
merchants in Yehud receives brief notice in the biblical narratives
(Tyrian fishmongers in Neh. 13.16), there is ample archaeological
evidence to point toward extensive and protracted exchange relationships with the larger Mediterranean world.

A primary form of evidence is the presence of imported ceramics,
mainly of Athenian manufacture, that appear at virtually every
excavated site in Yehud. Places as diverse as Bethel (Kelso 1968: 38),
En-Gedi (Mazar and Dunayevsky 1967: 137-38), and Beth-Gubrin
(Clairmont 1954-55: 117) have all yielded Attic ware sherds, usually
of the fifth century BCE. In contrast to ruralization that seemed to be
targeted at Yehud, commercialization was widespread throughout the
Levant, as evidenced by the quality and quantity of imported Aegean
ceramics at a number of sites (Stern 1982: 137-41; see also the
summary in Auscher 1967).

This ceramic evidence for such expanding commercial activity has
received varying interpretations. For example, Clairmont claimed that
Aegean imports are only reflective of Phoenician mercantile activity
and are not indicative of direct trade between Athens and the various
Near Eastern cultures (1954-55: 90-91). On the other hand, in an
important analysis of some of this ceramic evidence, De Vries has
argued that the decorative themes and peculiar distribution of vessel
types revealed that these wares were being produced for a specifically
eastern market (De Vries 1977). Stern characteristically tries to steer
a middle course, claiming on the one hand that direct trade links with
the Aegean world did exist (1982: 140) but that the 'chief carriers' of
this trade were Phoenicians (1982: 236; see also Stern 1984a: 112).

Regardless of who actually controlled this trade, several factors
indicate that this commercial activity was a dominant element in the
economic life of the Levant in the Persian period. One factor is the
widening utilization of native ceramic jar types designed primarily as
containers for the transit of goods. While concentrated along the

Levantine coast, such jars have also been found within the Judaean territory (Stern 1982: 109-10), suggesting that some form of agrarian product (such as grains, wine, oil, etc.) was being exported. A second factor indicating the importance of this commercial activity in the postexilic world is the foundation of a number of new entrepots, such as Shiqmona (Elgavish 1968), located along the coast, whose entire existence was predicated on exchange with the Mediterranean trading sphere. In sum, whether controlled by Greeks, Phoenicians, or Palestinians, commercial activity with the rest of the Mediterranean region permeated the economic life of the postexilic community. There is considerable room for further research on this matter of Yehud's, and the Levant's, economic interaction with the West. De Vries and others have argued that the Attic wares found in the Levant indicate that the trade was carried on to obtain the vessels themselves, not for any specific contents, though this conclusion has yet to be demonstrated with any finality (De Vries 1977: 545). Moreover, many social historians of the Greek world have emphasized that the Greek city-states were based on import trade, not the exportation of manufactured goods (Austin and Vidal-Naquet 1977: 113). If the wide distribution of Attic wares in Yehud points to some sort of exchange relationship with the Aegean world, either direct or through intermediaries, there remains the unaddressed issue of just what Yehud was offering of marketable value for trade.

All this leads to some basic observations regarding Kippenberg's explanatory model for the development of class differentiation in the postexilic community. Part of his argument relies on the need for the payment of imperial taxes in silver coinage, a mechanism which he contends led to a growing gap between the 'haves' and the 'have-nots' (Kippenberg 1978: 49-53). However, the evidence from several areas of the Persian empire goes directly contrary to this assertion. For example, the textual evidence from Mesopotamia demonstrates that Achaemenid practices of utilizing a silver standard for collection of taxes simply followed neo-Babylonian precedents (Oppenheim 1985: 572). Moreover, as Frye and others have noted, taxes were usually paid in kind, the value of such payments being accounted for in monetary equivalents (Frye 1984: 116; Hallock 1985: 604-605; Tuplin 1987a: 141-42). Indeed, Achaemenid coinage was not viewed in modern terms, but was still weighed out as a convenient form of bullion (Oppenheim 1985: 578-79). In sum, the introduction of official monetary standards under the Persians did not lead to the partial monetary economy envisioned by Kippenberg.

While the introduction of official coinage may not have led to social differentiation within the postexilic community, the process of commercialization may well have. In general terms imperial systems encouraged commercialization within their territories for two reasons. First, taxation by means of road tariffs, taxes on central markets, and other revenues derived from the transport and exchange of goods provided lucrative sources of imperial income without requiring substantive imperial investments. In the specific case of the Achaemenid empire, several such revenue-generating schemes were employed (Frye 1984: 117). Secondly, it was in the interest of the empire to break down traditional patterns of economic self-sufficiency in favor of interdependent economic systems, engendering the perspective that economic well-being relied on continued allegiance to the empire (Eisenstadt 1963: 33). Moreover, it can be demonstrated that protracted exchange patterns stimulate specialized production on the part of the parties involved in the exchange as each seeks to maximize the viability of the relationship (Eisenstadt 1963: 33-34; Bates and Lee 1977).

It may be that some elements of the postexilic community saw the economic advantages to be gained by entering this commercialized imperial environment and accordingly tailored their agrarian activities to maximize their participation in commercial interaction. Others were unable to take as full an advantage of these opportunities, either because of alienation from the means of commerce or because of the inability to conform their production to marketable commodities. Those who did enter the commercial sphere would have been able to accumulate wealth and prestige, and it is difficult to reconstruct a means for the accumulation of wealth by some within the postexilic community apart from exchange with sources of wealth outside of the community. The commercialization of the Levant in general during the Persian period would certainly have had some impact on the social dynamics of Yehud, even if the particular means remain less than clear.

Militarization

A third mechanism at work in the postexilic community was a process of militarization. Throughout Yehud, surveys have revealed a number of distinctive fortresses of the Persian period, usually square in design and frequently measuring approximately 30 × 30 meters in size. In several publications, Stern has drawn attention to these forts, arguing that they constitute 'a clear line of border fortresses' delineating the boundaries of Yehud (Stern 1977: 20; see also Stern 1984b: 86; 1982: 250). This interpretation, however, disregards the geographic and chronological character of these military installations. For example, Stern regards Khirbet ez-Zawiyye as a border garrison to defend Yehud from the Edomites to the south (Stern 1984b: 86). In fact, Khirbet ez-Zawiyye is situated on the northern slope of the ridge it sits upon, and faces northward toward Yehud and away from the Edomites (Kochavi 1972: 51).

Forts of this same design and size have been found throughout the Levant, from the Palestinian coast to the Jordan Valley and down into the Negev. Where these structures have been excavated, they are all apparently founded in the mid-5th century BCE (for example, Cohen 1986; Derfler 1987; Porath 1974; Pritchard 1985: 60, 79-80). Additionally, these forts are all situated so as to control major trade routes throughout the Levantine region, and when the Yehud forts are plotted in relation to the road systems of the late Iron Age, it is apparent that they, too, are situated with reference to the roadways. Consequently it is clear that the fortresses in Yehud are part of a larger imperial strategic interest, and not an effort to defend imaginary borders (a full discussion of the archaeological and geographical setting of these garrisons appears in Hoglund 1989).

While the garrisoning of imperial troops along the *via maris* apparently took place early in the Persian period, as evidenced at sites like Tell el-Ḥesi (Doermann and Fargo 1985), the military presence of imperial troops throughout the Levant was greatly intensified in the mid-5th century (Blakely and Horton 1986). There is every reason to conclude that this process of militarization represents one aspect of the imperial response to an Athenian challenge for control of the eastern Mediterranean during the Second Egyptian Revolt (464–c.450 BCE). With equal certainty it can be concluded that there is no evidence for an abortive revolt by Megabyzos, the satrap of 'Across the River', an event alleged in a fictional account by the Greek writer Ctesias (Bigwood 1975: 18; a fuller argument against Ctesias's narrative may be found in Hoglund 1989), and sadly followed in completely uncritical fashion by Olmstead and a host of equally esteemed historians of Syria-Palestine (Olmstead 1931: 588 and 1948: 312-13; for example, see Noth 1960: 318; Bright 1981: 375; Herrmann 1981: 308; Ackroyd 1984: 154).

The appearance of these imperial garrisons during the mid-5th century carries with it a number of new social and economic conditions for the postexilic community. Garrisons within the Achaemenid empire were maintained by imperial military forces composed of various nationalities and ethnic groups (Frye 1984: 119-20; Bresciani 1984: 518-19; Tuplin 1987b: 219-22). The situation was presumably no different in Yehud, especially since ostraca from both Arad (Aharoni 1981: 176) and Beer-sheba (Aharoni 1973: 82) mention individuals with non-Hebrew names in connection with the Persian garrisons at those sites. Also, within the empire local populations were obligated to raise additional revenues through taxation to support such garrisons since, in the official rationale for these installations, the troops were present to 'protect' the imperial territories from outside enemies (Xenophon, *Cyropaedia* 7.5.69; Bresciani 1984: 514). Moreover, the relatively sudden appearance of these garrisons within Yehud suggests a new interest on the part of the central imperial authorities in the administration of the region.

The militarization of Yehud in the mid-5th century provides the context within which Nehemiah's epochal mission of 445 BCE took place. In the light of this pervasive imperial development in the Levant, it is essential that exegetes take seriously the military and strategic dimensions of Nehemiah's task. The order of his request for imperial supplies in Neh. 2.8 begins with an appeal for timber for the 'fortress of the Temple', that is, the garrison within Jerusalem's boundaries. The 'commander' (Hebrew *sar*) of the fortress is given shared responsibility for controlling entry into Jerusalem in Neh. 7.2. The rebuilding of the walls of Jerusalem was in itself a refortification of the urban center, enabling greater independence from imperial control. It is this fact that was ultimately the grounds for Nehemiah's opponents to charge him with plotting against the interests of the empire (Neh. 6.6-7). The opposition that Nehemiah encountered from the surrounding provincial authorities may indicate that the militarization of Jerusalem and the surrounding Judaean hill country carried with it new social and economic arrangements that other districts in the region viewed as potentially threatening to their own well-being.

Ethnic Collectivization

The fourth and final imperial mechanism for consideration is a process of forming collective economic units out of ethnically distinct groups. Unlike the previous mechanisms, this process of ethnic collectivization is difficult to reconstruct from the material culture of the postexilic period, though the biblical narratives, once set in their imperial context, strongly point in this direction.

One begins the consideration of this mechanism by reflecting on that long-established Near Eastern practice of deporting subject populations. As Kuhrt has reminded biblical scholarship, despite their frequent modern characterization as 'benevolent', the Persians, like the Assyrians and Babylonians before them, did employ wholesale deportation of populations when it suited their purposes (Kuhrt 1983: 94). Though it is traditional within biblical studies to focus on the initial step, the removal of a population (or a select portion) from its homeland, the practice entailed much more than this.

Once a population was under imperial coercion, it would be taken to a territory where additional population was needed to improve the productivity of the region. As the Assyrian commander promised the besieged inhabitants of Jerusalem during Hezekiah's abortive revolt, if they yielded to the empire they would be given a land like their own, 'a land of grain and wine, a land of bread and vineyards, a land of olive trees and honey' (2 Kgs 18.32). This resettlement process in a new region was not without its costs. The transplanted population was supplied with a territory to inhabit and till, along with military protection, provided the population remained loyal to the empire. Disloyalty carried with it the loss of the population's right of access to the land. A group in this situation is perhaps best termed a 'dependent population', since deprived of autonomous self-sufficiency in a homeland and prohibited from insuring its own territorial security, the population was dependent upon the empire for such necessities (Oded 1979: 46-48, 91-99).

The Persians, like their Assyrian and Babylonian predecessors, utilized deportations and the establishment of dependent populations as a means of maximizing the agrarian potential of the vast territory under their control (Briant 1981). The Achaemenid imperial system added a new element to this basic mechanism by restructuring some dependent communities into collective entities, often groupings of villages (Briant 1975: 176-77). As collectives, these groups were administered, taxed and regulated as a corporate unit. Moreover, there is evidence that the empire sought to maintain the administrative identity of such collectives by insuring their ethnic distinction from the surrounding populations by relegating them to specific enclaves. Herodotus, for example, records a group of Paeonians living as an ethnically separate, dependent community some fourteen years after their deportation by Darius I (*Histories* 5.15; 5.98). And among the Persepolis Fortification tablets, there are monthly rations issued to several different ethnic groups inhabiting small villages (Hallock 1969: 306-308 [PF 1054, 1055, 1056, 1060]).

When we turn to the biblical narratives of Ezra–Nehemiah, several elements in these materials appear to relate to this imperial mechanism of ethnic collectivization. For example, regarding the status of the postexilic community, it is clear that despite the positive recognition of Cyrus's role in the community's history (Ezra 1.1) and God's actions on Artaxerxes I (Ezra 6.22; Neh. 2.8), another perspective is given voice in the narratives. The community's status is termed one of 'bondage' (Ezra 9.8-9), and the community members are 'slaves' (Neh. 9.36). The rich yield of the land is not the community's, but the Achaemenid rulers' who also 'have power over our bodies and over our cattle at their whim' (Neh. 9.37). These sentiments are comprehensible if Yehud was a dependent community, allowed access to a land under imperial domain, but denied ultimate control over its own destiny.

The collective nature of the postexilic community appears to be reflected in the use of the expression 'the assembly of the Exile' (*qāhāl haggōlâ*), or sometimes shortened to simply 'the Exile' (as in Ezra 9.4; 10.6). The use of *qāhāl haggōlâ* is unique to Ezra–Nehemiah, and is suggestive of a corporate identity not definable by a territorial or political referent, since such referents also appear in the narratives (for example, Ezra 10.7; Neh. 5.1). More to the point is the curious context for this term—a community that has returned to its traditional homeland, re-established its national cult, and interpreted this process as the work of God in history continued to call itself the 'assembly of the Exile' many decades after the first groups returned from Babylon.

There was an economic dimension to this entity, a dimension connected to the issue of ethnic exclusion from the postexilic community. While both Ezra and Nehemiah are presented as forcibly opposing intermarriage, the penalties for refusing to divorce a spouse are never spelled out. However, in Ezra 10.8 several penalties are described for those who fail to attend an assembly called to deal with intermarriage, including the divestiture of the individual's moveable property by the *qāhāl* and exclusion from participation in the 'assembly of the Exile' (a more detailed analysis appears in Hoglund 1989).

Marriage, in any community, functions on a variety of levels, including an economic one. Marriage presumes some right of partial ownership by both parties of the legally defined relationship, and when a mixed marriage occurs, it raises the potential for the transfer of one ethnic group's property to the control of another. That this was more than a potential condition in the Achaemenid empire is amply illustrated in the multiple property settlements of the Mibtaḥiah archive from Elephantine. For this reason, the reformulation of laws governing marriage often accompanies legal changes in the economic relationships within an ethnically or religiously diverse community.

Both Ezra and Nehemiah, in their roles as imperial officials, opposed intermarriage. Their opposition was justified, not by an appeal to some pre-existing definition of the community instituted when the first exiles returned to the Judaean territory, but on a radically new interpretation of Mosaic tradition (Neh. 10.29). This new interpretation appears for the first time in Israel's experience in the mid-5th century setting of the missions of Ezra and Nehemiah (Cohen 1983).

Given the social dimensions of the issue of intermarriage and the economic penalties prescribed in Ezra 10 for ignoring the corporate concern over this issue, coupled with the importance of this matter for both Ezra and Nehemiah, it seems that there was more than religious purity at stake. Conceivably, the 'assembly of the Exile' was a collective, treated by the imperial bureaucracy as a unit. Membership in the assembly was contingent on one's ethnic identity as a 'Yehudian', or a 'Jew'. Loss of such ethnic distinction carried with it the possible diminution of collective privileges or property and subsequent impoverishment of the assembly.

The new rules against intermarriage promulgated, and presumably enforced, by Ezra and Nehemiah may be reflective of the larger imperial concerns over security in the region signaled by the intensive militarization of the entire Levant in the mid-5th century. As such, the effort to circumscribe the postexilic community ethnically may have been necessary to insure the continued physical survival of the socioeconomic cohesiveness of the 'assembly of the Exile'. If so, the insistence by imperial officials on the community's ethnic separation from surrounding groups generated a self-definition that has become the lasting legacy of the Achaemenid empire on the descendants of that community.

There are few who would question the assertion that the Second Temple period in general was a time of dramatic transformations for the remnant that carried the torch of Israel's pre-exilic traditions. Moreover, these transformations are commonly assumed to have had their origins, if not their primary impact, during the Persian period. The extent to which deliberate imperial policies contributed to these changes will remain obscured until students of the biblical corpus recognize the necessity of understanding both the theoretical concerns of imperial systems, and the actual applications of these concerns within the Judaean territories as revealed by the data derived from the material culture. The task of compiling this information and bringing it to bear upon the biblical materials is not an easy one, but it holds the promise of giving modern readers a clearer consciousness of the delicate interplay of social, economic and political forces within the biblical narratives.

BIBLIOGRAPHY

Ackroyd, P.
  1984   The Jewish Community in Palestine in the Persian Period. In Davies and
              Finkelstein 1984: 130-61.
Aharoni, Y.
  1973   *Beer-sheba*. I. *Excavations at Tel Beer-sheba, 1969-71 Seasons*. Tel Aviv
              University, Publications of the Institute of Archaeology, 2. Tel Aviv:
              Institute of Archaeology.
  1981   *Arad Inscriptions*. Jerusalem: Israel Exploration Society.
Auscher, D.
  1967   Les relations entre la Grèce et la Palestine avant la conquête d'Alexandre.
              VT 17: 9-30.
Austin, M. and P. Vidal-Naquet
  1977   *Economic and Social History of Ancient Greece: An Introduction*. Trans.
              and rev. M. Austin. Berkeley: University of California Press.
Bates, D. and S. Lee
  1977   The Role of Exchange in Productive Specialization. *American
              Anthropologist* 79: 824-41.

Bigwood, J.
1976   Ctesias' Account of the Revolt of Inarus. *Phoenix* 30: 1-25.
Blakely, J. and F. Horton
1986   South Palestinian Bes Vessels of the Persian Period. *Levant* 18: 111-19.
Bresciani, E.
1984   The Diaspora: Egypt, Persian Satrapy. In Davies and Finkelstein 1984: 358-72.
Briant, P.
1975   Villages et communautés villageoises d'Asie achéménide et hellénistique. *Journal for Economic and Social History of the Orient* 18: 165-88.
1981   Appareils d'état et développement des forces productives au moyen-orient ancien: le cas de l'empire achéménide. *La Pensée* (Feb.): 475-89.
Bright, J.
1981   *A History of Israel*. 3rd edn. Philadelphia: Westminster Press.
Clairmont, C.
1954/55   Greek Pottery from the Near East. *Berytus* 11:85-139.
Cohen, R.
1986   Solomon's Negev Defense Line Contained Three Fewer Fortresses. *BARev* 12/4: 40-45.
Cohen, S.
1983   From the Bible to the Talmud: The Prohibition of Intermarriage. *HAR* 7: 15-39.
Davies, W. and L. Finkelstein (eds.)
1984   *The Cambridge History of Judaism*. I. *Introduction, The Persian Period*. Cambridge: Cambridge University Press.
Derfler, S.
1987   The Persian Fortress of Naḥal Yattir and Its Relationship to the Regional Center of Tel Beersheva. Paper delivered at the ASOR Annual Meeting, December 5, 1987.
De Vries, K.
1977   Attic Pottery in the Achaemenid Empire. *AJA* 81: 544-48.
Doermann, R. and V. Fargo,
1985   Tell el-Ḥesi, 1983. *PEQ* 117: 1-24.
Dendamaev, M.
1974   The Domain-lands of Achaemenes in Babylonia. *Altorientalische Forschungen* 1: 123-27.
Duverger, M.
1980   Le concept d'empire. In M. Duverger (ed.), *Le concept d'empire*, 5-23. Paris: Presses Universitaires de France.
Eisenstadt, S.
1963   *The Political Systems of Empires*. New York: Free Press of Glencoe.
1986   *A Sociological Approach to Comparative Civilizations: The Development and Directions of a Research Program*. Jerusalem: Department of Sociology and Social Anthropology, Hebrew University.
Elgavish, J.
1968   *Archaeological Excavations at Shiqmona, Field Report No. 1: The Levels of the Persian Period*. Haifa: City Museum of Ancient Art [Hebrew].

70 *Second Temple Studies*

Frye, R.
1984   *The History of Ancient Iran*. Handbuch der Altertumswissenschaft, Abt. 3
          T. 7. Munich: Beck.
Gershevitch, I. (ed.)
1985   *The Cambridge History of Iran*. II. *The Median and Achaemenian Periods*.
          Cambridge: Cambridge University Press.
Hallock, R.
1969   *Persepolis Fortification Tablets*. Oriental Institute Publications, 92.
          Chicago: University of Chicago Press.
1985   The Evidence of the Persepolis Tablets. In Gershevitch 1985: 588-609.
Herrmann, S.
1981   *A History of Israel in Old Testament Times*. Rev. and enlarged edn.
          Philadelphia: Fortress Press.
Hoglund, K.
1986   'We Are in Great Distress': Reconstructing the Social Context of Ezra–
          Nehemiah. Paper delivered at the Society of Biblical Literature Annual
          Meeting, November 26, 1986.
1989   Achaemenid Imperial Administration in Syria-Palestine in the Mid-fifth
          Century and the Missions of Ezra and Nehemiah. PhD dissertation, Duke
          University.
Kautzky, K.
1982   *The Politics of Aristocratic Empires*. Chapel Hill: University of North
          Carolina Press.
Kelso, J.
1968   *The Excavation of Bethel (1934-1960)*. AASOR, 39. Cambridge, MA:
          American Schools of Oriental Research.
Kippenberg, H.
1978   *Religion und Klassenbildung im antiken Judäa*. SUNT, 14. Göttingen:
          Vandenhoeck & Ruprecht.
Kochavi, M. (ed.)
1972   *Judaea, Samaria, and the Golan: Archaeological Survey 1967-1968*.
          Jerusalem: The Survey of Israel [Hebrew].
Kreissig, H.
1973   *Die sozialökonomische Situation im Juda zur Achämenidenzeit*. Schriften
          zur Geschichte und Kultur des Alten Orients, 7. Berlin: Akademie Verlag.
1984   Eine beachtenswerte Theorie zur Organisation altvorderorientalischer
          Tempelgemeinden im Achämenidenreich. *Klio* 66: 35-39.
Kuhrt, A.
1983   The Cyrus Cylinder and Achaemenid Imperial Policy. *JSOT* 25: 83-97.
Lapp, P.
1970   The Pottery of Palestine in the Persian Period. In A. Kuschke and
          E. Kutsch (eds.), *Archäologie und Altes Testament*, 179-97. Tübingen:
          Mohr.
Mazar, B. and I. Dunayevsky
1967   En-Gedi: Fourth and Fifth Seasons of Excavations, Preliminary Report.
          IEJ 17: 133-43.

Momigliano, A.
1979   Persian Empire and Greek Freedom. In A. Ryan (ed.), *The Idea of Freedom: Essays in Honour of Isaiah Berlin*, 139-51. Oxford: Oxford University Press.

Noth, M.
1960   *The History of Israel*. 2nd edn. New York: Harper & Row.

Oded, B.
1979   *Mass Deportations and Deportees in the Neo-Assyrian Empire*. Wiesbaden: L. Reichert.

Olmstead, A.
1931   *History of Palestine and Syria to the Macedonian Conquest*. New York: Charles Scribner's Sons.
1948   *History of the Persian Empire*. Chicago: University of Chicago Press.

Oppenheim, A.
1985   The Babylonian Evidence of Achaemenian Rule in Mesopotamia. In Gershevitch 1985: 529-87.

Petersen, D.
1984   *Haggai and Zechariah 1-8: A Commentary*. OTL. Philadelphia: Westminster Press.

Porath, J.
1974   A Fortress of the Persian Period Above Ashdod. *Atiqot* 7: 43-55 [Hebrew Series].

Pritchard, J.
1985   *Tell es-Sa'idiyeh: Excavations on the Tell, 1964-1966*. University Museum Monograph, 60. Philadelphia: University Museum.

Schottroff, W.
1974   Zur Sozialgeschichte Israels in der Perserzeit. *Verkündigung und Forschung* 19/2: 46-66.

Stern, E.
1977   Yehud: The Vision and the Reality. *Cathedra* 4: 13-25.
1982   *Material Culture of the Land of the Bible in the Persian Period 538-332 BC*. Warminster: Aris & Phillips.
1984a   The Archaeology of Persian Palestine. In Davies and Finkelstein 1984: 88-114.
1984b   The Persian Empire and the Political and Social History of Palestine in the Persian Period. In Davies and Finkelstein 1984: 70-87.

Tuplin, C.
1987a   The Administration of the Achaemenid Empire. In I. Carradice (ed.), *Coinage and Administration in the Athenian and Achaemenid Empires*, 109-66. BAR International Series 343. Oxford: British Archaeological Reports.
1987b   Xenophon and the Garrisons of the Achaemenid Empire. *Archäologische Mitteilungen aus Iran* 20: 167-245.

Weinberg, J.
1973a   Das *beit 'abot* im 6-4 Jh. v.u.z.. *VT* 23: 400-14.
1973b   Probleme der sozialökonomischen Struktur Judäas vom 6. Jahrhundert

v.u.Z. bis zum 1. Jahrhundert u.Z. *Jahrbuch für Wirtschaftsgeschichte*: 237-51.

1976　　Die Agrarverhältnisse in der Bürger-Tempel-Gemeinde der Achämenidenzeit. In *Wirtschaft und Gesellschaft im alten Vorderasien*. Nachdruck aus den Acta Antiqua Academiae Scientiarum Hungaricae, 22. Budapest: Akademiai Kiado.

THE POLITICS OF EZRA:
SOCIOLOGICAL INDICATORS OF POSTEXILIC JUDAEAN SOCIETY

Daniel L. Smith

It is the purpose of this paper to survey briefly some textual and archaeological evidence from exilic–postexilic sources that can be subjected to sociological or anthropological analysis. It is hoped that sociological analysis may remove some of the mystery surrounding the Persian period of Jewish history. But before I consider some of the texts and arguments, let me clarify that I am limiting my comments to biblical texts whose chronological locations in the exilic period have been determined with a reasonable amount of scholarly consensus. That being the case, I have not considered the otherwise very provocative suggestions by Schmid, Thompson, and Van Seters that major sections of the 'J' narrative of the Pentateuch (Hexateuch?) are in fact postexilic.[1] I can say, however, that some of my own brief investigations on, for example, the history and provenance of institutions of confinement in the ancient Near East have also led me to have questions about the appearance of houses of confinement or bondage (בית משמר, בית אסרים; Gen. 40.3; 42.19; Judg. 16.21; etc.) in the stories of Joseph and Samson. There is little evidence before the exilic period that such forms of punishment existed in the monarchical period.[2] There are also the clearly impressive lexical parallels that were already noted by Rosenthal in 1895 with regard to the stories of

---

1.   On this, see John van Seters, *Abraham in History and Tradition* (Yale, 1975); H.H. Schmid, *Der sogenannte Jahwist* (Zurich, 1976); T.L. Thompson, *The Historicity of the Patriarchal Narratives* (Berlin, 1974). I have a brief discussion of this matter in my *The Religion of the Landless: A Sociology of the Babylonian Exile* (Bloomington, 1989), pp. 42-43.

2.   See *The Religion of the Landless*, pp. 171-74

74 Second Temple Studies

Daniel, Esther, and Joseph.[1] The evidence marshalled by van Seters and Schmid of a literary nature, and by Thompson of a historical nature, is more substantial and convincing.

I also refrain from extensive reference to the recent work on archaeological material, specifically coins and clay seals, from the Persian Period. This material has been subject to very important analyses by Avigad, Meshorer and most recently (to my knowledge) by Betylon.[2] These scholars are trying to reconstruct lists of leaders in the postexilic community up to the Hellenistic period. Finally, R. Zadok, N. Cohen, and M.D. Coogan have attempted to apply a more sophisticated methodology to the study of Hebrew onamastica in the 'Murashu Archives'—a line of investigation first suggested by S. Daiches in 1912.[3] Onomastic studies may be able to suggest social indicators of ethnicity by observing, for example, how frequently the 'pious' names of Haggai and Sabbtai appear. Porten, in his studies of the Elephantine Documents, has even made similar arguments about another foreign colony of Jews. But it seems a risky business to conclude, as Coogan attempts, that the frequency of names created, for example, from the root šlm is a possible reflection of the desire of the exilic/postexilic community for peace.[4] Socio logical analysis is under enough suspicion for building castles out of

1. L. Rosenthal, 'Die Josephgeschichte mit den Büchern Ester und Daniel verglichen', *ZAW* 15 (1895), pp. 274-84 and 'Nochmals der Vergleich Ester, Joseph-Daniel', *ZAW* 17 (1897), pp. 125-28. See also D. Redford, *A Study of the Biblical Story of Joseph (Gen. 37-50)* (Leiden: Brill, 1970).

2. See N. Avigad, 'Bullae and Seals from a Post-Exilic Judean Archive', *Qedem* 4 (1976), pp.1-36, and 'A New Class of Yehud Stamps', *IEJ* 7 (1957), pp. 146-53; Y. Meshorer, *Ancient Jewish Coinage. I. Persian Period through Hasmoneans* (New York, 1982); *idem*, 'Yehud, A Preliminary Study of the Provincial Coinage of Judea', in *Greek Numismatics and Archaeology. Essays in Honor of Margaret Thompson* (ed O. Markholm and N. Waggoner; Wetteren, 1979); J.W. Betylon, 'The Provincial Government of Persian Period Judea and the Yehud Coins', *JBL* 105 (1986), pp. 633-42.

3. S. Daiches, *The Jews in Babylonia in the Time of Ezra and Nehemiah according to Babylonian Inscriptions* (London, 1912); cf. R. Zadok, *The Jews in Babylonia during the Chaldean and Achaemenid Periods* (Haifa, 1979); N. Cohen, 'Jewish Names as Cultural Indicators in Antiquity', *JSJ* 7 (1976-77), pp. 97-128; M.D. Coogan, *West Semitic Personal Names in the Murashu Documents* (Chico, CA, 1976).

4. Coogan, *Personal Names*, p. 85.

sand, so I shall not add these observations to the ramparts.

Background to a Sociology of the Exilic Community

The most sociologically significant event is precisely the military defeat and mass deportation of Judaeans to a foreign environment composed of a dominant Babylonian population and other conquered peoples. In his very important study of mass deportation in the neo-Assyrian Empire (which includes observations about neo-Babylonian practice as well), Oded estimated that four and a half million people were forcibly moved by the neo-Assyrian war machine. The single largest deportation comprised some 208,000 taken from the Babylonian heartland to Assyrian territory in northern Mesopotamia.[1] Clearly, these numbers dwarf even the highest figures for the Judaean exile at the hand of the Babylonians, and caution us against hasty conclusions about what numbers could be 'too large to be credible'. According to 2 Kgs 24.14, 10,000 captives were taken, but in v. 16 the numbers of 'men of valour' (גבורי החיל) and 'craftsmen and smiths' (החרש והמסגר) are given as 7,000 and 1,000 respectively. Jeremiah gives three figures, usually considered to be more reliable, although the most common reason I have seen for this conclusion is simply that they do not appear to be rounded off, and look like accurately copied figures. Jer. 52.28 lists 3,023 in Nebuchadnezzar's seventh year, 832 in his eighteenth year and 745 in his twenty-third year (the last date and figure is a deportation not referred to elsewhere in the Bible). The total, 4,600, probably comprises mature men only, and perhaps only the most important men. So, if we multiply the figure of 4,600 by four, to take account of family members, we are already approaching a total of 20,000 exiles as a minimum number. Albright had estimated that Judah's population in the 8th century was approximately 250,000 and fell to 'roughly half that number' between 597-86.[2] In an unpublished doctoral dissertation on the exile, Heinrich Wurz suggested that Jeremiah's first figure of 3,023 represented exile from outside Jerusalem ('cities of Judah'), while the 7,000 of 2 Kgs

1. B. Oded, *Mass Deportations and Deportees in the Neo-Assyrian Empire* (Wiesbaden: Otto, Harrassowitz, 1979), pp. 20-21.
2. Quoted in S.S. Weinberg, 'Post-Exilic Palestine: An Archaeological Report', *Proceedings of the Israel Academy of Science and Humanities* 4 (1971), pp. 78ff.

Second Temple Studies

24.16 represent exiles from Jerusalem. The two figures together, suggests Wurz, may be the basis for the figure of 10,000 given in 2 Kgs 24.14.[1] Finally, let us keep in mind that the 'Golah List' of Ezra 2/Nehemiah 7 numbers the returning exiles at 42,360, again most likely only mature males of the *bᵉnê 'abôt*—a social structure that we will consider below. The numbers in the 'Golah List' obviously do not include those Jewish exiles who apparently liked the Persian political climate and remained behind.[2] But sociologically speaking, the only point that we need to make is that the exile community was certainly numerous enough to be settled in communities large enough to maintain a clear communal identity, and to have sufficient numbers to reproduce such traditional forms of self-governance as elders, heads of families, and gatherings of elders to hear, and in the case of Ezekiel 5 to watch, the prophets who continued to deliver their messages from God. On this evidence alone, a sociological picture begins to emerge of the exilic community; yet it is far from complete without further consideration of the actual circumstances of exile.

The exilic community survived both military defeat and mass deportation. The significance of both aspects is partially explained by what we now understand about the importance that ancient Near Eastern generals and rulers attached to the psychology, and indeed spirituality, of dominance.[3] This was clearly a major element in neo-Assyrian and neo-Babylonian warfare. neo-Assyrian tactics are famous for including the terrorism of public executions,[4] and public

1. H. Wurz, 'Die Wegführung der Juden durch König Nebukadnezzar II' (ThD dissertation, University of Vienna, 1958).

2. This reluctance of many Jews to return may have been connected with the political intentions of the Persians in authorizing the 'return'. If Jewish subjects loyal to the Persian crown were sent to provide a 'buffer' against the Greeks, then the less hearty may have chosen to avoid the assignment. See O. Margalith, 'The Political Role of Ezra as Persian Governor', *ZAW* 98 (1986), pp. 110-12 and J. Blenkinsopp, 'The Mission of Udjahorresnet and those of Ezra and Nehemiah', *JBL* 106 (1987), pp. 409-21.

3. See the following: M. Liverani, 'The Ideology of the Assyrian Empire', in *Power and Propaganda: A Symposium on Ancient Empires* (Mesopotamia, 7; Copenhagen, 1979), pp. 297-318; H. Spieckerman, *Juda unter Assur in der Sargonidenzeit* (Göttingen: Vandenhoeck & Ruprecht, 1982).

4. See H.W.F. Saggs, 'Assyrian Warfare in the Sargonid Period', *Iraq* 25 (1963), pp. 145-54.

addresses like the speech before the city gates during the siege of Jerusalem in Hezekiah's reign. Renaming captives or client rulers, as Nebuchadnezzar did in the case of Zedekiah (which recalls details in the stories of Daniel), erecting stone tributes to military prowess in the conquered territories, and displaying power in the home country, as well as publicly humiliating the gods and temples of conquered peoples, were all tactics familiar to neo-Babylonian rulers. The act of carrying away Temple furniture and treasures, but not destroying the objects (in cases of non-Jewish conquests including the act of carrying away cult statues[1]) reveals a psychological intention beyond simply looting. The spiritual morale of the exiles in the light of such daily reminders that they are not home, and that 'their god' appeared to have failed them, are theological problems to which the exilic prophets Deutero-Isaiah and Ezekiel clearly address themselves. Speculation on the time of deliverance is clearly an issue between Jeremiah and Hananiah (Jer. 26–29), a prophetic struggle that was known to the first exiles as well as those still in the land before the second major deportation.

Oded, on the basis of cuneiform texts, reliefs and administrative texts, suggested that in the neo-Assyrian practice the use of chains was rare, but also cited warnings to soldiers to protect the exiles from abuse. Exiles are depicted in Assyrian reliefs accompanied by animals and family members as well as carrying supplies. There is clear evidence that neo-Babylonian practice was similar. The Weidner Text, the only cuneiform document we have from Babylon that explicitly mentions Jehoiachin,[2] is a ration list that refers to the king's sons which (according to 2 Kings) he did not have when he first left Jerusalem. Secondly, we know that Jeremiah advised the exiles in the famous 'letter' of ch. 29, to let their sons and daughters marry, and we presume that he was not advocating mixed marriages. But Jer. 40.1 *does* refer to chains (cf. Nah. 3.10) and the oracles against Babylon in Jeremiah 50–51 condemn severity. This lends

1. See D.L. Weisberg, *Guild Structure and Political Allegiance in Early Achaemenid Mesopotamia* (Yale, 1967); M. Cogan, *Imperialism and Religion* (Chico, CA: Scholars Press, 1974), pp. 34-40.

2. E.F. Weidner, 'Jojachin, König von Juda, in Babylonischen Keilschrifttexten', in *Mélanges Syriens offerts à monsieur René Dussaud* (Paris, 1939), II, pp. 923-35.

some credibility to Josephus's later reference to exiles in chains.[1]
J.M. Wilkie believes that the treatment of the exiles was increasingly
severe, noting the references in Deutero-Isaiah, especially 42.22, but
including 40.2; 41.11-12; 42.7; 47.6; 49.9, 13, 24-26, which all seem
to refer to serious suffering and confinement.[2] Finally, one can
consider the term for 'yoke', עֹל. In only a minority of cases does עֹל
refer to working animals. In Isa. 10.27; 14.25 and notably 9.4, all
probably exilic–postexilic, there is a clear reference to forced labour
or confinement. In any case, עֹל as a reference to the conditions of
exile becomes common, in connection with 'those that have enslaved
you' in Ezek. 34.27, in Jer. 28.48, and Isa. 47.6. And certainly, one
must keep in mind the canonical legacy of Babylon as the archetypal
symbol for the oppressor, a symbol that remained viable even for
early Christian radicals who intended a reference to Rome (as in the
book of Revelation). Dandamaev has admittedly concluded that there
is no evidence for chattel slavery in this period,[3] but while this may
certainly be the case, there is other evidence that the need for the
concentration of captive populations in the Babylonian heartland was
as much for labour as for discouraging revolt in the defeated territories. In short, deportees may not have become slaves in the technical
or conceptual sense that we understand this term, especially under
the influence of images of post-Civil War American slavery, but
centralized work forces are another matter. McAdams's survey of
ancient settlements in the central flood plain of the Euphrates in 1981
led him to conclude that

> there is no doubt about the rapid, continued growth that got under way
> during, or perhaps even slightly before, the Neo-Babylonian Period. This
> is most simply shown by the rising number of sites. . . the total increases
> from 143 in the Middle Babylonian period to 182 in the Neo-Babylonian
> period, to 221 of Achaemenid date. . . the available documentary evidence
> suggests that large masses of people were involuntarily transferred as part

1.   Josephus, *Ant.* 10.100-103 (p. 212 in Loeb, VI).
2.   J.M. Wilkie, 'Nabonidus and the Later Jewish Exiles', *JTS* ns 2 (1951),
pp. 36-44.
3.   M. Dandamaev, 'Social Stratification in Babylonia, 7th to 4th Century B.C.',
in J. Harmatta and G. Komoroczy (eds.), *Wirtschaft und Gesellschaft im alten
Vorderasien* (Budapest, 1976), pp. 433-44.

of intensive Neo-Babylonian efforts to rehabilitate the central region of a domain that previously had suffered severely. . . [1]

Furthermore, we have cuneiform inscriptions suggesting that Nebuchadnezzar II did initiate building campaigns using labour from conquered territories. The following text refers explicitly to the lands including Palestine and the cedars of Lebanon:

> [after a long series of location names]. . . the lands of Hattim, from the upper sea to the lower sea, the land of Sumer and Akkad, the land between the two rivers. . . the rulers of the lands of Hattim across the Euphrates where the sun sets, whose rulers, at the bidding of Marduk my Lord, I conquered, and the mighty cedars of the mountain of Lebanon were brought to the city of Babylon, the whole of the races, peoples from far places, whom Marduk my Lord delivered to me, I put them to work on the building of Etemenanki, I imposed on them the brick-basket. [2]

Finally, we now have very interesting evidence to suggest that Jews were included in the armies of Nabonidus, and that the stories of the 'mad ruler' which contributed to our canonical Daniel may well have had their *Sitz im Leben* among the Jewish soldiers of the last neo-Babylonian ruler. [3]

The cumulative force of this evidence is that the Babylonian exile was no holiday as long as the Chaldaean rulers were in charge, however much conditions changed with the arrival of the Persians. [4] This background information, then, allows us to appreciate more fully the sociological factors in the formation of exilic–postexilic society.

1. R. McAdams, *Heartland of Cities. Surveys of Ancient Settlement and Land Use on the Central Floodplain of the Euphrates* (Chicago, 1981), p. 177.

2. F.H. Weissbach, *Das Hauptheiligtum des Marduk in Babylon* (Leipzig, 1938). I am not a cuneiformist, so I have checked my conclusion from this passage with a colleague at Oxford University. I am furthermore aware of the difficulty of concluding, on the basis of temple work, that work was performed on wider projects as well. I clarified, however, that this argument is speculative at this stage.

3. So says C.J. Gadd, 'The Harran Inscriptions of Nabonidus', *Anatolian Studies* 8 (1958), pp. 35-92; see also J.T. Milik, '"Prière de Nabonide" et autres écrits d'un cycle de Daniel, fragments de Qumrân 4', *RB* 63 (1956), pp. 407-15 and D.N. Freedman, 'The Prayer of Nabonidus', *BASOR* 145 (1957), pp. 31-32.

4. This would be against opinions such as the following: 'Once settled, however, it appears that they enjoyed considerable economic well-being. This may be gathered from Jeremiah's letter...' (I. Zeitlin, *Ancient Judaism* [Oxford: Polity Press, 1984], p. 259).

The Formation of a 'Culture of Resistance'

Survival of a disaster (as the exile was) requires the achievement of social solidarity. We need therefore to ask: are there indications of such a solidarity in the exilic community during and after the exile?[1] To begin with, the presence of elders gathering to consult the prophet Ezekiel is, as I have mentioned, significant. Elders acting as communal leaders are a very old institution in ancient Israelite society, although Rost has suggested that they grew less prominent with the increasing bureaucratic divisions associated with the Solomonic and post-Solomonic monarchy.[2] Their presence in Ezekiel, and their prominence in Ezra–Nehemiah, suggests self-government. The gathering at the city gate to hear cases was apparently replaced by gatherings in homes, as we find in Ezekiel. But beyond the presence of elders, there is considerable uncertainty about the precise nature of the communal leadership attested in the exilic literature. Among his fascinating studies of postexilic Judaean society, Weinberg has pointed out that the *bêt 'ābôt* emerged as one of the central characteristic components of the postexilic community.[3] Weinberg has shown that *bêt 'ābôt*, or simply *ābôt*, are characteristic of the postexilic literature, and further elucidates this social constituent of the postexilic, as opposed to pre-exilic, social formation. The most intriguing problem in relation to the *bêt 'ābôt* is the numbers of its members indicated by the 'Golah List'. This text, which appears in Ezra 2/Nehemiah 7 (as well as in 1 Esd. 5) is considered by many scholars to be a genuine indication of the exilic communal structure in the decades after the liberation by Cyrus. In his commentary on Ezra–Nehemiah, Rudolph argues for an early date for the list, based on his observations of the internal evidence in the list itself.[4] It appears to have a clear beginning and ending as a separate document, it is associated most clearly with Zerubbabel, and it refers to the banning of the family of Hakkoz from priestly functions, while elsewhere in Ezra–Nehemiah (Neh. 3.4, 21

---

1. See I. Eph'al, 'The Western Minorities in Babylonia in the 6th to 5th Centuries BC: Maintenance and Cohesion', *Orientalia* ns 47 (1978), pp. 74-90.
2. L. Rost, *Vorstufen zur Kirche und Synagoge im Alten Testament* (Stuttgart, 1938).
3. J. Weinberg, 'Das Beit-'Abot im 6-4 Jh. v.u.Z.', *VT* 23 (1973), pp. 400-14.
4. W. Rudolph, *Ezra und Nehemia* (Tübingen: Mohr, 1949), pp. 7-17.

and Ezra 8.33) Uriah, a son of Hakkoz, is clearly restored. Alt, and more recently Galling, have associated the list with the rebuilding of the Temple, which they date to approximately 525–520 or 18 years after the traditional date for the liberation by Cyrus in 538.[1] But what we are specifically interested in is the *bêt 'ābôt* in the Golah List, and most specifically, the numbers associated with them. Batten doubted the authenticity of the list, owing in part to his doubts about the large numbers for families when compared to the pre-exilic *bêt 'āb*. Agreeing with Meyer, who wrote before the turn of the century, Batten speculated that the confusion of the numbers may be associated with an apparent confusion between family names, and names of places of residence, indicated by the variation between the terms 'sons of' and 'residents of' (בני and אנשי).[2] But let us review briefly why the numbers of the constituent units appear to present a problem by considering work on pre-exilic forms. The classic exposition of pre-exilic Judaean society is given in Joshua 7. J. Scharbert,[3] considering this and other textual references to the 'House of the Father', believes that the *bêt 'āb*, a blood-related family of a living eldest male, could conceivably consist of four generations. On the basis of Judges 9, Scharbert calculated that Gideon's family could have been composed of as many as seventy adult males (although the Judges passage is problematic, since there is a clear emphasis on unusual circumstances and epic-sized events). Gottwald concluded that a single *bêt 'āb* could consist of 150 persons or more.[4] Finally, Stager's interesting archaeological contributions to this debate resulted in his postulation

---

1. See K. Galling, 'The "Gola-List" According to Ezra 2//Neh 7', *JBL* 70 (1971), pp. 149-58 and *Studien zur Geschichte Israels im persischen Zeitalter* (Tübingen: Mohr, 1964). Alt wanted to date the return to the era of Cambyses' invasion of Egypt, while Galling prefers a time when Darius had successfully put down the revolt of the self-proclaimed 'Nebuchadnezzar III'. At this time Zerubbabel could go to Darius and point out that the Jews remained loyal and deserved to be allowed to rebuild in Palestine.
2. L. Batten, *Ezra and Nehemiah* (ICC; Edinburgh: T. & T. Clark, 1913), pp. 71-81.
3. J. Scharbert, 'Beyt Ab als soziologische Grösse im Alten Testament', in W. Delsman, J. Peters and W. Romer (eds.), *Von Kanaan bis Kerala* (FS J. van der Ploeg; Berlin, 1972) pp. 213-38 .
4. N.K. Gottwald, *The Tribes of Yahweh. A Sociology of Liberated Israel* (New York: Orbis, 1979), pp. 285ff.

of a dwelling unit that was conceivably based on the *bêt 'āb*:

> it is likely that the spatially isolated clusters of dwellings—the compounds—housed the minimal *bêt 'āb*... if we assume that a honeycomb pattern prevailed at Raddana, i.e. an even distribution of contiguous, multiple family compounds throughout the settlement, there might have been 20 or more such households in the village, totalling ca. 200 persons under high fertility–low mortality conditions. But this projection may be too high... These upper estimates do not take into account the various phases of the family cycle within established multiple family households, the establishment of new nuclear households, and the dissolution of others... [1]

In any case, it is a long stretch between the numbers of the *bêt 'āb* familial unit in either Gottwald, Stager or Scharbert's estimates, and the numbers given for the postexilic *bêt 'ābôt*. As I have indicated, many scholars have suggested that the List itself is of dubious authority. Others have suggested that the *bêt 'ābôt* is simply a continuation of the pre-exilic *mišpāhôt*, rather than of the *bêt 'āb*.[2] But I think that Mowinckel was on the right track when he suggested that what we have are, in fact, fictionalized family units.[3] More recently, Robert Wilson suggested that genealogical reformation often reflects changed social circumstances,[4] and this is further illustrated in the anthropological work of Tait and Middleton.[5] If we follow this line of reasoning, then we must ask what kind of social circumstances would give rise to such a suggested 'rearrangement' of the basic familial unit in the exile?

I would like to submit three interrelated possibilities that are suggested by biblical texts. They are: (1) the creation of social solidarity in order to preserve the integrity of the social unit under

1. L. Stager, 'The Archaeology of the Family in Ancient Israel', *BASOR* 260 (1985), pp. 1-36 (22-23).

2. There is, however, a rather stubborn insistence in Numbers (P) to associate *bêt 'āb* with larger social units, and never with the *mišpāhôt*. The point is that the term *bêt 'ābôt* was coined to equate the solidarity of the smaller unit with the size of the larger unit.

3. S. Mowinckel, 'Die Listen', in *Studien zum Buch Esra–Nehemiah*, I (Oslo, 1964), pp. 62-162.

4. R. Wilson, *Genealogy and History in the Biblical World* (New Haven: Yale University Press, 1977).

5. D. Tait and J. Middleton, *Tribes Without Rulers* (London, 1958).

pressure, reflected in (2) the creation of a minority group conscious-ness characterized by social borders delimiting the 'inside' and 'outside' of the group, and also by concerns for purity and group integrity, and (3) the possible results of adaptation to organizational units imposed from outside the social group, perhaps in order to facilitate centrally assigned work duties. The last point is the most speculative, and I must admit that I am still in the process of formula-ting it. In outline, what I want to suggest is that a possible explanation of who ended up with what group among the exiles in a settlement or neighbourhood (which was then fictionalized into a familial unit) may have been partially determined by a central authority whose main interest was the organization of groups to provide work crews. This possibility was suggested to me not only by the evidence I have already cited for work among the neo-Babylonian captive populations, but also on at least two biblical precedents. First, Solomon's building programme required strict bureaucratic social organization (see 2 Chron. 7.17, relating Solomon's census to David's earlier census). Even though 1 Kgs 9.22 claims that Hebrews were not made workers (but cf. 1 Kgs 5.13), part of the revolt of Jeroboam after Solomon's death was fuelled by the complaints of Northerners with regard to the severity of the yoke imposed upon them by Solomon. Secondly, Nehemiah's work assignments (Neh. 3) in Jerusalem were centrally directed by crews provided by strictly recorded units, some of whom appeared to resemble the units of the Golah List while others were apparently guilds of specialized workers—although those two features may not have been exclusive. The frequency of the 'yoke' image, in relation to the exile itself, as well as Solomon's work assignments (1 Kgs 12.4), has already been alluded to. Finally, we have the (admittedly very late) passage from Josephus that the Jews were 'settled' by the Babylonians according to 'allotments'.[1]

We know, at any rate, that there was a tendency among the exiles to identify themselves as a special community, a kind of 'hibakusha' community (borrowing the term used by Japanese survivors of the atom bomb) with a marked particularism. Still in the time of Ezra, probably 70-90 years after the liberation of Cyrus, the community was using terms like 'children of the Golah', and 'the holy seed' (זרע קדש, בני הגלה, Ezra 9.2). The break-up of mixed marriages is

---

1. *Apion* 1.128-42 (Loeb, I), quoting Berossus.

only the most dramatic example among many others that we could
cite, of a community very much concerned with what the Norwegian
anthropologist Frederick Barth has called 'boundary maintenance' and
Bernard Siegel refers to as 'defense structuring'.[1] The break-up of
mixed marriages, as a sociological as well as theological phenomenon,
has caused a great deal of anxiety among scholars who anguish over
the theological implications of exclusivity.[2] This is to miss the point,
however. From the socio-psychological and anthropological work that
has been done on the sociology of refugee behaviour and the survival
of disaster, we know that the ability of a group to reconstruct its identity is essential to its survival in a foreign cultural environment. One
can cite, for example, the work of Elise Brenner, Richard Clemmer,
and Edward Spicer on American Indian cultural strategies for
survival. The wider anthropological work of Frederick Barth and
Nelson Graburn on strategies of boundary maintenance mechanisms
allows us to see that the social forms that a minority, exiled, or
refugee community creates can be the result not of a desperate attempt
to cling to pointless and antiquated traditions from a previous era or
homeland, but rather a creative construction of a 'culture of resistance' that preserves group solidarity and cultural identity.[3]

Seen in this way, the work of the priests (the Priestly revisers of the
Pentateuch, the prophet-priest Ezekiel and Ezra) is to be understood
in a new light. Indeed, Weinberg's argument that the priests emerged
as the leaders of the postexilic community would tend to be supported

1.   F. Barth, *Ethnic Groups and Boundaries. The Social Organization of Cultural Difference* (Bergen, 1969); B. Siegel, 'Defense Structuring and Environmental Stress', *AJS* 76 (1970-71), pp. 11-32.

2.   J.G. Vink bends over backwards to make Ezra 'ecumenical', but in doing so must deny the historicity of the break-up of marriages. See 'The Date and Origin of the Priestly Code in the Old Testament', *OS* 15 (1969), pp. 30-33.

3.   As a beginning see M. Barkun, *Disaster and the Millenium* (New Haven: Yale University Press, 1974); A. Wallace, 'Revitalization Movements', *American Anthropologist* 58 (1956), pp. 264-81; W. Peterson, 'A General Typology of Migration', *American Sociological Review* 23 (1958), pp. 256-65; E. Kunz, 'Exile and Resettlement: Refugee Theory', *International Migration Review* 15 (1981), pp. 42-51; H.B.M. Murphy, 'Flight and Resettlement: The Camps' (Geneva: UNESCO, 1955); L. Baskauskas, 'The Lithuanian Refugee Experience and Grief', *International Migration Review* 15 (1981), pp. 276-91; N. Graburn, *Ethnic and Tourist Arts Cultural Expressions from the Fourth World* (Berkeley: University of California Press, 1976) especially the Introduction.

in this way.[1] A sociological analysis would challenge the Wellhausean prejudice of a sacerdotal decline from prophetic majesty, by pointing to the creation of a culture of resistance by priests who faced very real political and social threats in a massive disaster like the Babylonian exile. Part of this culture, as Mary Douglas has so help-fully illustrated in her analysis of Leviticus,[2] is a concern for ritual purity that expresses, symbolically, the concern to preserve the integrity of the social group:

> When rituals express anxiety about the body's orifices, the sociological counterpart of this anxiety is a care to protect the political and cultural unity of a minority group. . .
> . . . pollution behaviour is the reaction which condemns any object or idea likely to confuse or contradict cherished classifications (pp. 36, 124).

The revision of the older priestly laws, wherein we see the main con-cern with the transfer of pollution, becomes a characteristic concern of the exilic period. This can be illustrated briefly by a consideration of the redactional history of a passage like Leviticus 11, and a brief consideration of the term בדל. In their form-critical studies of levitical priestly law, Elliger, Reventlow, Koch, and Rendtorff have proved that the priestly redactors of the exilic–postexilic period reworked older cultic traditions.[3] An example is Lev. 11.2-23, which appears in Deut. 14.1-20, suggesting an earlier source. But only Leviticus continues with detailed passages on the *transfer* of pollution in vv. 24-47. According to Elliger, vv. 46-47 are the final additions to this passage, a summary of the concerns of the entire passage.[4] The key term here is בדל, 'make a separation'. Apart from its strictly cultic uses, P employs this term to refer to separation between *peoples* (Num. 16.21; Lev. 20.24, 26). In Ezra–Nehemiah it applies always to the separation of the 'holy community' (Neh. 13.3)—from foreign

---

1. Weinberg, 'Das Beit-'Abot ', n. 4.
2. M. Douglas, *Purity and Danger* (New York: Proeger, 1966).
3. See K. Elliger, 'Sinn und Ursprung der priesterlichen Geschichtserzahlung', *Kleine Schriften* (München, 1966); H.G. Reventlow, *Das Heiligkeitsgesetz formgeschichtliche Untersucht* (WMANT; Berlin, 1961); K. Koch, *Die Priesterschrift von Ex. 25 bis Lev. 16: eine überlieferungsgeschichtliche und literarkritische Untersuchung* (Göttingen: Vandenhoeck & Ruprecht, 1959); R. Rendtorff, *Die Gesetz in der Priesterschrift* (Göttingen: Vandenhoeck & Ruprecht, 1963).
4. 'Sinn und Ursprung', pp. 148ff.

wives (Ezra 10.11), the *'am hā'āretz* (Ezra 9.1; Neh. 10.21) and the *gōy hā'āretz* (Ezra 6.21). This use of בדל is a key to discovering the Priestly theology of a 'culture of resistance' (or a 'spirituality of resistance) which uses a religious term to accomplish social ends, namely the avoidance of social 'pollution'.

To return to the *bêt 'ābōt*, and conclude this section on communal formation, I want to suggest that what has occurred in the expansion of the basic familial unit for pre-exilic society (the *bêt 'āb*) is a fictionalized family unit. Thus far I follow Mowinckel. But I want to argue further that this expansion is yet another example of creating a 'culture of resistance' by increasing the level of social solidarity and communal protection: the drawing inward in a fictionalized familial unit in response to the pressures of a hostile foreign environment, and the teaching of a theology of separation to protect boundaries. It is important to note that Frederick Barth's research revealed that the creation of 'boundary maintenance' social responses was not in any way mitigated by the mutual intelligibility of spoken languages or similarity of cultures.

The Return from Exile and Social Conflict with 'Outsiders'

One final area of investigation remains. If such a 'hibakusha' group as suggested above was created, we would expect to see evidence of that group's interaction with, or tensions with, those outside the group. There are a number of theories about just such tensions in the post-exilic community, which we can briefly summarize. It is here that we bring into our analysis an important sociological element which we have not mentioned before, namely those Jews who were not taken into exile and remained in the land.

As a starting point, I take Hag. 2.10-14. The debate surrounding this passage reveals many related issues. Inequality between those who were in an advantaged position at the restoration and those who were disadvantaged, conflict with the Samaritans, and the dispute about the rebuilding of the Temple, all rise from this particular passage. The final phrase is crucial:

> Haggai then spoke out, It is the same with this people, he said, the same with this nation as I see it—it is Yahweh who speaks—the same with everything they turn their hands to, and what they offer there is unclean. . .

The LXX adds the following curious phrase, part of which echoes Amos 5.10:

> because of their quickly won gains, they will suffer for their labours and you hated those dispensing justice at the city gate. . .

The context in Amos 5 is an oracle against economic injustice that is detrimental to the poor. Could this addition be here because of an early interpretation of this passage as referring to those repressing the poor of the 'Return'?

Rothstein had already argued in 1908[1] that this passage represents yet another example of the break between the postexilic Judaic community and the Samaritans, that is, those who began their syncretistic religion because of the exchange of populations by the Assyrian conquerors, as particularly reported in the annals of Sargon (*ANET*, p. 284). This view has many supporters including Rudolph, Koch, Elliger and Bowman.

Rothstein's original assumption that Hag. 2.10-14 refers to the Samaritan split is open to question. Coggins has convincingly shown that the identification of the group theoretically opposed to the Jerusalem Temple community as Samaritans involves a significant assumption about the Samaritan community itself. That is, Samaritanism could hardly be considered heathen or syncretistic if their main trait came to be precisely their *conservatism*:

> the basic features of Samaritan belief and practice have been seen to be very closely akin to those of Judaism, the differences being only of a kind which mark out the Samaritans as more conservative than Rabbinic Judaism came to be. One might well feel compelled to ask why Samaritans and Jews ever parted, and what distinguished them from each other. . .[2]

Commentators such as Morton Smith[3] still maintain that such an evolution is possible, although I think Coggins has given good reason to believe that this is unlikely. As Coggins concludes:

1. J.W. Rothstein, *Juden und Samaritaner* (Leipzig, 1908).
2. R.J. Coggins, *Samaritans and Jews. The Origins of Samaritanism Reconsidered* (Oxford, 1975), p. 138.
3. Morton Smith, *Palestinian Parties and Politics that Shaped the Old Testament* (New York: Columbia University Press, 1971), p. 92: 'the Samaritan cult on Mt Gerizim is probably a survival of one practiced during the Israelite monarchy. . . '

> The simple truth is. . .that there is no reference to the Samaritans in the
> Hebrew Old Testament. . .Samaritanism is part of that larger complex
> which constitutes the Judaism of the last pre-Christian centuries. . .
> (p. 163)

Another scholarly tradition, seen especially in the work of Mitchell, Bloomhardt, Welch, Ackroyd and May[1] sees Hag. 2.10-14 as a condemnation of the returning Jewish community itself in the same vein as the first chapter, and for the same reason: the building of the Temple. Ackroyd states: 'if their offerings are unclean—that is, unacceptable—then so is their whole life and condition'.[2] May has argued that there are many prophetic analogies both to the arguments of the prophets that the people can be unclean, and to the double use of the reference 'nation' and 'people', and thus does not accept that Haggai himself made any references to the separation of communities in Palestine by using the term 'remnant' (which he would say belongs to a later redactor under the influence of the Chronicler[3]). He continues, 'the burden of proof lies on those who presume [the reference to another people in 2.14] and would therefore make a distinction between "the people" in 2.14 and "this people" in 1.2, which refers to the Judean community'. May attempts to deal with the use together of עם and גוי. For this purpose, he cites other examples, from Isa. 1.4; 10.6; Exod. 33.13; and Ps. 33.12. None of these cases, however, employs the same construction as Haggai. There is a difficulty, of course, in the determination of technical use for עם and גוי. If the use is technical, May's references might be valid; but if not, there is little point in such argumentation, for the meaning of non-technical, common terms must surely be determined by the context in which they are used.

1. H.G. Mitchell, *Haggai and Zechariah* (ICC; Edinburgh: T. & T. Clark, 1912); P. Bloomhardt, 'The Poems of Haggai', *HUCA* 5 (1928), pp. 153-95; A.C. Welch, *Post-Exilic Judaism* (Edinburgh: T. & T. Clark, 1935); P.R. Ackroyd, *Exile and Restoration* (London: SCM Press, 1968); H.G. May, '"This People" and "This Nation" in Haggai', *VT* 18 (1968), pp. 190-97.

2. *Exile and Restoration*, p. 168. As we shall see, the claim that Israel was not yet holy without its Temple is an assumption based largely on Haggai, but even Haggai's earlier warning about the absence of the Temple was based on misfortunes such as drought and not fear of unatoned 'impurity'. Where, then, is this idea corroborated?

3. ' "This People" and "This Nation"', p. 192.

May believes, further, that Haggai's charge of Israelites being unclean is comparable with Isa. 64.56: 'we have all become like the one who is unclean'. But May then *contrasts* this with Isa. 52.1ff., where the threat of pollution comes from foreigners, specifically the Babylonians.[1] Why cannot this argument be reversed? I believe that Isaiah 52 *is* comparable with Hag. 2.10-14, but *contrasts* with Isa. 64.56, for the simple reason that the metaphorical language is about contact between two peoples or entities in Isaiah 52, and about a state of being in Isaiah 64. Hag. 2.10-14, too, involves a comparison of entities and peoples, and not a state of being. Thus May's arguments do not seem to counter the force of the analogy in Hag. 2.10-13, and his choice of 'contrasting' and 'comparative' passages appears arbitrary.

The symbolic logic of the metaphor is not usually given attention. The metaphor does *not* deal with a single entity that is in a particular 'state of being', that is, 'pure' or 'impure' (such as the passage quoted by May in Isa. 64.56). One would have expected a single substance or people in the metaphor if *one body* of people is meant here. The prophet, however, refers to two substances in relation to each other, *transferring purity or impurity from one to the other*. The metaphor refers to groups of actual people, for the text plainly makes the transition from v. 14: 'so it is with this people...'. There is a strain in the logic of the argument if one does not make this transition from 'relations between substances' to 'relations between peoples'. A separation between pure and impure groups (food or bodies) implies a schism between those that are addressed by Haggai, and those that are referred to as עם and גוי.

We have already made reference to the work of Mary Douglas, and her arguments are relevant here also, especially her assertion that purity fears relate to ritualistic anxiety about classification and protection of boundaries. Douglas's theory that pollution fears are related to societal strains, I submit, is strikingly confirmed by the passage we are considering, where the two themes of purity and group integrity are explicitly integrated. We must recall that the exile itself

---

1. In neither Isaiah passage are we in the context of the cult and the need for sacrifice to make the unclean people clean again. Indeed, in Isaiah, the point is that uncleanness comes from injustice, and thus the metaphor is yet another example of a prophetic anti-Temple polemic.

was frequently considered by Ezekiel to be the result of the 'pure' Jewish people allowing themselves to be defiled by 'Gentiles', thus again emphasizing the dangers of social intercourse—which is indeed often compared to sexual intercourse in the graphic language of prophecy. In Ezekiel 20, which highlights the theme of God's action 'for the sake of my name', defilement is declared a result of contact with enemy nations. The theme of exile as punishment for defilement is found in ch. 22 as well.

I thus believe that the grounds for seeing Hag. 2.10-14 as reflecting social conflict are strong, for whenever defilement was discussed in the context of defilement by inanimate and living things and enemy nations, these discussions were exilic or postexilic. But even if Haggai *is* referring to the Jewish community itself as those who are defiled, surely the reason cannot be that the Temple had not yet been built so as to remove pollution—which would have meant that pollution was unalterably universal at the destruction of the Temple! In Leviticus 18 and 20, where clear references to the exile are also contained in the postexilic punishment clauses, we find again warnings against defilement (Lev. 18.28; 28.22). Without a sociological analysis, such warnings seem to be foreign to the subjects of the chapters themselves, dealing as they do with familial relations.

However, if, as I believe, Haggai is referring to pollution from some group outside the community he is addressing, who is this group? A number of possibilities have already been suggested in the literature.

a. *Religious Conflict after the Exile*
This first view comes from those scholars who are a part of what E.W. Nicholson has referred to as the 'back-to-Wellhausen' movement. This tendency is seen in Morton Smith's *Palestinian Parties and Politics that Shaped the Old Testament* and Bernhard Lang's *Der Einzige Gott*.[1] Lang and Smith believe that Hosea is the most significant early exponent of the monotheistic theology of the 'Yahweh Alone Movement'. The significance of this background becomes clear when both Smith and Lang refer to a conflict between 'parties'. The 'Yahweh Alone Movement' continued as a minority which struggled

1. Translated into English as *Monotheism and the Prophetic Minority* (Sheffield: Almond Press, 1983).

against the continued syncretism all around, and among, the Jewish people. Citing the constant anti-idolatry messages of the prophets (Jer. 44.15ff.) through the exile (Ezek. 14.1ff.) and even into the Persian period (Zech 10.2; 13.2), Smith points out that it was a constant struggle in all periods. Lang, largely agreeing with this reading of 'monolatry' arising from a 'Yahweh Alone' sect, uses more direct sociological terms in describing it: 'Yahweh Alone worship can be understood as a crisis cult which continued beyond the actual crisis situation. Or, rather, the crisis situation is perceived as permanent...' (p. 23).

Thus, one can talk about a conflict between 'Yahweh Alonists' and 'Syncretists'. But does this line follow the division between 'exiles' and those left in Palestine during the exile? Smith does not think the matter is so simple. Syncretists were clearly among the exiles, if one interprets intermarriage of the priests in Ezra 10.18-28 as motivated by such a syncretistic mood (or at least not prevented by a monotheistic one). That economic interests were involved between the exiles as former landlords, and those *dallat hā-'āretz* left behind, is also suggested by Smith.[1] But Smith believes that the main lines of the religious conflict, noted in Hag. 2.10-19, refer to the religious community of those left in the land; namely, a large number of people who represent the kind of syncretistic worship which so horrified Ezekiel in his vision of his return to the Temple (Ezek 8.1ff.).

b. *Religious/Class Conflict in the Restoration*
Paul Hanson's *The Dawn of Apocalyptic*[2] approaches the problems of the beginning of apocalyptic literature in our period by positing social tensions between two groups during and after the exile. Early in Hanson's work, we see that he is drawing a distinction between those who dream visions and those who face the pragmatic decisions of power and control, especially with regard to the cult. This opposition, Hanson believes, continues from even earlier struggles between Zadokites and Levites, and Isa. 63.18 suggests that this conflict was 'internal' and therefore between rivals within the community of Israelites, not between Israelites and non-Israelites or 'syncretists'.

---

1. *Palestinian Parties and Politics*, pp. 55ff.
2. P.D. Hanson, *The Dawn of Apocalyptic* (Philadelphia: Fortress Press, 1975).

As far as the conflict between Zadokites and Levites is concerned, there is little doubt that the two groups fell out. But the evidence, especially the chronological evidence, can be interpreted in different ways. In his recent history of the priesthood, for example, Cody points out that, contrary to Hanson's interpretation, Ezekiel's restoration programme represents an important compromise between the two groups, with Levites gaining some advantages they did not previously have.[1] Furthermore, contrary to supporting exclusive claims of either Levite or Zadokite, Trito-Isaiah shows signs of a profound *generalization* of the priesthood; in 61.6 *all Israelites are priests to the rest of the world*. Moreover, 66.21 states that even some from foreign nations will be taken to be priests and levites. Cody notes that by the time of Ezra 8.2, both groups are called 'sons of Aaron'.

A different theory along similar lines, but with more attention to the formative nature of the exile itself, is provided by Hugo Mantel.[2] Mantel believes that the conflicts of the Hellenistic era between the Pharisees and Sadducees can be traced to the 6th and 5th centuries in conflicts along similar sociopolitical lines, and thus he works backwards into the time we are concerned with. Mantel's main sources are Ezra and Nehemiah. Ezra 7.25-26 interestingly implies that the law which Ezra metes out applies only to those who 'know the law' (having been taught?) and punishment also applies only to them. Who, then, are those to whom Ezra speaks? Precisely to that community, states Mantel, which called itself, again and again, the 'sons of the Golah'. Mantel thus develops the very interesting theory that the returned exiles formed an autonomous community on the strength of the social bonds created during the exile.

In conclusion, Mantel believes that the religion of the 'Sons of the Golah' was different from the Temple religion of the high priests. Certainly Neh. 10.55 refers to 'extra Laws'. What was the nature of this 'separate religion'? Mantel lists his suggested outline:

1.   there was an obligation for all to study Torah;
2.   authorities for interpretation were not priests;

1.   A. Cody, *A History of the Old Testament Priesthood* (Rome: Pontifical Biblical Institute, 1969), p. 166.
2.   H. Mantel, 'The Dichotomy of Judaism during the Second Temple', *HUCA* 44 (1973), pp. 56-87.

3. the beginnings of midrash—the Torah had to be 'interpreted' and translated;
4. prohibition of intermarriage beyond the merely priestly prohibitions of Exod. 34.16; Deut. 7.4
5. prohibition of even transport of goods on sabbath;
6. celebration of the Feast of Booths which transfers the piety of believing into the individual home;
7. rules that were not from the law of Moses (Neh. 10.55);
8. the institution of Nehemiah's reforms, and debt remissions.

c. *Class Conflict: Materialist Theories*
An important aspect of this argument is the potential conflict between the large population that remained behind, and the returning, old 'aristocracy', which provides the material for a 'class'-aligned conflict, as suggested by Janssen.[1] Janssen points to the cordial relationships between Jeremiah and the Babylonians, the latter apparently well aware of Jeremiah's implicitly pro-Babylonian stand. The possibility of a Jerusalemite 'fifth column' within the late pre-exilic community may have had some influence on the redistribution of the land among those left behind on the land (Jer. 40), although as 'workers' and not owners, a view taken also by Alt.[2] Janssen makes the interesting point that the threat of 'foreigners' possessing the lands and fields of Israelites is a common warning used by the prophets (Amos 5.11; Mic. 6.15; Jer. 5.17). In the situation of the exile, one might imagine the foreigners to be Babylonians, but Janssen refers to the internal conflict of Trito-Isaiah to suggest that the 'foreigners' were other Israelites, who were the 'new *'am-hā'āretz*' since they now possessed the land and enjoyed its fruit. This replacement policy is reflected in passages such as 1 Kgs 8.33 and Deut. 28.43 (which warns of others 'in your land'). Thus Hag. 2.10-14, 19) with its impure people, and the mention of robbers in Zech. 4.1-5; 5.11, all reflect the problem of loss of land by those in exile.

In selected biblical texts, we can see what a significant issue land possession was for the exiles:

1. E. Janssen, *Juda in der Exilszeit: Ein Beitrag zur Frage der Entstehung des Judentums* (FRLANT, 69; Göttingen: Vandenhoeck & Ruprecht, 1956), especially ch. 1, 'Die Bevorzugung der *Dallath Ha'Aretz* durch die Babylonier'.
2. A. Alt, 'Die Rolle Samarias bei der Entstehung des Judentums', in *Kleine Schriften zur Geschichte des Volkes Israel*, II (Munich, 1953), pp. 316-37.

The word of Yahweh was then addressed to me as follows, 'Son of man, your brothers, your kinsmen, the whole house of Israel, these are told by the citizens of Jerusalem, You have been sent away from Yahweh, it is to us that the land was given as our domain. Say therefore, The Lord Yahweh says this – Yes, I have sent them far away among the nations and I have dispersed them to foreign countries, and for a while I have been a sanctuary for them in the country to which they have gone. Then say, The Lord Yahweh says this: I will gather you together from the peoples. I will bring you all back from the countries where you have been scattered and will give you the land of Israel. They will come and will purge it of all the horrors and filthy practices. . . '(Ezek. 11.14-18).

The word of Yahweh was then addressed to me as follows, 'Son of man, the people living in those ruins in the land of Israel, say, Abraham was alone when he was given possession of this land, now we are many and we hold the country as our domain.

Very well, then, tell them, The Lord Yahweh says this: You eat blood (or 'you eat on the mountains') you raise your eyes to your idols, you shed blood, are you likely to keep possession of the land? You rely on your swords, you engage in filthy practices, you each commit adultery with your neighbours' wives: are you likely to retain possession of the land?' (Ezek. 33.23-27).

These sentiments should also be seen in the context of Jeremiah's redemption of family lands, after which he states, 'Fields and vineyards will once again be bought in this land' (32.6-15). On the basis of these texts, and the reported redistribution of lands of the people among the *dallat hā-'āretz*, it is obvious that one must consider the possible implications of land dispossession in relation to the return of the exiles. The most important theorists of class conflict working on this period are Joel Weinberg and Heinz Kreissig.[1] Kreissig's

1. J. Weinberg, 'Probleme der sozialökonomischen Struktur Judäas vom 6. Jahrhundert v.u.Z. bis zum 1. Jahrhundert v.u.Z. (Zu einigen wirtschaftshistorischen Untersuchungen von Heinz Kreissig)', *Jahrbuch für Wirtschaftsgeschichte* 1 (1973), pp. 237-51; H. Kreissig, *Die sozialökonomische Situation in Juda zur Achämenidenzeit* (Schriften zur Geschichte und Kultur des alten Orients, 7; Berlin, 1973) (see also B. Funck's review of Kreissig, 'Zur Bürger-Tempel Gemeinde im nachexilischen Juda', *Klio* 59 [1977], pp. 491-96); H. Kippenberg, *Religion und Klassenbildung im antiken Judäa. Eine religionssoziologische Studie zum Verhältnis von Tradition und gesellschaftlicher Entwicklung* (Göttingen: Vandenhoeck & Ruprecht, 1973). In a recent article comparing the reforms of Solon to Nehemiah, Yamauchi claims that this comparison was 'to his knowledge' suggested by Morton Smith. In fact, these three, Weinberg, Kippenberg, and Kreissig, as well as

monograph is more concerned with the Achaemenid period, but his ideas about formation and struggle in the Jewish community depend on his analysis of the pre-exilic period, specifically in relation to the monarchy. Kreissig's view is that monarchy in Israel approached a kind of despotic control by the king over massive proportions of the land, which was previously held in the ownership of the *mišpāḥôt*.[1] If this was the case, as Kreissig states, 'In terms of the agricultural forms of production in Judah, there could hardly have been a greater change from the Monarchical period' (p. 26).

Thus, the population of Judah may have struggled on as best they could after the conquest, in small settlements rather than the destroyed cities, as suggested by archaeological evidence, and others may have formed new main population centres, as implied by the movement of Gedaliah to Mizpah (Jer. 40). One could easily assume that many of these people did very well, creating a new 'upper class' on its own terms. Nehemiah's later efforts to repopulate Jerusalem as a centre of power may well reflect the diversified settlement pattern as a result of the destruction on exile. The rise of a new upper class answerable to the Babylonians is furthermore proved by the neo-Babylonian involvement in Gedaliah's resettlement, and Zedekiah's earlier appointment. In other words, *contra* Alt, there does not seem to be a need to posit a foreign aristocracy, in order for an 'upper class' to exist in the area of Palestine after the exile.

Kreissig raises two important points in his analysis. One is that an internal aristocracy existed within Palestine, and even possibly within the Golah community itself, as indicated by Ezra–Nehemiah. The other is that there is also a presence of an external aristocracy, indicated not only by the 'Samaritans' and their interest in Judaean affairs, but also implied by the intermarriage of the 'chief men and priests' (Ezra 9.1-3). Kreissig supposes that material motivation to regain land was high among the returning Jews from Mesopotamia, and fuelled the class conflict. There may be further hints about the

Eisenstadt, have considered such a comparison. See E. Yamauchi, 'Two Reformers Compared: Solon of Athens, and Nehemiah of Jerusalem', in G. Rendsburg (ed.), *The Bible World* (FS Cyrus Gordon; ed. G. Rendsburg, *et al.*; New York: Ktav, 1980), pp. 269-92.

1. See Gottwald's helpful analysis of social structure and function in *The Tribes of Yahweh*, pp. 237-344.

economic domination of an internal hierarchy or aristocracy. Kippenberg suggests that the Darian innovation of silver currency throughout the Persian empire, as reported by Herodotus (*Hist.* 111.89) may have brought about a growing impoverishment of farmers who had to produce more surplus to exchange for silver (explicitly mentioned in Nehemiah 5) to pay taxes, and thus encourage the independence of small families who could produce more surplus rather than be responsible for more mouths to feed. The failure of some families would then lead to debt-bondage, also reported in Nehemiah 5. Nehemiah's reforms thus sought to deal with this growing economic problem among the Golah community.

We see that there are many lines that inter-communal conflict could follow, and there is greater or lesser evidence for each of them. But the majority of arguments support the suggestion that the Sons of the Golah returned to Palestine only to find their land in the hands of a new *'am-hā'āretz* which may have included some of the Samaritan upper-class, or the previous 'fifth column' supported by Jeremiah and Gedaliah, or former debtors and even slaves. Some of the families were able to re-establish themselves quickly, by intermarriage or by independent means, such as those whom Haggai scolds for building their own homes before attending to the Temple. But the larger group created, whether intentionally or as a result of their ideology, a separate community with an independent ethos. This community also found itself engaged in a largely class-oriented conflict with both the aristocracy from the 'return', and those who were able to intermarry and regain their former status. Attention to social mechanisms for survival, however, cautions against a predominantly materialist basis for postexilic conflict. I would argue that the separate religious, social and structural development of the exiles, apart from those that stayed behind, was antagonized by the arguments over property and finances, but that such conflicts had many other causes as well. In any case, all the evidence, as we have seen, does not lead to an exclusively religious explanation, either[1].

---

1. I am now working on the problem of intermarriage in the Ezra–Nehemiah material. After consulting some of the contemporary literature on the sociology of cross-cultural, cross-racial and cross-class marriage, I again see that new questions must be asked about the implications of this problem for the self-consciousness of the postexilic 'Sons of the Golah', and the economic complications of intermarriage.

Summary

There is little doubt that Ezra's constant use of the exclusive terms regarding these 'sons of the Golah', the frequent exhortations against intermarriage with the impure of the land, thus possibly corrupting the 'pure seed', the priestly reforms (as seen in Lev. 11 and the discussion of בדל), and Nehemiah 5, all add up to a self-conscious community that is occupied with self-preservation, both as a pure community in a religious sense, and also in a material sense, a self-consciousness that continued at least two generations after the liberation of c. 520 BCE. Haggai's use of the term 'remnant of the people' has its sociological–theological parallel in Ezra's use of 'holy seed'—both terms that are important not only for those they include, but also for those they exclude. Social boundaries erected as a mechanism for survival led to conflicts upon returning to Palestine. The exiles formed a community not only self-consciously defined—a 'Hibakusha' community—a community of 'survivors' who returned to Palestine, but who also formulated a theology of innocence and purity against the defilement of those who remained behind complete with social structures to accommodate the communal solidarity requirements. To be troubled by what appears to be 'exclusivism' on the part of Haggai, or to feel a need to put an acceptable face on the separation of the marriages in Ezra–Nehemiah, is to misunderstand profoundly the nature of group solidarity and survival of minorities. Sociological literature, as we have seen, alerts the biblical exegete towards a possibility of a creative response to the threat of domination and minority existence. We are invited to look at Ezra–Nehemiah, Haggai, and others from an 'exilic consciousness', from the perspective of their worries and experiences in order to understand fully the 'politics of Ezra'.

RECONSTRUCTING HISTORY FROM THE BOOK OF EZRA

Lester L. Grabbe

For much of this century we can refer to a basic consensus about the books of Ezra and Nehemiah. Despite differences on matters of detail, it can be found in commentaries from Batten in 1913, through Rudolph, and on to the recent major commentaries of Williamson, Clines and Blenkinsopp.[1] Included in that consensus, apart from the Nehemiah memoir, is a basic agreement on the authenticity of the Aramaic documents of Ezra 4–7 and the Ezra source or memoir in Ezra 7–10 and Nehemiah 8. Many questions about editing and the like remain and have been much debated, but the consensus is demonstrated by the fact that one of the main points of dispute is the time of Ezra's mission.

However, that consensus has now been seriously challenged in the new commentary on Ezra by Gunneweg.[2] One can perhaps summarize

1. L.W. Batten, *A Critical and Exegetical Commentary on Ezra and Nehemiah* (ICC; Edinburgh: T. & T. Clark, 1913); W. Rudolph, *Esra und Nehemia*. III. *Esra* (HAT; Tübingen: Mohr [Paul Siebeck], 1949); D.J.A. Clines, *Ezra, Nehemiah, Esther* (CBC; London: Marshall, Morgan & Scott, 1984); H.G.M. Williamson, *Ezra, Nehemiah* (WBC; Waco, TX: Word Books, 1985); J. Blenkinsopp, *Ezra–Nehemiah* (OTL; London: SCM Press, 1988). This does not suggest that there have not been dissenting voices, though these have been mostly in German-language scholarship; see the review in L.C.H. Lebram, 'Die Traditionsgeschichte der Esragestalt und die Frage nach dem historischen Esra', in H. Sancisi-Weerdenburg (ed.), *Achaemenid History*. I. *Sources, Structures, and Synthesis* (Proceeding of the Groningen 1983 Achaemenid History Workshop; Leiden: Nederlands Instituut voor het Nabije Oosten, 1987), pp. 103-38, esp. 104-17. Cf. P.R. Ackroyd, 'Problems in the Handling of Biblical and Related Sources in the Achaemenid Period', in A. Kuhrt and H. Sancisi-Weerdenburg (eds.), *Achaemenid History*. III. *Method and Theory* (Proceedings of the London 1985 Achaemenid History Workshop; Leiden: Nederlands Instituut voor het Nabije Oosten, 1987), pp. 33-54.

2. A.H.J. Gunneweg, *Esra* (KAT; Gütersloh: Mohn, 1985); cf. also his

his conclusions as a return to a position not all that distant from C.C. Torrey's—a position long thought dead and buried by the prevailing consensus.[1]

Naturally one can debate these points at great length, but the problem has become acute to me because I am engaged in writing a history of the Jews in the Second Temple period.[2] In the original draft of my chapter on the Persian period, I happily trotted along behind the basic consensus and found that one of the weightiest problems was the order of Ezra and Nehemiah. Now after reading Gunneweg, I have become convinced that more fundamental questions must be asked and that my original cosy reconstruction should be consigned to the waste paper basket. In this paper, therefore, I go back to the basics of sources and ask where we should go from here.

The Problem of Sources

There are several possible sources for the book of Ezra: the list in Ezra 2 (= Neh. 7), the books of Haggai and Zechariah, an Aramaic narrative in Ezra 4–7, the Aramaic documents in Ezra 4–7, and the (Hebrew) 'Ezra Memoir' (EM) in Ezra 7–10. My aim here is to concentrate on the question of the Aramaic documents, although there is also a brief glance at the EM.

The Aramaic Documents

Most recent commentaries and OT introductions accept that the Aramaic documents are to be taken as basically authentic. Indeed, since Bickerman's well-known article, even the Hebrew proclamation

---

Nehemiah (KAT; Gütersloh: Mohn, 1987). Unfortunately Gunneweg's introduction is quite brief and most of his important assumptions and conclusions must be gleaned from the detailed commentary; however, a useful summary of some of these appears in his 'Zur Interpretation der Bücher Esra-Nehemiah: Zugleich ein Beitrag zur Methode der Exegese', in *Congress Volume, Vienna 1980* (VTSup, 32; Leiden: Brill, 1981), pp. 146-61.

1.   The main works of C.C. Torrey on the subject include *The Composition and Historical Value of Ezra–Nehemiah* (BZAW, 2; Giessen: Ricker, 1896) and *Ezra Studies* (1910; repr. New York: Ktav, 1970), edited with a Prolegomenon by W.F. Stinespring. This includes in revised form a series of articles which appeared in *AJSL* 23–25 (1906-1909).

2.   L.L. Grabbe, *Judaism from Cyrus to Hadrian: Sources, History, Synthesis* (Minneapolis, MN: Fortress Press, 1991).

of 1.2-4 has been widely accepted as genuine.[1] It has usually been asserted that Meyer and Schaeder demonstrated the authenticity of the Aramaic documents.[2] However, it should be noted that all Schaeder did was show that the problematic orthography *could have been* updated by scribes. As for Meyer's more detailed examination, it is quite short, and presented as answering objections. As we all know, it is not an easy matter to demonstrate authenticity, even where there is abundant comparative documentation, much less for the Persian period where at most a handful of comparable documents is available. The few extant include the Elephantine papyri (primarily Cowley nos. 30-32),[3] the Gadatas inscription and the recent trilingual from Xanthos.[4] Meyer had already made use of the Gadatas inscription in his comparison, and it is often cited in recent commentaries, but one should note that the authenticity of this too is still disputed.[5] Thus, one

1. E.J. Bickerman, 'The Edict of Cyrus in Ezra 1', in *Studies in Jewish and Christian History* (AGJU, 9; Leiden: Brill, 1976), I, pp. 72-108 (a partial revision of *JBL* 65 [1946], pp. 244-75). However, the authenticity of the decree has not been universally accepted; cf. Blenkinsopp, *Ezra–Nehemiah,* pp. 74-76.

2. E. Meyer, *Die Entstehung des Judenthums; eine historische Untersuchung* (Halle: Niemeyer, 1896; repr. Hildesheim: Olms, 1965); H.H. Schaeder, *Iranische Beiträge,* I (Schriften der Königsberger gelehrten Gesellschaft, 6. Jahr: Geistes-wissenschaftliche Kl., Heft 5; Halle: Niemeyer, 1930). For a recent assertion of this position, see G. Widengren, 'The Persian Period', in J. Hayes and J.M. Miller (eds.), *Israelite and Judaean History* (Philadelphia: Fortress Press, 1977), pp. 489-538 [496-99].

3. Collections of these include A.E. Cowley, *Aramaic Papyri of the Fifth Century BC* (Oxford: Clarendon Press, 1923; repr. Osnabrück: Otto Zeller, 1967) and E.G. Kraeling *The Brooklyn Museum Aramaic Papyri* (New Haven: Yale University Press, 1953). Other papyri from Egypt were published by G.R. Driver, *Aramaic Documents of the Fifth Century BC* (rev. edn; Oxford: Clarendon Press, 1957) and E. Bresciana and M. Kamil, 'Le lettere aramaiche di Hermopoli', *Atti della Accademia Nazionale dei Lincei* Series 8, vol. 12 (1965-66), pp. 358-428. The most recent edition of some of the more important Elephantine papyri is B. Porten and A. Yardeni, *Textbook of Aramaic Documents from Ancient Egypt. I. Letters* (Department of the History of the Jewish People, Texts and Studies for Students; Jerusalem: Hebrew University, 1986).

4. H. Metzger *et al., La stèle trilingue du Létôon* (Fouilles de Xanthos, VI; Institute français d'études anatoliennes; Paris: Klincksieck, 1979).

5. The two most recent studies are O. Hansen, 'The Purported Letter of Darius to Gadatas', *Rheinisches Museum* 129 (1986), pp. 95-96 (against its authenticity) and J. Wiesehöfer, 'Zur Frage der Echtheit des Dareios-Briefes an Gadatas', *Rheinisches Museum* 130 (1987), pp. 396-98 (in favor of it). Other studies include

of our few parallel documents is itself of uncertain value.

A detailed study of the Ezra documents in light of Persian inscriptions is beyond the scope of this paper, but one might object that their authenticity should be accepted unless reasons are found to doubt them. However, it is precisely because such reasons do exist that the question must be opened. First of all, the passages in question are often referred to as 'Aramaic documents', yet this is not as significant as the designation might suggest, since with the exception of 7.12-26 these are not Aramaic entities imbedded in a Hebrew narrative, but sections of an Aramaic narrative. If these *are* archive sources used by the author of Ezra, why are they not inserted in the appropriate place in his Hebrew narrative?[1] Similarly, why is the supposed Persian decree (1.2-4) within a Hebrew narrative itself in Hebrew?

Secondly, even many of those who accept the Aramaic documents as genuine also find editorial intervention—even a good deal of editorial intervention—within them.[2] The significance of this seems too frequently overlooked. We all know that editorial work can completely change the message of a passage, even when the changes are small. And from information of later times, doctoring of documents to make them more pro-Jewish seems to have been a minor cottage industry.[3] Thus, even if the documents are genuine in their

the translation and study by W. Brandstein and M. Mayrhofer (*Handbuch des Altpersischen* [Wiesbaden: Otto Harrassowitz, 1964], pp. 91-98), which assumes its genuineness, and M. van den Hout, 'Studies in Early Greek Letter-Writing', *Mnemosyne* 2 (4th series) (1949), pp. 19-41, 138-53, esp. 144-45 (against its authenticity).

1. It is because of such questions that many scholars have postulated an Aramaic source used by the author which already contained the documents as a part of it (e.g. Rudolph, *Esra*, pp. xxiii, 47; Blenkinsopp, *Ezra-Nehemiah*, pp. 116-17). Williamson (*Ezra-Nehemiah*, pp. xxiii-iv) thinks the author of Ezra 1–6 had the documents before him but himself wrote the Aramaic connecting passages—a less convincing hypothesis. Nevertheless, under either supposition the basic problem remains.

2. E.g. Blenkinsopp, *Ezra-Nehemiah*, pp. 119-23, 126-27

3. A good example of this can be found in Josephus, *Ant.* 19.5.2.280-285, who gives a decree of Claudius about Jewish citizenship in Alexandria. An original decree of Claudius has now been found among the papyri which gives a rather different picture; see V. Tcherikover, A. Fuks and M. Stern, *Corpus Papyrorum Iudaicarum* (3 vols.; Cambridge, MA: Harvard University Press and Jerusalem: Magnes Press, 1957-64), II, pp. 36-60. It is now generally agreed that Josephus did indeed have a genuine decree of Claudius (whether the extant one or one similar), but

original form, we cannot assume that their present form still conveys their original message.

Thirdly, and most importantly, some of the documents have a large element of Jewish theology in them. To take one example: it has long been recognized that 7.12-26 has a number of Jewish elements and concerns which would not normally be expected in such a document.[1] These have been defended by the argument that the official commissioning of Ezra was written by Ezra the scribe himself and that, therefore, the Jewish coloring is hardly surprising.[2] We might admit this as a possibility, but such a thesis can easily cover a multitude of scribal sins. Indeed, it is difficult to falsify a hypothesis like this, which makes it somewhat useless as an argument—not to mention the circular reasoning of using the existence of Ezra and his office to demonstrate the originality of the very document from which the information comes!

The Ezra Memoir

I make only a brief comment here. The existence of such a source has been extensively debated with, as so often with source theories, no consensus. What bothers me about the situation is that so much seems to be dependent on an *a priori* tendency on the part of the scholar. Gunneweg dismisses such a source with little discussion.[3] On the other side, those who accept it also often do so with little discussion, usually being content with a brief answer to objections.[4] One replies to

it has sufficient Jewish reworkings to change the meaning basically to its opposite (V. Tcherikover, *Hellenistic Civilization and the Jews* [New York: Jewish Publication Society, 1959], pp. 409-15; D.R. Schwartz, *Agrippa I: The Last King of Judaea* [TSAJ, 23; Tübingen: Mohr {Paul Siebeck}, 1990], pp. 99-106). The attempt by A. Kasher (*The Jews in Hellenistic and Roman Egypt: The Struggle for Equal Rights* [TSAJ, 7; Tübingen: Mohr {Paul Siebeck}, 1985], pp. 262-309) to refute this cannot be considered successful; see the discussion in Schwartz.

1. In addition to Gunneweg (*Esra*, pp. 119-41) on the passage, see Lebram, 'Traditionsgeschichte', pp. 117-25.

2. This is the basic defense of the document used by Meyer, *Entstehung*, pp. 63-65.

3. *Esra*, p. 141.

4. An exception is Williamson, who devotes several pages to the question in his introduction (*Ezra, Nehemiah*, pp. xxviii-xxxii), though much of this is only a survey of scholarship. His actual defense comprises only one long paragraph, though other details are found in the commentary itself.

objections only after having decided the answer already, but why come to the assumption of an EM in the first place? Even more basic, though, seem the remarkable parallels between the activities of Ezra and those of Nehemiah.[1] These go far beyond the situation over mixed marriages which occurs twice (Ezra 9–10; Neh. 9–10, 13). For the historian this subject is too important to be left to a few comments in a commentary and a very subjective decision either for or against. An even-handed evaluation of the question would be very much in order.

Where Do We Go from Here?

The picture so far given has been somewhat negative. This is not to suggest that the consensus is necessarily wrong, but to emphasize the need for a fundamental reassessment of the question of sources. If we do not accept the Aramaic documents and the EM, what sources do we have for the history of the Jews in the Persian period?

All is not lost. Even Gunneweg has accepted the originality and value of the Nehemiah memorial. Even recognizing its one-sided and self-serving nature,[2] we still find it an important and data-rich account. There is also other material by common consent from the Persian period: Isaiah 56–66 may have interesting things to tell us, though the interpretation of it is is both difficult and controversial.[3]

1. Cf. M. Noth, *The Chronicler's History* (JSOTSup, 50; trans. and ed. H.G.M. Williamson; Sheffield: JSOT Press, 1987), pp. 62-66; U. Kellermann, *Nehemiah: Quellen, Überlieferung und Geschichte* (BZAW, 102; Berlin: Töpelmann, 1967), pp. 56-69; Lebram, 'Traditionsgeschichte', pp. 120-22; W.T. In der Smitten, *Esra: Quellen, Überlieferung und Geschichte* (SSN, 15; Assen: Van Gorcum, 1973), pp. 63-66.
2. Cf. D.J.A. Clines, 'The Nehemiah Memoir: The Perils of Autobiography', in *What Does Eve Do To Help? And Other Readerly Questions to the Old Testament* (JSOTSup, 94; Sheffield: JSOT Press, 1990), pp. 124-64.
3. Cf. J. Blenkinsopp, 'Interpretation and the Tendency to Sectarianism', in E.P. Sanders *et al.* (eds.), *Jewish and Christian Self-Definition. II. Aspects of Judaism in the Graeco-Roman Period* (London: SCM Press, 1981), pp. 1-26; *idem*, 'A Jewish Sect of the Persian Period', *CBQ* 52 (1990), pp. 5-20; A. Rofé, 'Isaiah 66.1-4: Judean Sects in the Persian Period as Viewed by Trito-Isaiah', in A. Kort and S. Morschauser (eds.), *Biblical and Related Studies Presented to Samuel Iwry* (Winona Lake, IN: Eisenbrauns, 1985), pp. 205-17; P.D. Hanson, *The Dawn of Apocalyptic* (Philadelphia: Fortress Press, 1975). On Hanson's thesis see especially the review article by R.P. Carroll, 'Twilight of Prophecy or Dawn of Apocalyptic?', *JSOT* 14 (1979), pp. 3-35; cf. also L.L. Grabbe, 'The Social Setting of Early Jewish

Better are Haggai and Zechariah. Indeed, if the Meyers's recent dating of the books to before the completion of the Second Temple (c. 515 BCE) is correct, these would also be extremely important contemporary sources.[1] However, even though few reviews have yet appeared, one suspects that specialists will not fall over themselves in a scramble to embrace this new thesis.

But perhaps we are rightly being forced back onto the original data from the Persian period itself: the Persian inscriptions, papyri and coins, and the archaeology. Although many of the papyri have been long known, there is recent new inscriptional material, as well as a useful archaeological survey.[2] When we look back at the consensus, we see a tendency to fit the inscriptional and archaeological data into the picture given by the book of Ezra. While this is understandable, perhaps the time has come to let the non-biblical sources speak more loudly in their own right and not have their voices swallowed up by the cacophony of the biblical literature. It is too easy to find a convenient background in Persian history for one's particular interpretation of the biblical data.[3]

Apocalypticism', *JSP* 4 (1989), pp. 32-33.

 1. E. and C. Meyers, *Haggai, Zechariah 1-8* (AB; Garden City, NY: Doubleday, 1987), p. xlvii.

 2. For the archaeology, see E. Stern, *Material Culture of the Land of the Bible in the Persian Period 538-332 BC* (Jerusalem: Israel Exploration Society and Warminster: Aris & Phillips, 1982); H. Weippert, *Palästina in vorhellenistischer Zeit* (HdA, Vorderasien 2.1; Munich: Beck, 1988), pp. 682-728. For the coins, see Y. Meshorer, *Ancient Jewish Coinage. I. Persian Period through Hasmonaeans* (New York: Amphora, 1982); L. Mildenberg, '*Yehud* Münzen', in Weippert, *Palästina*, pp. 721-28. For the papyri and inscriptions, see p. 78 nn. 2-4 above. For a guide to the published cuneiform texts from the Achaemenid period, see A.L. Oppenheim, 'The Babylonian Evidence of Achaemenian Rule in Mesopotamia', in *Cambridge History of Iran* (Cambridge: Cambridge University Press, 1985), II, pp. 529-87; A. Kuhrt, 'Babylonia from Cyrus to Xerxes', in *CAH* (2nd edn; Cambridge: Cambridge University Press, 1988), IV, pp. 112-38, and especially the accompanying bibliographies.

 3. A good example of this is the recent article by O. Margalith, 'The Political Role of Ezra as Persian Governor', *ZAW* 98 (1986), pp. 110-12 which 'proves' that Ezra came to Jerusalem in 458 BCE because this date fits the situation in the Persian empire. This argument overlooks the fact that one can find similar evidence for a dating in 398 BCE or many other potential dates for Ezra, if one is so inclined—not to mention the fact that Ezra is never called 'governor' nor is any political role assigned to him in the biblical narrative.

Conclusions

Of course, all the foregoing points are no doubt ripe for debate; indeed, few of them are really new, but most can be found in the literature and commentaries over many decades. What is surprising, however, is the extent to which the dominance of the consensus has prevented their full impact from being felt. Dare one say that their appearance primarily in German-language scholarship has been a part of the reason? Whatever the reason, fuller consideration of these arguments has led me to revise my thinking on the subject. A reading of Gunneweg demonstrates an important truth: *there is nothing like the impact of a sustained skeptical argument from a true believer.*

Thus, two conclusions have forced themselves upon me. First, the question of the supposed Persian documents in Ezra 1–7 is in urgent need of re-evaluation, and their authenticity should no longer be taken for granted as is currently the custom, at least in English-speaking scholarship. Secondly, we should cease to write the history of Judah in the first part of the Persian period by lightly paraphrasing the book of Ezra, with the occasional Elephantine papyrus tossed in plus a spoonful or two of Olmstead for leavening.[1]

There may be protests at this seemingly radical stance, and such epithets as 'hypercritical' and 'unduly skeptical' may be forthcoming, not to mention the anguished question, 'How can we write an history of the Jews in the Achaemenid period with such an approach?' As to the former: I have not prejudged the answer to the question. We *may* end up agreeing with the consensus, but such a conclusion can be reached only after a more thorough debate than has occurred in recent years. As to the latter problem, historians have to use what data there are and be content with them. After all, scholars today generally accept that we cannot use Joshua to reconstruct the settlement of Israel in the land, even though this has meant drawing back from any narrative history of that period. Similarly, if some of our few sources for the history of Israel in the Persian period turn out to be untrust-

---

1. This is not to suggest that all those whom I have labeled as supporters of the consensus have necessarily done this, since many of them are good critical scholars. However, there are recent clear examples of just such an attempt to write history, J. Bright (*A History of Israel* [3rd edn; Philadelphia: Westminster Press, 1980], pp. 373-402) being especially obvious.

worthy, no amount of arbitrary traditionalism will change the situation. The job of a modern historian is to write history, not invent it.

This paper was originally read at the SBL International Meeting, Vienna, August 1990. I thank the British Academy for financial assistance in attending that meeting.

LITERATURE AND SOCIETY

Textual Strategies and Ideology in the Second Temple Period

Robert P. Carroll

> To say the very least, historiography as well as fiction is a house of a million windows, but all giving on the real world.
> (Meir Sternberg)[1]

> The reconstruction of the past through literature is almost always misleading in terms of historical objectivity. Literary truth is one thing, historical truth another. But, although it is full of fabrication—or for that very reason—literature presents us with a side of history which cannot be found in history books. For literature does not lie gratuitously. Its deceits, devices, and hyperbole all serve to express those deep-seated and disturbing truths which only come to light in this oblique way.
> (Mario Vargas Llosa)[2]

The Hebrew Bible is the product of the Second Temple period. This ought to be an uncontentious statement, but I imagine some unreconstructed biblical scholars may wish to contest it in favour of a First Temple period origin for the Bible with some appendices from the time of the Second Temple. While I can see that there *may* be something to be said for the view that the Bible contains fragments of material from before the collapse of the temple in the sixth century, the claim that the Bible *as we know it* (i.e. the fully redacted final form of the various books constituting it) comes from the Second Temple period seems to me to be quite ungainsayable.[3] That claim of

1. *The Poetics of Biblical Narrative: Ideological Literature and the Drama of Reading* (Bloomington, IN: Indiana University Press, 1985), p. 28. His section on 'Fiction and History' (pp. 23-35) is very germane to this paper; as also is H.N. Schneidau, *Sacred Discontent: The Bible and Western Tradition* (Berkeley: University of California Press, 1977).
2. 'The Power of Lies', *Encounter* 69/5 (1987), pp. 28-30; citing from p. 28.
3. Space prevents argumentation for this viewpoint, but once biblical studies

course solves no real problems but leaves open to discussion all the specific issues about the relation of texts to their mooted socio-historical backgrounds and the discernment of the ideological holdings of which the texts are products. So little is known about the social and historical background of the early Second Temple period that many scholars have recourse to ideologically constructed social structures often drawn from the classical world.[1] Applied to the biblical world, such theories entail fundamental problems of a technical and methodological nature.[2] While I refuse to privilege theory or ideology in its application to biblical texts—Fredric Jameson notwith-standing![3]—this paper is not the place to produce a critique of ideological analysis of the Second Temple period. I wish only to

enters the twentieth century and gets its act together this may become the consensus view. In the meantime see G. Garbini, *History and Ideology in Ancient Israel* (London: SCM Press, 1988) and M. Smith, *Palestinian Parties and Politics that Shaped the Old Testament* (London: SCM Press, 1987).

1.   This technique involves using what is sometimes called 'proxy-data'. See H. Kressig, *Wirtschaft und Gesellschaft im Seleukidenreich: Die Eigentums- und die Abhängigkeitsverhältnisse* (Schriften zur Geschichte und Kultur der Antike, 16; Berlin: Akademie Verlag, 1978); and especially the work of H.G. Kippenberg, *Religion und Klassenbildung im antiken Judäa: eine religionssoziologische Studie zum Verhältnis von Tradition und gesellschaftlicher Entwicklung* (Göttingen: Vandenhoeck & Ruprecht, 1978); *idem* (ed.), *Seminar: die Entstehung der antiken Klassengesellschaft* (Frankfurt: Suhrkamp, 1977). Extremely useful is G.E.M. de Ste Croix, *The Class Struggle in the Ancient Greek World from the Archaic Age to the Arab Conquests* (London: Duckworth, 1981).

2.   This is not the place for a critique of 'proxy-data' and the Marxian approaches to biblical studies. Some useful observations on the Second Temple period are to be found in S.J.D. Cohen, 'The Political and Social History of the Jews in Greco-Roman Antiquity: The State of the Question', in R.A. Kraft and G.W.E. Nickelsburg (eds.), *Early Judaism and its Modern Interpreters* (Philadelphia: Fortress Press, 1986), pp. 33-56. The points made about methodological issues apply just as much to the Persian period as to the Graeco-Roman era. On the earlier period see H.G.M. Williamson, 'Post-exilic Historiography', in R.E. Friedman and H.G.M. Williamson (eds.), *The Future of Biblical Studies: The Hebrew Scriptures* (SBL Semeia Studies; Atlanta: Scholars Press, 1987), pp. 189-207. The unpublished seminar paper by P.R. Davies, 'Taking up Social Scientific Investigations of the Second Temple Period' makes many good procedural points for the study of this period.

3.   This oblique aside intimates the serious need for an *ideologiekritische* approach to theoretical Marxian approaches to texts. Another paper perhaps.

consider a few texts for what they may have to contribute to an understanding of social background and ideological activity in the period under scrutiny. Taken together the texts may throw some light on the complex and perennial issues of land exchange in biblical times, with an element of the equally problematic exchange of women in the background. Now these are very big topics, and nothing short of a book-length treatment could do justice to them, so this paper must be regarded as an attempt to do injustice to these texts and their backing ideologies. The chosen texts and topics are: 1) Jeremiah the landowner (Jer. 32); 2) the inheritance, sale and redemption of land (Lev. 25–27); 3) the murder of Naboth (1 Kgs 21; 2 Kgs 9.17-26). Nothing here is simple and the selection of texts has been made in order to highlight certain features of the Second Temple period rather than to provide a comprehensive analysis of lengthy and difficult biblical texts.

1. *Jeremiah the Landowner*

The simplest (the simplicity is very much a relative one!) of the texts, though hardly the shortest, is the story of how Jeremiah became a landowner during the siege of Jerusalem. Technically only vv. 6-15 of ch. 32 tell the story, but like so much of the prose of the book of Jeremiah this simple story is complicated by its present redactional position in that book. The standard commentaries may be consulted for analysis of the chapter, as its forty-four verses make it too long to be analysed usefully here.[1] Redaction and expansion complicate the story and transform it from a 'simple' land transaction deal into a statement about the siege, the future, Jeremiah as a great figure of prayer, a history of Jerusalem as the object of divine wrath since its foundation, and the restoration of the land. These are all features of other Second Temple literature and so the chapter becomes an important guide to some central issues of that period. The standard approach to vv. 6-15 is to read them as a 'symbolic action' of Jeremiah's and to

---

1. By standard commentaries I mean those of Duhm, Volz, Condamin, Rudolph, Weiser, Lamparter, Bright, Thompson and Carroll. My treatment of Jeremiah 32 in this paper does not reiterate Carroll, *Jeremiah: A Commentary* (OTL; Philadelphia: Westminster Press, 1986), pp. 618-32, but moves on from there.

classify this with the other 'symbolic actions' in the book.[1] None of these 'symbolic actions' is as simple or as straight-forward as commentators imagine, and a good deal of misprision is involved in the standard treatments of them.[2] Bearing such hermeneutical complications in mind it may still be possible to treat the land sale incident by itself for temporary purposes. However, the redactional presentation of the story helps to underline the difficulties of reading the transaction as if it were a literal or historical event in the life of the 'historical' Jeremiah. The textual or literary Jeremiah (i.e. the fictional or fabricated figure in the book) may buy and sell land while 'shut up in the court of the guard' (v. 2) and while holding court 'in the presence of all the Jews who were sitting in the court of the guard' (v. 12).[3] Hanamel ben Shallum may easily break through the Babylonian siege of Jerusalem to sell land to his cousin in prison and then return home through the siegeworks to Anathoth! Like Socrates before the hemlock break holding court among his friends, the fictional Jeremiah, imprisoned as a traitor to his nation, behaves like a clan chief commanding and transacting. The ostensible reason for Jeremiah's purchase of the land is that 'the right of redemption' is his (v. 7). This is not so much a case of buying and selling land as it is an example of land redemption. Land which once belonged to Jeremiah is here sold back to him by Hanamel. That at least explains why Shallum did not just pass the land on to his son who had the right to inherit his father's land. The rule operating here is that of land redemption, keeping the land in the family of its original owner (cf. Lev. 25.23-24). So, although the book never presents Jeremiah as a landowner, he

---

1. Cf. S. Amsler, *Les actes des prophètes* (Essais Bibliques, 9; Geneva: Labor & Fides, 1985), especially pp. 29-31; G. Fohrer, *Die symbolischen Handlungen der Propheten* (ATANT, 54; Zürich: Zwingli Verlag, 2nd edn, 1968) esp. pp. 33-47.

2. I have discussed these matters in my unpublished papers, delivered under various circumstances in Sheffield: 'Street Theatre in the Book of Jeremiah: the Intractability of Reading Biblical Texts' (staff seminar, 7th March 1988); 'Septennial Proclamations and Street Theatre in the Book of Jeremiah' (SBL International Meeting, 3rd August 1988). The notion of 'misprision' is very much influenced by H. Bloom, *A Map of Misreading* (New York: Oxford University Press, 1975) and the chapter 'The Necessity of Misreading' in his *Kabbalah and Criticism* (New York: Seabury Press, 1975), pp. 95-126.

3. Cf. the image of Ezekiel among the exiles or in his house with the elders of Judah sitting before him (Ezek. 1.1; 8.1; 33.31).

is most certainly that in this story. Not simply because he buys land from Shallum's representative, but because it is land that once he owned and which is now reverting to him. That is the logic of the rules of redemption and, although commentators do not usually read it that way, that is how we must understand it. Otherwise we must ask the question, 'why did Shallum not pass his own land on to his son Hanamel?' No wonder Jeremiah is known as 'Jeremiah of Anathoth' (29.27; cf. 11.21-23; 37.12; a different understanding of his association with Anathoth appears in 1.1).

Leaving aside all these implications of the redaction of 32.1-15, what makes the story a symbolic or performative gesture is the statement in v. 15 attributed to Yahweh, 'houses and fields and vineyards shall *again* be bought in this land' (expanded in vv. 42-44). Jeremiah's redemption of family land becomes in this way a token or earnest of future transactions in the land of Judah. Just as Jeremiah had the right to redeem his field in Anathoth so Yahweh had the right to redeem the land of Judah, a redemption enacted by the re-emergence of land transactions in the future. Jeremiah *prefigures* the communal activity of the future. That makes his purchase symbolical as well as an actual redemption of a field. The field stands for 'this land' which is then spelled out in v. 44 as 'the land of Benjamin...places about Jerusalem...the cities of Judah...cities of the hill country...cities of the Shephelah...cities of the Negev'. Thus the act is equivalent to the counsel of 29.5 to the exiles in Babylon: 'build houses...plant gardens', but should be associated with the pro-Judaean strand in the book (cf. 30–31; 42.7-12) in contrast to the pro-Babylonian strand in 24; 29.4-19. The emphasis on 'right of redemption' ($mi\check{s}pat\ hagg^{e'}ullah$, v. 7; cf. v. 8) may incorporate the notion of restored land and restituted rights of commercial and real estate transactions, and this concept of 'redemption' may simply be derived from the levitical rules of land inheritance and redemption ($g^{e'}ullah$, Lev. 25.24). It may well be the case that the writer of Jer. 32.6-15 did not mean to imply that Jeremiah was buying back (i.e. redeeming) *his own land*, but understood 'rights of redemption' to mean 'the right to purchase in the first place'. This would account for the writer's overlooking the fact that Hanamel was entitled to inherit his father's land and explain why (s)he failed to notify the reader of prior ownership on the part of Jeremiah. In the story Jeremiah just buys a field in Anathoth and this transaction presages future land deals throughout Judah/Judaea. It does not anticipate the buying *back* of property but the acquisition (*qnh*) of land within the context of normal transactional procedures.[1]

The legal transaction enacted by Jeremiah (vv. 9-14) is made the sign of the re-emergence in the future of similar legal transactions (v. 44). These exchanges of land, money and deeds will be the good Yahweh will do to his people which will constitute his restitution of their fortunes (the restoring of the fortunes is the central motif and theme holding together the disparate elements in chs. 30–33). But whereas Jeremiah buys land in the midst of an already crowded (even besieged!) territory, these future transactions will take place in a land characterized by the people as 'a desolation, *without man and beast*' (v. 43). To an empty land there shall come immigrants and refugees who once had been dispersed throughout many countries (v. 37). These are the people who will buy and sell land! The fully redacted story envisages a land under the control of the Chaldaeans where no Judaeans dwell (v. 43b). In the restoration all the scattered people will flock back to their own land, settle there and begin again the procedures of buying fields with due process and this will signify Yahweh's great instauration of land and people. This seems to be the sense of ch. 32. Yet the reader of the book of Jeremiah cannot help feeling uneasy about this story. It seems to presuppose an empty and derelict land, but the reader knows that according to 39.10 and 52.16 (2 Kgs 25.12) that land was not empty. The vineyards and fields (the term used for 'fields' is different from 32.15) were *given* to the poor by the Babylonians and this gift by conquest presumably made the poor the owners of the land. Also, the reader knows from chs. 40–42 that Gedaliah, his followers and all those associated with him worked the land and enjoyed its harvests (40.12). If the reader is endowed with common sense then it will be obvious also that, from the fall of Jerusalem until whenever the restoration of 32.37-41, 42-44 was imagined to have taken place, the land must have been occupied and worked by somebody or other. Yet ch. 32 is blithely ignorant of such occupiers, or chooses to ignore them.

1. An alternative explanation would be to say that the writer of 32.6-15 simply did not understand the law of redemption but used the phrase in a midrashic manner in order to introduce the topic of Jeremiah the landowner. Similar midrashic elements appear in the story of the cancelled *berît* of Jer. 34.8-22.

What I think may be read from the story of Jeremiah the landowner, among other things, is this: the grounds for owning land in the
restored territory (its boundaries are outlined and defined in v. 44; cf.
33.13) are the possession of legal deeds which demonstrate purchase
of fields from the time of the repossession of the land. Implicit in that
ruling would be the view that those who had 'occupied' the land since
the fall of Jerusalem were not the legitimate owners of that land. Only
those who had come 'back' from foreign lands could claim by right of
purchase an entitlement to the land. Is this a case of reading too much
into the text? Is this detection of an ideology of land claims and rights
behind the story of Jeremiah the landowner too subtle a reading of it?
To see ch. 32 as a textual strategy *reflecting* a social practice of land-
purchasing[1] may be regarded by some readers of Jeremiah as
assuming too much connection between texts and society. Perhaps it is,
and I acknowledge the necessary gap that there must be between a text
and whatever social situation may be regarded as giving rise to that
text.[2] But this reading of ch. 32 fits quite well with those strands in the
book which address themselves to the legitimacy of relationship to
Yahweh and Jerusalem in combative terms (eg. chs. 24; 29.10-14). It
makes the point made by 32.37-41 (cf. 24.6-7; 29.14) that only return
from dispersal to a foreign country counts as warranting Yahweh's
favour. This effectively rules out those who never left the land or who
imagined that their possession of the land could prevail against the
newcomers. Stories about such conflicts are to be found in Nehemiah
and Ezra[3] as well as the book of Jeremiah and may also be detected

1. The mode of acquisition of land in biblical times remains beyond our
knowledge, though the remarks in Isa. 5.8-10; Mic. 2.1-5 have led some scholars to
argue for the practice of latifundialization in the eighth century. Cf. J.A. Dearman,
Property Rights in the Eighth-Century Prophets: The Conflict and Its Background
(SBLDS, 106; Atlanta: Scholars Press, 1988); D.N. Premnath, 'Latifundialization
and Isaiah 5.8-10', *JSOT* 40 (1988), pp. 49-60. Such texts could be dated to the
Second Temple period because the books in which they appear belong as *redacted*
works to that era. I persist in my folly of refusing traditional interpretations of the
prophets which have not considered seriously alternative possibilities. I refuse to
accept such 'rationalizing paraphrases' (to use N.-P. Lemche's happy phrase) of
what passes for scholarship in much of modern biblical studies!
2. Texts are not photographs of social reality, but complex social constructions
generated by such reality in conjunction with various ideological factors controlling
their production.
3. Another cluster of problems is associated with the historicity or fictionality of

throughout Isaiah 40–66 (40–55 make claims for the newcomers who have returned to Zion and 56–66 are dominated by internecine quarrels relating to Jerusalem). I suspect therefore (to go no further than the hermeneutics of suspicion but in a positive direction!) that we should read the story of Jeremiah the landowner as a textual strategy helping to enforce the ideological claim to land on the part of those who could trace or claim association with Babylonian Jews. No precise date can be put on such a strategy except the general period of the Second Temple when communities of Jews in Egypt, Babylonia and Judah/Judaea had dealings with each other, often of a hostile nature (e.g. Jer. 44; the Elephantine papyri; Neh. 13).

2. *Inheritance, Sale and Redemption of Land*

How was land acquired in ancient Israel? Presumably by the usual means of purchase, or acquisition in time of war, by gift or inheritance, families acquired territorial holdings. There are various stories of individuals buying land (cf. Gen. 23; 2 Sam. 24.18-24) and these represent the matter as gift or simple purchase. Only Jeremiah 32 offers any evidence of the legal procedures which may have accompanied such transactions (vv. 9-14, 24, 44) and this text has very limited value for determining the actual processes of acquiring land. As the *only* story of such a procedure it cannot be used as a paradigm of land transactions and then referred to as a warrant for explaining Jeremiah 32. This would be to argue in a circle—a feature of much commentary writing on the book of Jeremiah (cf. the use of ch. 26 as paradigmatic evidence for trial procedure in ancient Israel and ch. 36 as the paradigm for writing prophetic texts)—and a vicious circle at that! It may well be the case that when land changed hands money also was exchanged and the transactions were witnessed by other parties, and substantiated by the writing of legal documents, but

Ezra the scribe. Garbini (*History and Ideology*, pp. 151-69) offers a number of arguments against the traditional view of Ezra and relates the name to the great liturgical reform of c. 159 BCE. Arguments for the conventional view may be found in H.G.M. Williamson, *Ezra, Nehemiah* (WBC, 16; Waco, TX: Word Books, 1985). C.C. Torrey's judgment that Ezra and Neh. 7–13 'has no value whatever, as history' (*The Composition and Historical Value of Ezra–Nehemiah* [BZAW, 2; Giessen: J. Ricker'sche Buchhandlung, 1896], p. 65) remains a good starting point for the discussion.

the biblical stories of land purchases ignore such procedures. The paradigmatic status of Jeremiah 32 cannot be established without a good deal of further evidence which we unfortunately do not possess.

Leviticus 25 is the *locus classicus* of the inheritance of land in the Bible. The other chapters, Leviticus 26–27, contain important pericopae about land and so the three chapters bear on the general subject of land in the Second Temple period. Little in these chapters is simple or capable of being discussed within the limits of a brief paper, but there are a number of significant features in this material to which I wish to draw attention by way of exploring textual strategy in this period. If Leviticus 25 is about 'the rights of ownership', especially with reference to the Jubilee Year legislation,[1] then we must note the potential opposition between such rights and the well-known claim that the land belongs to Yahweh (v. 23). The prohibition 'the land shall not be sold in perpetuity,[2] *for the land is mine*; for you are strangers (*gērîm*) and sojourners with me' posits the owner of the land to be Yahweh, not the people, and therefore we may well ask about statements elsewhere in the chapter which regard the land as the permanent property of the cities (e.g. v. 34). One true but trivial explanation for such conflicting principles would be a theory of sources making up the chapter.[3] Discrete and disparate rulings and customs having been brought together in Leviticus 25–27 (indeed throughout Leviticus), so we must not expect coherence or sense to be made of the whole book. Taking that as read, I want to push some of the distinctions in Leviticus 25 a little further in order to discern certain ideological factors at work in the text. Think about the claim, 'the land belongs to Yahweh'. What is going on in such a claim? Is it a trace of older Canaanite myths of a chthonic nature? The land of the Baals has now become the land of Yahweh? Or does it belong with

1. M. Noth, *Leviticus: A Commentary* (OTL; London: SCM Press, 1965), p. 84.
2. The Hebrew word לצמתת is not easily translated: צמתת has the sense of 'finality, completion' and so may mean here that land cannot be sold outright (cf. NEB). It can only be sold temporarily; hence the ruling about permitting sold land to be redeemed in v. 24. Noth (*Leviticus*, p. 18) understands צמתת as 'pledge to silence' and the ruling to mean that land sales could not take place to the exclusion of a claim of ownership.
3. See the analysis in K. Elliger, *Leviticus* (HAT, 4; Tübingen: Mohr, 1966), pp. 335-60.

other familiar beliefs from the Second Temple period about the holy land and the holy city? Does Yahweh's ownership of the land make the people of Israel tenants of landlord Yahweh? Or is it more a case of Yahweh's ownership of the land underwriting land ownership in Israel? Because Yahweh owns the land individual Israelite families may (or may not?) own land? What is stated in Lev. 25.23 is only an implication of Yahweh's ownership: the land may not be sold permanently or, perhaps more precisely, without the recognition of its human owner's rights.[1] But the glossing of this prohibition with the statement '*because* you are aliens and sojourners with me' makes the reason for such lack of selling the temporariness of the people's dwelling in the land! Where so many of the laws and exhortations in Torah command Israelites to behave well towards strangers and aliens (*gērîm*), here it is the Israelites themselves who are the sojourners in the land. Such aliens cannot own land and so the implication of Yahweh's ownership of the land is that Israelites are not the owners!

Consonant with this interpretation of Lev. 25.23 is the material in ch. 26, where activities contrary to Yahweh's commandments will result in expulsion from the land itself (see esp. vv. 14-39). A major consequence of that mass expulsion of the people from Yahweh's land (though 26.33 does designate the territory 'your land' because the logic of 25.23 is never carried through in the biblical text) will be the desolation of the land emptied of people. During this period of desolation the land will pay off (תרצה) its sabbaths and even keep sabbath (חשבת; vv. 34, 43; cf. 2 Chron. 36.21). Implicit in the concept of the land keeping sabbath while the people suffer in their enemies' lands is the notion of *the empty land of Israel*. The entire populace of aliens and sojourners is removed from Yahweh's land to foreign lands and the *emptied* land keeps sabbath! We have here yet again an allusion to the myth of the empty land which appears to be behind so much of Jeremiah and other ideological readings of the Babylonian destruction of Jerusalem. This is the logic of the assertion that the owner of the land is Yahweh and *not* the people of Israel. So there can be no land claims by the people. Aliens in their own land and prey to invading forces, they are but sojourners *with* Yahweh in *his* land and subject to instant dismissal from that land if they do not heed his commandments. If Yahweh owns the land, then temporary occupation

1. Noth, *Leviticus*, p. 189.

of any part of it is entirely in his gift and he may give it to one and remove it from another (cf. Dan. 4.35). There can be no permanent land claims in Israel. If we then ask, 'who benefits from such an ideology of land possession as is embodied in the claim that the land belongs to Yahweh?' we shall have to enquire about the social roots of the belief itself.

Most of the elements in Leviticus 25 run counter to the claim that the land belongs to Yahweh, so it may be the case that 25.23-24 is an addition to the section on problems with the sabbatical year (25.18-22). Yet running through these closing chapters of Leviticus are elements relating to Yahweh's sacral property (eg. 27.14-15, 16ff., 28ff.) in which the role of the priest is fundamentally important. The sanctuary governs via the priests and the priests determine matters in the name of Yahweh. So a claim that the land belongs to Yahweh rather than the people is a claim more likely to be made by the priests than the people. Apart from the levitical ownership of the houses in the cities of the Levites (25.32-33), the priestly control of vows and dedications to Yahweh, as well as their assessments of valuation, gave them considerable power in the community. The entitlement to redemption of land (cf. 25.24) is not as comprehensive as is some-times imagined to be the case on the strength of 25.24. It does not apply to houses (25.29-30) nor to fields dedicated to Yahweh under certain conditions (27.16-21). These fields in the Jubilee year came into the possession of the priest (27.21). So a careful reading of the various clauses in Leviticus 25–27, especially in ch. 27, shows an economic favouring of the sanctuary staff which may justify inter-preting the general assertion 'the land is mine' (25.33) as a priestly regulative device for controlling the land. As a principle the claim must have given great power to those who are recognized as speaking for and of Yahweh. Control of land exchanges in the Second Temple period may well have come under the control of the temple authorities, though it is difficult to be sure what implications are packed into the claim of Lev. 25.23.

I shall not attempt to deal with the differentiation of regulation of land possession or debt bondage in Exodus, Leviticus and Deuteronomy. No real agreement can be found between the traditions and therefore diversity of practice must have been the inevitable out-come of treating these texts as normative in the Second Temple period. The interpreters of such texts will have therefore enjoyed great power and manipulative influence. If Yahweh is the landowner then those who speak for him (i.e. the priests) will in reality hold the land, enjoy it and benefit from it. The alternative notion of families occupying and therefore 'owning' land which cannot be alienated *permanently* from them (except for good theological reasons!) lies behind the rule of redemption (25.24 and following cases). A necessary implication of the familial duty of redemption is the prevention of the *accumulation of land*. Nobody could buy up other people's land for more than temporary periods before selling it back to the original family. Except for land not owned by families (e.g. the land that could be accumulated by the sanctuary, 27.21; for the distinction between purchased land and land owned by inheritance, cf. 27.22), land could not be alienated from families. This would necessarily prevent latifundialism—though whether anything in Leviticus 25–27 should be regarded as actual and real *or* ideal and literary cannot now be established. If carried out rigorously these rulings about land acquisition and familial retention of such land would favour the sanctuary as the arbitrator of deals, valuations and the ultimate acquirer of released devoted fields. The function, if not the intention, of the practice of these land regulations would be to make the sanctuary more powerful and to weaken the capacity of families to acquire more land.

This looks like a powerful strategy of control in the service of the sanctuary's ideology of Yahweh as owner of the land, with tight rules for controlling access to land by the families living under the jurisdiction of that sanctuary (the Second Temple?). At least it looks like that in the final redaction of that section of Torah which we call 'Leviticus' in the Second Temple period.

Accepting the myth of the empty land as a textual reality for the sake of argument, we may ask the questions which arise from the emptying of the land (26.33-39). What happened to it? Did actual sabbaths and Jubilees operate or accumulate? Are those categories post-invasion rationalizations and constructions? Did the rulings of redemption and inalienability of land hold 'unoccupied' land for the descendants of those who went away? In the fifth century (or later) could a stranger turn up in Judaea and claim family land on the grounds that their ancestors had been taken away to Babylonia and the land was now theirs by right? Do such rulings seek to dispossess the people of Jerusalem who never left their lands in favour of so-called 'returning' immigrants? These questions all feed into the larger and more important question: how was land acquired and retained in the Second Temple period? What textual strategies are going on in these regulations and what ideology of land occupation may be detected behind them? If I state the problem as a series of questions it is because a) I do not know the answers, and b) I wish to generate discussion around these issues as a way of reading Leviticus 25–27. Because what we do *not* know is so much more than what we *do* (or imagine we do) know, asking questions may be the best way to find out the relative amounts of knowledge and ignorance.

3. *The Murder of Naboth*

The famous story of Naboth's murder is a cluster of discrete and disparate elements which, and when taken with the 2 Kings 9 material, do not add up to a coherent story. In the shorter account Naboth's murder is the subject of a brief oracle intimating Yahweh's knowledge of the murder of him and his sons (2 Kgs 9.26). The occasion for this oracle being recalled by Jehu is the murder of Joram the son of Ahab, a killing which took place in the region of Naboth's property (*ḥelqat nābôt*, vv. 21, 25, 26 with the addition of the word *śᵉdēh* 'field of' in v. 25). For those who know only 1 Kings 21 and the topos 'Naboth's vineyard', 2 Kings 9 will make for strange reading. Joram pays for his father's crime but no mention is made of that famous vineyard nor of Jezebel's equally famous involvement in the conspiracy which caused Naboth's murder. The death of Joram takes place near the property of Naboth (whatever happened to that famous vineyard?) and that proximity triggers off the cited oracle. We may imagine a secretive killing of Naboth which only comes to light when an oracle declares it; even Elijah is absent from this account. I like Alexander Rofé's description of the deed: 'the Lord. . . swears that he saw it; he is the sole witness of a hidden murder, perpetrated at night, seen by nobody else. Thus, according to 2 Kings ix, Naboth died by the hand of murderers sent by the king, a murder after the manner of Macbeth.'[1] How very different is the story in 1 Kings 21!

---

1. 'The Vineyard of Naboth: The Origin and Message of the Story', *VT* 38 (1988), pp. 89-104 [p. 96]. The nocturnal aspect of the deed is implicit in the word אמשׁ, 'yesterday evening' or 'last night' used in v. 26; cf. Gen. 9.34; 31.29, 42.

My justification for including the story of Naboth in this paper lies more with the vineyard account than with the shorter tale (and more original, according to Rofé) of the murder of him and his sons. But that alternative story is necessary in order to appreciate the function of the radical changes introduced into the 'vineyard' version. In a paper on land acquisition, the gifting of Naboth's vineyard to Ahab by his wife Jezebel after a dispute about land transference principles is an appropriate story for consideration—especially as Naboth's reason for refusing Ahab's offer of purchase or exchange in the first place is due to the vineyard being 'the inheritance of (his) father' (21.3). The phrase 'inheritance of his fathers' (*naḥᵃlat 'ᵃbōtāyw*) occurs in Num. 36.7-8 in a section dealing with the conservation of inherited property within the individual tribal boundaries of territory (the daughters of Zelophehad case), so there are links between the Naboth story and the rules of land inheritance. Ostensibly these rules allow Naboth to resist the blandishments of Ahab. Without Naboth's refusal there would be no story, so perhaps it is not necessary to tie 1 Kings 21 in with Numbers 36 too tightly. The real villain of the fully edited story is not Ahab but Jezebel his Sidonian wife (cf. 2 Kgs 8.30-37 which tells the story of Jezebel's death but without referring to the Naboth story). 1 Kings 21 is such a skein of genres that only the figure of Jezebel can be focused on here.

In the story of Naboth's vineyard Jezebel represents at least two topoi: that of the foreign wife (who has power because she is queen— an Esther in reverse) who violates the integrity of Hebrew men, and also that of the deceiving woman who uses deceit to further her own (or somebody else's) ends (cf. 2 Sam. 14; Gen. 27). The genres which use these topoi cannot be investigated here, but the polemic against foreign wives is an important element in the Second Temple literature of Nehemiah and Ezra. In his reading of the story of Naboth's vineyard Rofé sees a retelling in the fifth–fourth century of the old story of Naboth in which the guilt is shifted from Ahab to Jezebel and the *ḥōrîm* (1 Kgs 21.8). The historical setting for this retelling is the polemic against intermarriage in Ezra and Nehemiah.[1] Rofé's point is only a general one and he does not insist on reading 1 Kings 21 as a polemic against the involvement of foreign wives in the manipulation

---

1. 'The Vineyard of Naboth', pp. 101-102. The-*ḥōrîm* 'nobles' also appear in Ezra 9.7; Neh. 6.17; 13.17.

of property. The influence of the foreigner Jezebel on the elders and nobles of Naboth's city (1 Kgs 21.8: Jezreel?) cannot be denied and undoubtedly the foreign wives bitched against in Ezra and Nehemiah were themselves influential in shaping what their men did by way of opposition to Nehemiah. Jezebel the Sidonian may well stand for the Canaanite wives of the Second Temple period (cf. Ezra 9.1-2; Neh. 13.23-27) and 1 Kings 21 may represent more a polemic against foreign wives than a straightforward story about land deals—the inherited land element may only be the connecting link with the property of Naboth motif in 2 Kings 9. Yet one cannot help but notice the connection between the foreign woman and a disregard for old family traditions in the story of how Naboth's property was filched from him by the deviousness of a foreign woman in conjunction with the leading males in the community. Make of that connection what you will!

At this point my paper has shifted from seeing in certain texts strategies for handling land to a more obvious detection of polemic against foreign wives. Both topics are features of the Second Temple period so neither is out of place in this paper. But it would be unwise to generalize from 1 Kings 21 on both topics together: there may be a case to be made out for arguing that the polemic against foreign wives in the books of Ezra and Nehemiah had as part of its motivation an attempt to control the inter-tribal connections of the people of Judaean territory. This control by means of divorce would weaken the links between the 'holy seed' and the 'peoples of the lands' (Ezra 9.2) and most probably involve the breaking up of territorial holdings. The smaller the territory controlled by the ideological masters of Jerusalem the more easily controllable it would be. This is speculation of course, but in the absence of fully documented evidence it is difficult to read Ezra and Nehemiah in terms of textual strategies of Second Temple politics. Rofé's claim that '1 Kings xxi appears to be an important source for the history of Judah in the midst of the Persian period'[1] may be correct, but I am sure that it cannot just be read as straight historiography. The hermeneutics of the matter is exceedingly complicated. I note the connection made between marriage to a foreign wife and property in Ezra 10.1-8 where the failure to put away such a wife would lead to the forfeiture of 'all his property'

---

1. 'The Vineyard of Naboth', p. 102.

(*kŏl-rᵉûŝ*, v.8). The text is silent about the precise nature of this property—moveable goods, though hardly land—and is equally reticent about who would be the beneficiaries of the forfeiture. Such a polemic against foreign wives where there was genuine affection and loyalty between the men and the women must have entailed a considerable forfeiture of property and a concomitant benefit to the central coffers of the Jerusalem ideologues. The anti-Canaanite ideology which informs the attack on the foreign wives confines the polemic to people from the neighbouring territories around Jerusalem and does not apply to foreign wives from further afield. At least, the books of Ezra and Nehemiah are silent about such wives and Deut. 20.10-18 (cf. Deut. 21.10-14) differentiates between (captive) women as potential wives who come from distant cities and the women of the neighbouring cities who are not eligible for marriage (only for slaughter). Whether anything in Deuteronomy 20–21 was ever practised in the Second Temple period I do not know, but what I find obvious from all these polemics against Canaanite people is this: having a Babylonian or a Persian wife was no obstacle to success in the Second Temple period! Now who could possibly benefit from such an ideology of prohibited relations and permissible marriages? The books of Ezra and Nehemiah represent their eponymous protagonists (whether fictional, textual or historical is neither here nor there) as coming from Babylonia (Ezra 7.6) and from Susa the Persian capital (Neh. 1.1). The chances of men from those areas having Canaanite wives must be considered very slight, so the ban on Canaanite wives did not apply to them or their like. I do not want to turn literature into history, so I will simply draw attention to the functions served by an ideology of negative and positive foreignness. Any pressure group in the Jerusalem of the Second Temple period whose roots were in Babylonia or Persia could control land and property there with an ideology which outlawed those with Canaanite wives and which exempted other kinds of foreign wives from such a control.

At this stage of the argument there are too many complicated strands of narrative and ideology for a simple picture of things to emerge. Whenever a woman or women appear in a biblical text the reader must sit up and take notice. Women—whether foreign or not—have little respect for conventions and rules, whether relating to property or people, and therefore transform situations. Jezebel in 1 Kings 21 is evidence for this at a textual level. Her Jewish equivalent, Esther, provides a reverse image of Jezebel's destructiveness—the enemies of the Jews are humiliated by her. The otherness of women radically alters the picture because biblical women are subversive of the order operating in any story (whether good, conventional or bad). Female subversiveness is fundamental to the way the Hebrew Bible is written so it may be the case that all those foreign wives discriminated against in Ezra–Nehemiah represent a textual strategy of control against alternative political ideologies. I do not know. Women are a problem, foreign women an even greater problem! Whether a *Kulturkampf* is to be detected in the Second Temple period at this point is difficult to say. Difficult because we are at the point of leaving the textual levels of meaning in order to make assertions about the real social world of the Second Temple and the steps in that switch from literary to 'real' meanings are too many and contentious to be taken in conclusion here. Texts and theories are safer places to be than the real world because they are more easily manipulated by readers and theoreticians. But the gap between texts and the real world remains as unbridgeable as ever and I hope this attempt at discerning textual strategies in the Second Temple period has confirmed once again the reality of that gap.[1]

1. For some useful remarks on the difficulty of extrapolating historical 'facts' from literature see P. Laslett, 'The Wrong Way through the Telescope: a Note on Literary Evidence in Sociology and in Historical Sociology', *British Journal of Sociology* 27 (1976), pp. 319-42. For the study of ancient texts see M. Liverani, 'Memorandum on the Approach to Historiographic Texts', *Orientalia* 42 (1973), pp. 178-94.

THE TEMPLE IN PERSIAN PERIOD PROPHETIC TEXTS

David L. Petersen

I

This is a preliminary draft for an essay about the significance of the temple according to Persian period prophetic texts. The essay has at its roots an interest in exploring the widely held notion that prophecy was subsumed or incorporated into the cult during the Persian period.[1] One way of testing that claim is to examine the role and significance of the temple, something surely central to Persian period Judaean Yahwism, in literature attributed to Persian period prophets. However, before examining this literature it is important to treat briefly other issues pertaining to this claim regarding the place of the temple in Persian period prophetic literature. Perhaps the most important related matter is the surprisingly understudied topic, the similarities and differences between the First and Second Temples. The temple rebuilt by, among others, Zerubbabel, and dedicated in 515 BCE surely embodied meanings different from those associated with the structure that Solomon built. The so-called Second Temple was no longer a royal chapel as had been the temple built by Solomon and which was sustained by Judaean royal patrons as an expression of their rule. It was a new structure, physically different from its Solomonic forerunner.[2] The Second Temple might still express the

---

1. So, e.g., J. Blenkinsopp: 'One of the most important aspects of the transformation that prophecy underwent after the loss of national independence was its reabsorption into the cult' (*A History of Prophecy in Israel* [Philadelphia: Westminster Press, 1983], p. 252). My own earlier analysis concerning the Levitical singers whom the Chronicler deems to be prophets could be construed in a way consistent with Blenkinsopp's thesis.

2. That the second temple was architecturally different from the Solomonic structure is clear. The most detailed discussion, if not always fully informed by

ideology of Yahweh's cosmic rule, but it no longer served as the shrine of a Judaean nation state.

Apart from architectural design, what were the differences between the First and Second Temples that one might discern in Persian period prophetic literature? A number of scholars have made some general observations regarding putative ideological differences between the First and Second Temples. For example, M. Haran maintained, 'it (the Second Temple) already shows signs of entirely new principles while the earlier features of the institution of the house of God are fading away. It marks a stage of transition to a new period which was preparing to give up the institution altogether in practice—even while clinging to it as an eschatological symbol.'[1] This opinion elicits a tantalizing series of questions. What were the 'new principles' operating in the Second Temple? What 'earlier features' were disappearing? Did the temple become an 'eschatological symbol'? If so, how did that symbol work?

Of these questions, there is, perhaps, greatest unanimity regarding the last one, at least to the extent that one may speak about the place of the Jerusalem temple in some eschatological literature. In the complex of traditions regarding the eschatological Jerusalem, one should expect to find a temple in that new-found city. As Clements put it when referring to the postexilic setting, 'In heaven existed the true Jerusalem and the true temple where men would enjoy the presence of God...Judaism resorted to its eschatology to provide the solution...to the question, "Will God in truth dwell on earth?"'[2] At some future time, when there is a new Jerusalem, there will be as well a

---

recent biblical scholarship, is Th. A. Busink, *Der Tempel von Jerusalem: von Salomo bis Herodes; eine archäologisch-historische Studie unter Berücksichtigung des westsemitischen Tempelbaus. II. Von Ezechiel bis Middot* (Leiden: Brill, 1980), pp. 776-841.

1. M. Haran, *Temples and Temple Service in Ancient Israel* (Oxford: Clarendon Press, 1978), p. 45. Cf. his discussion in 'Temple and Community in Ancient Israel', in M. Fox (ed.), *Temple in Society* (Winona Lake, IN: Eisenbrauns, 1988), pp. 17-25. In the latter work, Haran wrote, 'The temple was thus turned into an eschatological symbol, to be resurrected only at the end of days, while for the ongoing daily life new frameworks and channels of communal activity were found' (p. 22).

2. R.E. Clements, *God and Temple: The Presence of God in Israel's Worship* (Philadelphia: Fortress Press, 1965), p. 134.

new temple. More recently, E. Gaines has examined the eschatological Jerusalem traditions and has argued that these traditions are employed in four primary ways: as a response to the loss of the physical city, as a critique of the Jewish cultic center, as a theological apologetic, and as a motivation for righteousness. In the literature she surveyed, there is striking variety concerning the place of the temple in the eschatological Jerusalem. For example, in the book of Revelation, the vision of the new Jerusalem provides no place for the temple: 'And I saw no temple in the city' (Rev. 21.22). By way of contrast, she notes that in the third *Sibylline Oracle*, 'the image of the city itself has been entirely displaced by the temple as the place of divine presence'.[1] The Qumran literature provides an entirely different option, namely of construing the sectarian community as the true sanctuary in opposition to the profaned temple in Jerusalem. Just as there is variety in the function of eschatological Jerusalem traditions, there is also variety concerning the place of the temple in eschatological Jerusalem.

The penultimate question raised by Haran's statement involves the demise of 'earlier features'. What was lost? I have already had occasion to mention what some have deemed most important, namely the absence of the role of the temple as national and royal symbol. One might well expect to find greater attention devoted to the divine ruler, Yahweh, so as to replace the royal 'power vacuum'. And such appears to be the case in certain Persian period texts, particularly those that anticipate the day of Yahweh. In addition, one senses that the Second Temple was physically less glorious than its Solomonic predecessor, though such is not stated explicitly in Ezra 3.12, a text which reports that some old men wept when they saw the foundations of the Second Temple being laid.

Neither the absence of monarchic symbols nor the absence of physical splendor were that which the rabbis thought distinguished the First from the Second Temple. In various post-biblical Jewish texts, there were varying lists, typically of five items, which served to explain how the two temples differed from each other.[2] However, all these lists normally included one common element: the holy spirit,

---

1. E. Gaines, *The Eschatological Jerusalem: The Function of the Image in the Literature of the Biblical Period* (PhD dissertation, Princeton Theological Seminary, 1988), pp. 369-70.

2. I am indebted to Clements (*God and Temple*, p. 126), for this material.

viz. the indwelling presence of Yahweh. This is an astounding claim, one which strikes at the heart of the expectations concerning what the Second Temple would provide, namely the indwelling presence of Yahweh. Could it be that this later belief was also held by some Persian period Yahwists who construed the Second Temple as, in some measure, lacking the presence of Yahweh? If there were literature that spoke about a day on which Yahweh would appear, then one might infer that such expectations attested to convictions that Yahweh was not fully present at the temple in that writer's time.

As regards the first question that Haran's analysis prompts, namely what were the 'new principles', there is as yet, to my mind, no thoroughly worked-out answer. Haran himself contends that prayer in the temple courtyard was an increasingly prominent element in the early Second Temple period. And it is the case that only in an early Second Temple text does the phrase 'house of prayer' appear as a way of describing the temple (Isa. 56.7). Moreover, in this same period, certain Levites were designated as those who began 'the thanksgiving in prayer' (Neh. 11.17). Nonetheless, prayer, as such, does not require the temple—so the classical cases of 2 Sam. 7.27; Neh. 1.11; Jon. 2.2 (though this prayer does come to Yahweh who is in his 'holy temple'). Apart from such general indications, it is difficult to know what new forms of ritual behavior became prominent in the early Second Temple period.

It may well be that what is new as regards the Second Temple involves neither readily identifiable new forms of religious behavior nor a new theology of the temple. Rather, as Weinberg and now Blenkinsopp (above) have argued, what is new in the Second Temple period is the sort of social structure in which the Second Temple was embedded, namely the *Bürger-Tempel-Gemeinde*. And it is the working out of this structure, one in which not all inhabitants of Judah were equally enfranchised in the group that supported and benefited from the temple, that may be responsible for the new principles to which Haran has alluded.

II

Before pursuing either the main issue—how Persian period prophets viewed this temple, or the related issue—how the Second Temple was different from the First, I must be clear about three matters: (1) the notion of the Jerusalem temple in a religio-historical sense, (2) the corpus of prophetic literature that the title presumes, and (3) how one non-prophetic Persian period literary corpus, Ezra–Nehemiah, views the Second Temple.

A Religio-historical Perspective

How should one, using perspectives drawn from the disciplined study of religions, think about the meaning or significance of the temple in Jerusalem? Since at least the time of Eliade, there has been a consistent emphasis on the notion of holy space as the key notion to explain any temple. The concept of holy space, as something set apart from secular or profane space was, in Eliade's case, informed by the work of earlier ancient Near Eastern specialists, who had argued for the notion of the temple as a symbol for the *Weltberg*, the cosmic *omphalos*. This concept of a *Weltberg* has been repudiated by ancient Near Eastern scholars.[1] As a result, Eliade's concept of holy space has recently been subjected to a thorough-going reassessment by Jonathan Z. Smith. Though it would be a gross oversimplification, I risk stating that Smith has made a plausible case for replacing the category of 'holy space' with that of 'holy place'. With this new phrase in mind, I cite Smith's religio-historical description of the Jerusalem temple, which is, in this case, primarily a description of the Solomonic temple:

> There is nothing inherent in the location of the temple of Jerusalem. Its location was simply where it happened to be built...The major narratives present the portrait of the Temple being built as a royal prerogative at a place of royal choosing. Its power over the populace, and with respect to its rival shrines, was maintained or reduced by the *imperium*.
>
> . . . the Temple in Jerusalem was the focus of a complex, self-referential system. It could, in principle, have been built anywhere else and still have been the same. It required no rationale beyond the obvious one that, once having been declared a temple and accepted as such (by YHWH, king priests, and people), it became a place of clarification—most particularly of the hierarchical rules and roles of sacred/profane, pure/impure. In an apparent paradox, its arbitrariness, its unmotivated character, guaranteed its ordering role. There was nothing to distract from the system.[2]

1. So, for example, the work of R. Clifford, *The Cosmic Mountain in Canaan and the Old Testament* (HSM, 4; Cambridge, MA: Harvard University Press, 1972).
2. J.Z. Smith, *To Take Place: Toward Theory in Ritual* (Chicago Studies in the

To use Smith's (as well as Wheatley's and Dumont's) categories in the first place helps us understand the significance of the temple in establishing or justifying various hierarchies, especially those involving power (using the vocabulary of sacred/profane) and status (using the vocabulary of pure/impure); and in the second place invites us to contemplate ways in which various Jerusalem temples might function within diverse social contexts. Temples involve more than just sacred space. They are part of, and symbolize, various forms of social interaction; and forms of social interaction change over time. As a result, one might expect the role of a temple to change as well. For example, if a set of hierarchies obtains during the Second Temple period which is different from the set of the First Temple period, then one may speak in a rather precise way about a significant contrast between the roles of the First and Second Temples.

In sum, one should be aware of a temple's religio-social function, symbolically expressing hierarchies of power and status, and not simply view the temple as holy space. I will use these categories in the conclusions to discern one major difference between the First and Second Temples.

Persian Period Prophetic Texts

What constitute Persian period prophetic texts? For the purposes of this paper, I include Deutero-Isaiah, Haggai, Zechariah 1-8, Trito-Isaiah, Malachi, Joel, and Deutero-Zechariah, and roughly in that order. For the purposes of completeness, I will include in my analysis brief references to the role of the Second Temple as envisioned in two earlier prophetic books, Jeremiah and Ezekiel.

Ezra–Nehemiah

One may achieve an important vantage point on the Second Temple by examining Ezra–Nehemiah's account of its construction and dedication.[1] This literature presents something of a control group with

History of Judaism; Chicago: University of Chicago Press, 1987), pp. 83-84.

1. A full discussion would take into account the Chronicler's view of the temple. I do think that the Chronicler, when read in an appropriately anachronistic fashion, presents a notion of the temple which is different from that of Ezra–Nehemiah. The Chronicler appears to be more interested in the matters of status and hierarchy than does Ezra–Nehemiah.

which to compare the prophetic texts. Ezra–Nehemiah begins with what Blenkinsopp has termed 'The Rescript of Cyrus'. In that document, we find the following statement placed in the mouth of Cyrus: 'The Lord, the God of Heaven, has given me all the kingdoms of the earth, and he has charged me to build him a house at Jerusalem, which is in Judah' (Ezra 1.2). Cyrus makes the proclamation because, according to this author, 'the Lord stirred up the spirit of Cyrus' (Ezra 1.1). God stirred up as well the spirits of certain Yahwists (Ezra 1.5) to return and build the temple. According to those first verses of the book, the fiscal resources for temple rebuilding are those provided by Yahwists in exile (so Ezra 1.4, 6). From here to the end of Ezra 6, the author provides a series of narratives that depict the construction of the house of God or the *hêkāl* (both terms are used). Of particular interest is the description of the financing provisions in Ezra 6, a matter which the author views as having been addressed by both Cyrus and Darius. The cost is to be defrayed by 'the royal treasury' (so the Cyrus edict, Ezra 6.4). Darius adds by way of specification, 'from the royal revenue, the tribute of the province from Beyond the River' (6.8). Moreover, Darius moves beyond construction to maintenance provisions: the cost of the sacrificial system as well is to be borne by royal revenue:

> And whatever is needed—young bulls, rams, or sheep for burnt offerings to the God of heaven, wheat salt, wine, or oil, as the priests at Jerusalem require—let that be given to them day by day without fail, that they offer pleasing sacrifices to the God of heaven, and pray for the life of the king and his sons.

As one looks at the description of temple construction in Ezra–Nehemiah, several things are apparent. First, the temple was built at the behest of Yahweh, in the service of the Persian imperial policy, and with the subvention of imperial tax revenue. If, as a number of scholars have suggested, this remarkable promissory note by Cyrus or Darius is historically implausible, then the author is creating a purposeful picture, namely to highlight the prominence of Persian support for the temple which may well be viewed happily by some Yahwists and with opprobrium by others. Secondly, according to Ezra 3.12-13 some Yahwists thought this temple to be a pale replica of the Solomonic edifice. These two considerations suggest that, at least for the author of Ezra 1–6, the temple could be described as a less than ideal physical structure.

A recent monograph by Tamara Eskenazi, which is essentially literary-critical in its approach, suggests one possible reason for this view of the temple. She argues that in Ezra–Nehemiah one must distinguish between 'the house of God' and 'the *hêkāl*'.[1] She maintains that (1) 'the house of God' may be used in Ezra–Nehemiah to describe both the temple (*hêkāl*) and the city of Jerusalem with its walls (Ezra 1.7–6.22); (2) 'building the house of God is not limited to structures in stone but refers to the process of building the community itself' (Ezra 7.1–10.44);[2] (3) to rebuild the city wall is to rebuild the temple (Neh. 1.1–7.5); (4) the completion of the house of God focuses on the role of the entire community (Neh. 8.1–10.40); and (5) the rededicated city as holy place is equated with the house of God (Neh. 12.27–13.3). If such judgments about the diverse connotations of the phrase 'house of God' are licit, then one Persian period canonical text presents a remarkable perspective on the notion of the temple, namely, one that distinguishes between what in pre-exilic times had been considered equivalent, the house of the deity and the *hêkāl*, and one that highlights the latter, and tends to de-emphasize the former.

Ezra–Nehemiah appears to present a highly nuanced view of the Second Temple using the vocabulary of 'house of God' and *hêkāl*. Such a literary version of Judaean existence would seem to stand in considerable contrast to the reality that one may construct using the model of the *Bürger-Tempel-Gemeinde*. Put another way, the *Gemeinde* notion implies an emphasis on the *hêkāl* and upon socio-economic distinctions within Judaean Yahwists, whereas Ezra–Nehemiah, as interpreted by Eskenazi, presents a literary vision that emphasizes the unity of the people and the people-city as the 'house of God'. If such is the case, how do Persian period prophetic texts fit into this complex set of notions about the Second Temple?

1. The salient sections are T. Eskenazi, *In an Age of Prose: A Literary Approach to Ezra–Nehemiah* (SBLMS, 36; Atlanta: Scholars Press, 1988), pp. 53-57, 71-73, 83-87, 104-109 and 119-21.
2. Eskenazi, *In an Age of Prose*, p. 73.

III

In order to answer this question, I must begin the overview of the
relevant prophetic literature with brief comments about Jeremiah and
Ezekiel. The pictures drawn by Jeremiah and Ezekiel are notably
different. One could argue that in the material which may reasonably
be attributed to Jeremiah there is no allusion to the rebuilding of the
temple. The absence of such concern might be construed as consistent
with Jeremiah's pointed rhetoric regarding the Jerusalem temple (Jer.
7.1-15; 26.1-6). Moreover, the so-called 'Book of Consolation' (Jer.
30–31) contains no explicit reference to the rebuilding of the temple,
though it does call for the reconstruction of the city and the palace
(30.18; 31.38-40).[1] Jeremiah 33, which is something of an appendage
to the Book of Consolation and which may date to the Persian period,
anticipates temple sacrifice under the aegis of Levitical priests: 'and
the Levitical priests shall never lack a man in my presence to offer
burnt offerings, to burn cereal offerings and to make sacrifices forever' (3.17-18). This promise is construed as similar to the promise of
a Davidic ruler forever available to Israel. The primary issue appears
to be the identity of the priestly house in charge of the ritual service,
that is, a question of hierarchical status. The Levites, and no other
priests, are those to whom Yahweh has promised, as he did to David,
everlasting prerogatives. In sum, the book of Jeremiah only refers
explicitly to the temple in a late stage of the book's composition. It is
concerned essentially with the Levitical priests, a concern shared by
the deuteronomistic tradition. The text involves a hierarchy of status,
in which the position of one priestly group is highlighted.

Ezekiel 40–48 provides a picture that stands in radical contrast with
the vignette in Jeremiah if only by reason of the former's length. The
restoration of Judah is tied to a vision of a new temple which is fundamentally different from the one built by Solomon.[2] I am unable to
deal fully with the purport of this vision here; suffice it to say that the

1. One might argue that Jer. 31.23, 'O Holy Hill', refers to the temple.
However, I would not maintain that any reference to Zion or *har* involves necessarily
such a reference.
2. The critical literature on Ezekiel's vision of restoration is vast. Apart from the
standard commentaries and monographs (e.g., Gese, Levenson, Zimmerli) Smith's
'To Put in Place' (*To Take Place*, pp. 47-73) is particularly useful.

vision is utopian, dealing however with real problems—for example, what will be the role of the various priestly houses in the restored Judah (hierarchy of status), and what role will the civil ruler have in the restoration polity (hierarchy of power)? That the vision does at its core provide something new is clear from the claim in Ezek. 43.12. The vision involves a new Torah; 'This is the law of the temple...Behold this is the law of the temple'. The new conditions of Judah in the mid-sixth century require something overtly new, not a continuation of the old, as was the case with Jeremiah 33. However, as with Jeremiah 33, questions of hierarchical status obtain, with an obvious emphasis in Ezekiel 40–48 upon the Zadokite line and an equally firm denial of certain ritual prerogatives to the Levites.[1]

If one may think about these texts in Jeremiah and Ezekiel as forbears of Persian period prophetic literature, then there was significant diversity within pre-Persian prophetic literature on the character of the Second Temple. However, there is also an important similarity, namely the reference to the temple with regard to the hierarchy of priestly status. Moreover, as one reviews the place of the temple in the aforementioned Persian prophetic literatures, several topics recur: admonitions to rebuild the temple, promises of weal attendant upon temple reconstruction, references to the temple as the site of ritual behavior, the temple as a place of social integration, the temple as a place of theophany, and issues of priestly status at the temple. Rather than attempt to create a synthetic treatment of these themes I will instead offer a brief summary for each of the relevant prophetic texts.

Deutero-Isaiah.
The evidence is minimal. The only clear reference to the temple occurs in 44.28. Isa. 44.24–45.13 provide the larger literary context, often characterized as a 'disputation', in which Yahweh is defined by a series of participial clauses (vv. 24-28). The first part of the verse refers to Cyrus by name as Yahweh's agent: 'who says of Cyrus, "He is my shepherd, and he shall fulfil all my purpose; saying of Jerusalem, She shall be built, and of the temple (*hêkāl*), Your foundation shall be laid"'. Though there is ambiguity, I think the

---

1. There is no consensus regarding the place of the Zadokite material in the restoration vision. Some view it as a late addition, others think it integral to the vision.

speaker who is quoted following the verb *lē'mōr* is Cyrus. He is the one who bears responsibility for announcing to Yahwists that their temple in Jerusalem will be rebuilt. In this text, the emphasis is clearly on beginnings, the ceremonial re-dedication of the temple's foundation. Deutero-Isaiah appears uninterested in the day of completions: the ceremonial re-dedication of the temple. If the issue of hierarchy is involved, it is a hierarchy of power. Yahweh, through his agent Cyrus, is in control. Other human agents, notably Yahwistic temple builders such as a Davidide, have no place.

Haggai

If there is any prophetic book that focuses expressly on the temple it is Haggai. This prophet, whose activity is dated by the book's editor to 520 BCE, calls in no uncertain terms for the reconstruction of the Jerusalem temple. He admonishes the people to undertake such action because, while they have prepared houses for themselves, the deity whom they venerate is without a dwelling place. Moreover, through Haggai's intermediation, Yahweh promises marvelous riches that will attend the completion of the temple: '"I will fill this house with splendor", says the Lord of hosts. "The silver is mine, and the gold is mine", says the Lord of hosts."' '"The latter splendor of this house shall be greater than the former", says the Lord of hosts.' (2.7b-9a). Moreover, such bounty is not something Haggai associates with the far distant future. Rather, beginning with the day upon which the temple was ritually re-dedicated, one may expect radical blessing, which Haggai describes using the vocabulary of marvelous fertility (2.18-19).

Here too, the issue of the hierarchy of power is at work. And now Yahwistic leaders, Zerubbabel and Joshua, as well as 'all the remnant of the people' have a place. They, rather than a Persian ruler, bear responsibility for the rebuilding of the temple. Nonetheless, one thread links Deutero-Isaiah with Haggai. Both focus on the *beginnings* of restoration. Unlike Ezekiel 40–48, which presents a polity for restored Israel, Deutero-Isaiah and Haggai advocate return and restoration respectively, without explicit attention to the morphology of the reformed Judaean community. As a result, these literatures do not address the issue of status, the key hierarchy at work when the temple-based community is envisioned.

Zechariah 1–8

As I have argued elsewhere, one may distinguish between the visions and the oracular material in Zechariah 1-8. Temple reconstruction as such is not an issue in the visions. Instead, they report the divine initiatives concerning, and general principles regarding, the reformed community in a way that challenges the perspectives of Ezekiel 40–48. It is clear that Zechariah's visionary world presumes the existence of a rebuilt temple (cf. Zech. 3.7). However, in the visions, there is remarkably little attention devoted to the temple itself. Rather, its functionaries, such as Joshua, or an object that might be present in the temple, such as the lampstand, are part of that peculiar visionary world. The hierarchy of power is addressed in one of the visions, Zechariah 3, which serves to enfranchise the role of the high priest in postexilic Judah. The issue was a critically important one: what role would a civil leader have? Would it be like the 'prince' in Ezekiel 40–48? What would be the power relation between the high priest and the Davidide? These are the questions addressed by Zechariah's lampstand vision. And the answer is a dyarchic polity, one of power shared between priest and ruler.

The situation in the non-visionary material is palpably different, and in many ways quite similar to the sentiments expressed in Haggai. In the oracles of Zechariah 1-8, the temple appears prominently. The priests are referred to as 'the priests of the house of the Lord of hosts' (7.3). For those preserving these oracles, it was obvious that the temple would be rebuilt (1.16: 'my house shall be built in it'). However, a question involving hierarchy of status is prominent here in a way it was not in Haggai. A major concern during this period was the relative status of those who had been in exile and those who had lived in the land. With which group would the seeds for restoration be planted? For the oracles in Zechariah 1-8, the answer is clear: 'Those who are far off shall come and help to build the temple of the Lord... (6.15)', viz. those in/from the diaspora will play an important role in temple reconstruction. One admonition, 6.9-13, the political implications of which are not wholly clear, suggests that the silver and gold which Haggai expected from 'the nations' (Hag. 2.7-8) was being provided, in a more mundane way, by some diaspora Yahwists who had returned to their homeland. It is perhaps not too much to say that, at this point, the oracular material in Zechariah represents the implementation of Haggai's expectations for temple reconstruction, and with particular attention to the diaspora group as the one with special status. One suspects that the admonitory language of Zech. 8.9 was directed to those Yahwists who had returned from diaspora.

In the Zechariah 1–8 oracular material that treats of the temple one finds surprising stress placed upon one individual as temple builder, namely Zerubbabel (4.6b-10a; 6.12-13). We should probably view this emphasis using Smith's analytical categories and, in so doing, think that these oracles are addressing the hierarchy of power in early postexilic Judah. On the one hand, the oracles treat the temple and view as significant Zerubbabel's role in temple restoration. On the other hand, the temple does not appear prominently in the visions while Joshua, the high priest, is prominent in the visions. As I have already suggested, one key issue for the polity of reformed Judah was the relative power of the civil and religious leaders. Zechariah's visions held for relative equality between the two: Davidic pretender and high priest. Not so the oracles, which highlight the role of the Davidide, in a way similar to Haggai (Hag. 2.20-23).

In sum, Zechariah 1–8 addresses both the hierarchy of status and the hierarchy of power. As regards the hierarchy of status, pride of place is given to those whose recent history involved diaspora. And as for the hierarchy of power, the oracles justify the prominence of the civil leader, Zerubbabel, by pointing to his role as celebrant in the temple re-dedication ceremony.[1] The visions postulate a new polity, with the ritual leader of the temple holding a position coequal to that of the civil leader, who remains a Davidide.

Trito-Isaiah
Unlike the previous three prophetic collections, Isaiah 56–66 presumes the existence of the temple. Hence, with this literature and that which follows it chronologically, we are in an new world, one which no longer looked forward to the rebuilding of the Second Temple. What was promised or anticipated by Deutero-Isaiah, Haggai and Zechariah was now in existence. The temple had been finished and re-dedicated in 515 BCE. Nonetheless, there are elements that link these chapters with the earlier collections. Trito-Isaiah includes pro-

---

1. It may well be that this notion is designed to challenge the view that Cyrus, as in Deutero-Isaiah, was the titular temple builder.

mises for splendor at Yahweh's house (60.7). Isa. 66.18-21 strikes a similar note. In both cases, these oracles of promise allude to the presence of ritual practice in Jerusalem, which allows us to infer that the writer is addressing a situation in which sacrifices are again being offered (see 60.13 for reference to the glory of the temple).

However, these texts suggest that not all is as had been anticipated by Trito-Isaiah's prophetic forbears. Isa. 60.6 suggests that the wealth which various prophets thought would follow the reconstruction of the temple had not arrived. Hence this hope is projected yet again into the future: 'they shall bring gold and frankincense...' In addition, despite Yahweh's presence at the temple, Trito-Isaiah also speaks of Yahweh's other habitation: 'Look down from heaven and see, from thy holy and glorious habitation' (63.15). This reference to the holy habitation, which was of course the cosmic prototype for the earthly dwelling, is linked to an apparent dislocation of Yahweh's 'holy people' from the sanctuary (*miqdāš*). In sum, it would appear that, for Trito-Isaiah, the temple did not embody the full scale of values which had been anticipated for it.

Finally, there are several curious references to the temple which provide something of an innovative claim. Both texts involve direct discourse, whether admonition or interrogation. The first, Isa. 56.3-8, is so unusual that some have construed it as redactional, and not part of the Trito-Isaianic corpus.[1] The subject is the place of the *ben hannēkār* and the *sārîs* within 'his people' and at his house. There are at least two hallmark elements in this text: the requirements for acceptance in the Yahwistic community, namely keeping the sabbath and observing the covenant, and the notion of the house of prayer. At the outset it is clear that the author of this text is not claiming that the temple is a 'house of prayer' in contrast to its being a 'house of sacrifice'. Isa. 56.7 has as one of its points the acceptance of the burnt offerings and sacrifices of the foreigner who appears at Yahweh's house of prayer. The notion of the 'house of prayer' is not a *replacement* of but a *synonym* for 'house of Yahweh' or temple. Nor is the innovation in this text the possibility of having a foreigner in some way involved in Yahwistic rites. This too is allowed in other places, for example, passover rites. The innovation occurs with regard to the

---

1. So P.D. Hanson, *The Dawn of Apocalyptic* (Philadelphia: Fortress Press, 1975). I follow Westermann in thinking that 56.1-2 make up a separate oracle.

temple as a symbol for religious integration. The non-Israelite and the 'imperfect' Israelite are enfranchised within Israel through obedience of sabbath requirements and 'holding fast Yahweh's covenant'. Should they accomplish these tasks successfully, then Yahweh would give them a prominent place in his house. However, it seems that the foreigner and the eunuch can observe the sabbath and hold fast the covenant without prior participation in temple sacrifice. Participation in temple ritual, viz. having one's burnt offerings and sacrifices accepted on Yahweh's altar, is the reward, not the means by which acceptance into the community is achieved.

The second text, Isa. 66.1-4 (and perhaps 5-6), is consistent with 63.15, to which I have already referred. In both instances, the prophetic writer refers to Yahweh's heavenly dwelling. However, instead of calling for Yahweh's presence, 66.1-4 raises a question: 'Heaven is my throne and the earth is my footstool; what is the house which you would build for me, and what is the place of my rest?' This question receives no answer—and it is not a rhetorical question. Instead, the author provides a description of actions Yahweh favors and does not favor. Those who are humble, contrite, and tremble at his word are the favored. Those who slaughter an ox, sacrifice a lamb, etc. are not favored. Do we have here a prophet who has rejected in paschal fashion the notion of temple and its sacrificial system? I doubt it. To achieve an appropriate angle of vision on this admittedly difficult text, we must note the prominence of word and speech in both Isa. 66.1-4 and 56.1-8. The temple is a place of utterance, human voice and the deity's voice (so also 66.6). The author of these two texts seems to be arguing that without the appropriate voices, the temple's sacrificial system is inadequate. Speech and act make up appropriate ritual behavior at the temple. Put another way, this author has argued in both ch. 66, implicitly, and ch. 56, explicitly, that the temple is a 'house of prayer'. The question in 66.1 reads: 'what is the house which you build for me?' The answer is not 'the temple', but 'a house of prayer'.

Isaiah 56 and 66, whatever their authorship, provide serious reflection about the nature of the recently completed temple. One senses that the role of the temple may well be undergoing a process of redefinition in these chapters. It is a house of utterance as well as a house of sacrifice. I think it fair to say that this author is addressing here the hierarchy of status. To designate the temple as the 'house of prayer' is to limit the status of any priestly class to control prayerful utterance. Moreover, as regards sacrifice itself, access to the temple is open to 'the other', whether an outcast in Israel or a foreigner. The issues of status are here being addressed in a way that calls into question not only the nature of priestly authority but also the very definition of what it is to be a member of the covenant community.

Joel

As with Isaiah 56–66, the book of Joel presumes the existence of the temple. Joel 1.13-14 refers explicitly to the temple and its priests (cf. 2.15-17). Due to some catastrophe, perhaps drought or locust onslaught, there has been a cessation in the cycle of calendrical offerings (so also 1.9). As a result, the book of Joel advocates various forms of communal lamentation in order to garner a response from the deity to the people's plight. The temple was the site at which such laments were undertaken. All such practices involve traditional responses to crisis in both pre- and postexilic Israel.

Joel does, however, present something unique. The last two chapters, which are made up of an agglomeration of 'day of Yahweh' traditions, do refer to the temple: 'a fountain shall come forth from the house of the Lord' (4.18). This mythic motif of fructifying water issuing forth from the temple is attested in one prophetic corpus we have already examined, Ezekiel 40–48. That was a vision written during a time when the temple existed only in ruins. As a result, a glorious future involving a rebuilt temple with water issuing from its door was in some ways natural, as an expectation for a marvelous new structure (Ezek. 47.1-12). However, once a temple has been rebuilt and had been in operation, one is less likely to freight that symbol with notions involving radical change from the status quo. To do so implies some concern with the temple in its current form. One may, therefore, infer that the last two chapters of Joel express some dissatisfaction with the way in which Yahweh is manifest in Jerusalem. It is, literally, a lamentable situation. And, despite the fact that one can use the temple for the appropriate lamentation procedures, it is possible to think about a vastly better situation—one in which a fountain flows from the temple when Yahweh finally acts on Israel's behalf. Therefore, for Joel, the temple functions in two distinct ways, as a means for ritual response to a contemporary crisis and as a symbol by means of which future weal is anticipated. To speak about the latter is to suggest that the former is not wholly adequate. If we put the matter in the vocabulary of hierarchy, it is that of power. Yahweh, and no human instrumentality, will engender a better future.

Malachi

The sacrificial system of the temple figures prominently in the book of Malachi. However, at least in the first two chapters, the standard vocabulary for the temple itself is not used. Rather, this prophet focuses on one element in the temple complex, the altar as well as ritual activity at the altar (so 1.6-14; 2.1-9; 2.10-17). Malachi admonishes the priests to comport themselves in accord with that which Yahweh requires, namely ritual purity. Conjointly, he pleads the cause of one group, the Levites, who have apparently been sullied by some other priestly house (2.4-9). To hear such language is to hear disputation regarding the hierarchy of power. For Malachi, the temple represents an institution which may stand under critique (see also 3.10) and about which the hierarchy of status may be argued.

There is another component. Malachi, like Joel, expects Yahweh to act. The 'day of Yahweh' traditions infuse this late prophetic book as well. And the temple has a role to play: 'Behold, I send my messenger to prepare the way before me, and the Lord (*hā'ādôn*) whom you seek will suddenly come to his temple' (3.1). There is considerable dispute about the identity of 'the Lord'. Is it Yahweh or is it some forerunner (cf. 3.23: 'Behold, I will send you Elijah the prophet before the great and terrible day of the Lord comes'). In either case, the individual appears at the temple as a part of the eschatological scenario. For Malachi, then, the temple remains important, both as a religio-social institution, with attendant concerns over status, and as a site in the future drama of judgment and salvation, which is ultimately concerned with the hierarchy of power—Yahweh's power.

Deutero-Zechariah

The motif that may be discerned in Joel and Malachi is even more pronounced in Deutero-Zechariah, viz. reflection about the temple on the 'day of Yahweh'. As a result, the matter of power is paramount. The author refers to the mundane temple only in an occasional way, though if the standard conjectural emendations are correct, such a reference involves the provincial bank (11.13). Elsewhere, in 9.8 and 14.20-21, we find ourselves again in the world of the eschatological

scenario. As was the case with Mal. 3.1, Zech. 9.8 treats the temple as
a place at which someone will appear. In 9.8 there is, however, no
ambiguity about the identity of the individual. It is Yahweh who will
stay at the temple and, in so doing, protect those loyal to him. Here
one senses standard Zion traditions, involving Yahweh as defender of
his royal mountain. In contrast, 14.20-21 treats the temple as does
Joel, as a place where something 'ideal' will occur. Again the text
refers to 'that day', a time when, according to this text, there will be
radical sacrality provided by temple basins. Unlike Ezekiel, which
continues to draw strict boundaries to distinguish the sacred from the
profane, Zech. 14.20-21 speaks of a time when holiness will suffuse
the city (cf. the notion of the city as the house of God in Ezra–
Nehemiah as well as the idea of the city which is filled with Yahweh's
kābôd [2.9]).

IV

In conclusion, Persian period prophetic texts provide a remarkable
variety of perspectives on the Jerusalem temple. In no case does it
seem obvious that the prophetic literature stood, in some straight-
forward way, in the service of, or as part of ritual activity at, the
temple. As a result, I find it difficult to maintain that prophetic
activity during this period has been subsumed into the cult. Just as the
pre-exilic prophets accepted the notion of monarchy and could
critique its abuses, so too, prophets in the postexilic period era could
accept the new-found prominence of the temple and still stand in a
stance critical of its operation or personnel.

There was a new temple, which embodied things both old and new.
Because it involved innovation, whether such innovation be viewed
sociologically (*Bürger-Tempel-Gemeinde*) or theologically ('what is
this house you would build for me?'), there were issues that had not
been prominent before, for example, 'who is to be construed as an
acceptable Yahwist?' With no national boundaries to define the matter,
and with Yahwists residing throughout the ancient Near East, Judaean
Yahwists had to develop new ways for thinking about eligibility and
participation in the temple system, whether as officiants or as
supplicants.

For those active in Judah c. 520 BCE, the Second Temple presented
a number of pragmatic problems, some of which are addressed

directly by the prophetic literature I have surveyed, for example, Isaiah 56–66 and Malachi. In addition, some Yahwists anticipated a future beyond that which was promised to occur with the completion of the temple. The silver and gold did not flow in, as Haggai and others had anticipated. This promise of riches is clearly thrust into the future, since it occurs in texts that postdate the construction of the temple. Moreover, if the thesis of the *Bürger-Tempel-Gemeinde* is licit, we could expect some Yahwists, who were not fully enfranchised, to envision, if not a different temple, a temple that would offer an alternate religio-social system, as in Isaiah 56 and 66.

Perhaps one should suggest that the early postexilic writers thought about two temples, the temple in Jerusalem, which Joel addresses in the call for communal lamentation, together with its personnel whom Malachi critiques radically; and the temple that will function on 'the day of the Lord', which Joel thinks will involve a marvelously fertile spring and which Deutero-Zechariah thinks will serve as the place of Yahweh's final theophany. However, there is no reason to think that a new temple need be built. Rather, during the eschatological drama, the Second Temple would assume certain mythic and theophanic capabilities for which it had always been, in theory, available.

How then are we to think about the differences—as manifest in the prophetic literature—between the First and Second Temples? I suggest that one fundamental difference involves the prominence of the hierarchy of status in the Second Temple. Since the hierarchy of power had been decided—Yahweh was cosmic deity, and the Persian emperor was his earthly regent—the issue of power was settled. Davidide governors were unimportant in the larger polity. 'Day of Yahweh' traditions did, however, provide an occasion for the renaissance of this hierarchy, in ways which emphasized that Yahweh was indeed the powerful high god. However, the issues of which priestly house would have supreme authority, whether diaspora Yahwists would have major leadership positions, or who could be full participants in the community loom large in Persian period prophetic texts. All three issues involve the hierarchy of status. The exigencies of existence in Second Temple Judah provided the issues about which intermediaries during this period were concerned. And since many of these issues are different from those in the Iron Age, Persian period prophets might appear to have a stance vis-à-vis the temple that was different from their predecessors. However, the differences are more readily explained as a function of the issues they confronted rather than as involving the enactment of their roles in the temple system.

CRITIQUE

NEHEMIAH 5:
BY WAY OF A RESPONSE TO HOGLUND AND SMITH

John M. Halligan

I have chosen the text of Nehemiah 5 as a test text for Hoglund's proposal that postexilic Judah be interpreted in the light of Achaemenid policy, and Smith's that the political climate of the Second Temple period contained a social group, the 'Sons of the Golah', shaped by the pressures of a 'culture of resistance' while in exile and maintained after the repatriation. I would like to take their insights to a reading of Nehemiah 5 to see what new understanding of this troublesome passage may emerge.

Hoglund refers to Nehemiah 5 once, in the context of his discussion concerning the $q^e h\bar{a}l$ $hagg\hat{o}l\hat{a}$, the unique name for the community nearly a century separated from the exilic band that actually returned to Judah from Babylon. Neh. 5.1 recounts the complaint of the 'people' ($'am$) against their fellow Judaeans to whom they have pledged their fields and children in return for food and tax payments. Who are these people? Are they the 'assembly of the exile'? If this people is within the $q^e h\bar{a}l$ $hagg\hat{o}l\hat{a}$, then do we have an instance of an intercommunal conflict, as Smith suggests?

Smith is much aware of the import of Nehemiah 5. He cites it indirectly through Kippenberg, who believes the impoverishment in question is due to the introduction of coinage during the reign of Darius. Silver was too dear for the peasant to secure as tax payment and thus could not meet demands. Smith discusses the measures taken by Nehemiah to rectify the crisis, in particular, to preserve a self-conscious community in the midst of a socially distinct 'other'. I propose to take the passage further, guided by the suggestions of Hoglund and Smith.

The text of Neh. 5.1-5 lists three critical conditions that the people had reached during the governorship of Nehemiah: 1) there was insufficient food for the numerous children born to them; 2) in order to get sufficient food to feed them, they had to mortgage their property; and 3) they had to borrow money to pay the imperial taxes.[1] A fourth matter concerns the violation by the Jewish creditor of the sentiment of Deuteronomy 15 wherein a Hebrew slave is not to be sold to foreigners. The people have handed over their children to the mortgagees who have subsequently sold them to the Gentiles (*goyim*).

The people, unable to feed their children, mortgage their property; unable to meet their mortgage, they forfeit their property; still unable to satisfy continuing debt, they forfeit their collateral, their sons and daughters. The lenders, in order to recover their investment, sell off the collateral either to fellow Judaean creditors or foreign parties. Nehemiah's humanitarian policy has been to redeem Judaean slaves according to his means. In Neh. 5.8 Nehemiah finds that he is buying recycled Judaean slaves; sons and daughters once redeemed have been re-enslaved and now re-redeemed.[2]

Hoglund posits, and I tend to agree, that there took place shortly after 538 BCE a resettlement of Judaean exiles, including relocation of resident populations, into new villages along Persian design to form ethnic collectives for the purposes of creating an international network of commercial exchange and transport. Hoglund's review of settlement patterns and ceramic chronology has pointed toward the Persian province of Yehud as structured along the lines of tributary modes of production administered by governors and other officials responsible to the crown in Susa.

The social and economic crisis in Nehemiah would have reached the magnitude reported somewhere midway through the Persian period. In fact, Nehemiah was a crown-appointed governor sent to strengthen the provincial capital, Jerusalem. While I accept Hoglund's suggestion that such an imperial plan was initiated in Yehud in the early days of Achaemenid rule, it remains to be seen whether it persisted through the time of Nehemiah.

1. I would argue that Nehemiah's testimony concerning the integrity of his term of office covers his conduct during the period of economic crisis rather than following it.

2. If I may use the gate opened by Carroll in his analysis of Jeremiah 32 as a 'textual strategy reflecting a social practice of land purchasing' in postexilic Judah, then I suggest that Jer. 34.8-22 may reflect the very condition Nehemiah is addressing here.

Let us suppose the Persians redistributed the Judaean exiles led by Sheshbazzar, who had in Babylon known the meaning of 'centralized work forces' (Smith), on new rural work sites throughout Yehud. In a subsequent wave led by Zerubbabel more exiles were added to the land if not the existing labor forces. A delegation of exiles visited Jerusalem during the reign of Artaxerxes I and reported through Hanani to Nehemiah at Susa that the walls of Jerusalem were breached, its gates were burnt, and its people were 'in great distress'. With the crown's blessing Nehemiah led what must have been a fourth delegation of exiles to Yehud to repair the condition of the people and the city. Later another group under Ezra would venture to Yehud. How were successive waves of exiles absorbed by the Achaemenid agrarian system? Were they assigned villages and work stations or permitted to seek out relatives or friends and settle nearby? What place was there for allowing the resident populace to rebuild centers of worship at Persian expense?

I submit that the original mechanisms have weakened or metamorphized by the time of Nehemiah's arrival. Whether this was due to neglect by the king due to expansionist dreams in Asia Minor, or Egyptian mischief to the south I do not know. But Nehemiah 5 reveals a desperate economic situation which would in no way credit imperial planning. If Hoglund is right, the *dallat hā'āreṣ* mentioned in Jeremiah 40 and the *beⁿê haggôlâ* and any other resident in Yehud had been collected, distributed and settled in work villages in the early Achaemenid period. Things have changed, the population density has increased, food is scarce, capital is frozen and the economy is caught in a downward spiral. Smith reckons a special cohesiveness forged by exilic pressures governed the *beⁿê haggôlâ* even though they were diverse in their roles. There were priests and levites, nobles and craftsmen, as well as field hands, merchants and military personnel among the *beⁿê haggôlâ*. The cry for help in Nehemiah 5 seems to come from within that broad group one might term 'peasants'. I am not prepared to identify them as 'peoples of the land' (*ᶜammê hā'āreṣ*).

Nehemiah 5 identifies the indigent as simply 'the people' and their creditors as 'brother Jews'. The financial crisis does not seem related to the work on the walls of Jerusalem (*contra* Myers); therefore, its epicenter is elsewhere in place and perhaps in time as well. Mention in Neh. 5.3-4 that they were mortgaging fields, vineyards and homes (*sic* LXX) to maintain subsistence levels and that they had borrowed money to meet imperial taxes indicates a cash-flow failure among the rural peasants.[1] In times of cash or crop shortage at the fund of power, the farmer, there is also failure expected at the level of the creditor. Nehemiah includes himself, his brothers, and his men among the class of creditors assisting the peasants. It remains for a lengthier study to offer a thorough look at the world of Achaemenid finance relative to the province of 'Beyond the River' and in particular the district of Yehud; however, I wish to venture a remark concerning credit which may throw some light on the situation at hand in Nehemiah 5. The cause of grain shortage appears to be natural, and no enemy is cited in the passage. In short-term crisis, short-term credit is attractive to debtor and creditor. That this crisis had advanced to a chronic stage seems indicated in Neh. 5.3 wherein fixed assets such as land and homes are used as security.

I agree with Hoglund that imperial domain meant that 'the land was the empire's, and could be possessed or dispossessed at imperial whim'. Thus in that ruralization period the land of Yehud—unless otherwise indicated by imperial edict—belonged to the crown. At some point thereafter was land privatized? Could land ownership have devolved to communal title such as that of the *bêt āb* as described by Gottwald relative to pre-monarchic Israel?[2] The text implies that individual families held title to the property. This transformation needs further study.

Ninety per cent of all the sales of all manufacturers, wholesalers, processors, and jobbers are today made on credit. It is the nature of business to exchange goods on a credit basis. I cannot prove that commerce in the Achaemenid empire was conducted on credit on the same scale but I feel safe to say it was greater than we usually allow for. Trade credit, or mercantile credit, is credit extended by sellers to buyers at all levels of the production and distribution process down to the retailer. Installment sale credit entails the purchaser signing a promissory note or series of notes for the amount of credit extended;

1. In a study of the economic plight of the Canaanite peasant during the Amarna period I had noted that such factors of production as control of his land, water, seed, draft animals, tools and labor may and do become debt titles. Cf. J.M. Halligan, 'The Role of the Peasant in the Amarna Period', in *Palestine in Transition: The Emergence of Ancient Israel* (SWBAS, 2; ed. D.N. Freedman and D.F. Graf; Sheffield: Almond Press, 1983), p. 19.

2. N.K. Gottwald, *The Tribes of Yahweh* (New York: Orbis, 1979), p. 292.

such notes are generally paid off in equal installments running for a specified period; the loan is secured by the goods sold; this is a secured loan.

The text of Nehemiah is witness that a class of creditors did arise in the Second Temple period in Yehud.[1] I submit they arise as trade creditors working the international commercial routes through Phoenician and Egyptian contacts and centers. They acted as agents, wholesalers, and regional marketers for the goods produced in the agricultural *bêt āb* of Yehud. They were Judaean not Persian; they made money, they were not born to it. Because internal or local trade needed less supervision a 'farmer's market' type of exchange proved adequate in rural Yehud.

Judaean farmers could buy seed on credit or with cash in hand. If by credit, it would be credit against the next harvest's yield. The expected harvest's yield itself could become an instrument of debt in that such a promissory note could be bought and sold among credit brokers, and it is not beyond the realm of possibility, given the sophistication of the Persian network of commerce, that a creditor might speculate in futures on commodities such as wine, oil and grain against not only yield but also where, when, and at what market price the goods could be delivered. In this system crop failure would not cripple the commodities trader because shortages could be anticipated and notes dumped or covered by the prudent. On the other hand the farmer could be devastated because there was less financial flexibility.

Farmers prosper as sellers if the yield is steady, they suffer as debtors if the yield is poor or erratic. The local creditor is attracted to extending credit to the farmer in hard times less for a profit motive than from custom or the belief that times will change. Postexilic Yehud does not seem to be organized in the manner of the *mišpāḥâ* so financial protection does not appear. Seasonal fluctuations in inventory affect debt size and the smaller the farmer the greater will be the relative use of credit.

Traditionally, a creditor considers, before investing, character,

---

1. I tend to seen Nehemiah 5 as a class conflict but not as described by Smith in terms of a large resident population (chiefly peasants) and a returning aristocracy. Granted that Nehemiah speaks of 'nobles and officials', I am not assured these are descendants of stock that knew Babylonian captivity, but arose in the commercial climate Persia created in Yehud.

capacity, and the capital of the borrower. It would be a serious error to see in Nehemiah 5 only the rapacious greed of the Judaean creditor repossessing fields, vineyards, houses, and children in order to make good on an error in investing judgment. The prudent creditor also considers three other matters before investing: collateral, (business) conditions, and coverage (insurance of any type). The surplus of children is exhausting the food available in Yehud; it is also the source of collateral for the beleaguered parents.

In the preceding remarks I have traced some of the financial parameters for the two actants in Nehemiah 5, the debtor and the creditor. In that the Judaean peasant was a high credit risk in times of crop failure he would not be eligible for unsecured loans. His only option was the secured loan whereby he had to pledge assets in case of default. Collateral is attractive to the creditor if its value exceeds the total loan figure so that if necessary it would be easy and profitable to sell. The pledge is normally a paper transaction with no physical transfer until such time as default occurs.[1] A secured pledge carries certain advantages to both parties: secured credit can gain higher amounts of credit to the borrower; a secured note is more valuable to the creditor because is negotiable; and funds are cheaper if secured.

The peasants of Nehemiah 5 have bought food and paid taxes through the use of secured loans. What security devices have the creditors chosen? Several were possible: (1) a receipt of goods in hand (did they take title to saleable items?); (2) a lien pledging all goods in bulk to the creditor (all oil from vineyards x and y); (3) a receipt to lodge title to goods held by the lender while the debtor makes payment; (4) a chattel mortgage on all moveable goods still held by the peasant such as herds; and finally (5) the physical surrender of the security to the lender until the debt is made good, such as children. There were in this case three groups of complainants, representing a range of such security devices.

Nehemiah identifies the nobles (*hahōrîm*) and the officials (*hassᵉgānîm*) as the villainous creditors. The specific charge is usury (*maśśâ*): not excessive interest, but any compensation for the loan. None of the complainants raises the issue of usury: it was their

---

1. A sworn verbal promise might be more in keeping with the agrarian community but I would not rule out the recording of the debt on some permanent and convenient material.

inability to meet principal that resulted in their loss of title to chattel and fixed assets. It would seem that the creditors had acted within the law governing lending among Jews but had not shown sufficient charity as enjoined by Deut. 15.7-11. The purpose of a charge of usury would be that it brings the creditors within the law's jurisdiction—even if it may not be applicable.

Nehemiah calls for the large assembly (*qehillâ gedôlâ*) so that the matter might be adjudicated. The trading of fellow Jews as slaves to Gentiles is the second public charge and one raised by the third group. However, the emphasis of Nehemiah is not on the fact of bondage but rather that these once redeemed were resold to Gentiles and still in need of redemption. The LXX adds that Nehemiah did redeem slaves, not because it was official policy to do so but rather of his own free will. While fellow Jews may voluntarily pledge themselves as slaves to other Jews to satisfy debt (Lev. 25.39; Exod. 21.1-6; Deut. 15.12-18), the slave envisioned in Leviticus 25 was not a Jew but rather a foreigner whom the Jewish master might sell, buy or give as inheritance. What became of the Jew sold to foreigners would not be bound by the Jewish law of Jubilee or Deut. 15.12, hence the concern of Nehemiah to redeem them as soon as feasible. However, the creditors were selling them right back to the Gentiles, so creating an industry of their own. (A further source of income may be alluded to in the scrambled phrasing of 5bα: 'some of our daughters are already enslaved and we are powerless'. This may refer to a special form of bondage, the employment of prostitutes. Nehemiah does not address this.)

The nobles and officials at fault promise to cease usury and return a hundredth of the money, grain, new wine and oil to their debtors. The priests are summoned to administer a solemn oath to the creditors, a divine sanction is enjoined by Nehemiah. The meeting ends with an 'Amen' from all the assembly (*kol haqqāhāl*). Frankly, this solution to the economic crisis defies reality. If the economy had deteriorated to the point described in 5.1-5, it could not have been restored instantly by forgiving all debt and returning all forms of security as well as a 1 per cent bonus. Commerce would come to a standstill, and work on the wall would be a luxury no one could afford. The instant removal of the credit system would jeopardize all other dependent commercial transactions in progress, and, no matter how distasteful to the deuteronomic palate they may be in character, these financial arrangements had to continue until relief for the economy arising from increase in production or trade occurred. These credit arrangements did not precipitate the famine but resulted from peasants' loss of power to produce saleable goods and in turn provide minimal subsistence for their dependents.

I have placed my analysis within the framework suggested by Hoglund, namely, the Achaemenid mechanisms of ruralization and commercialization. Ethnic collectivization may be hinted at 5.5 in the reference to 'flesh of us', that is, the creditors and the debtors being 'brothers'. Militarization may also be discerned if one is willing to view the rebuilding of the walls of Jerusalem in the way that Sanballat, Tobiah and Geshem do. A healthy Jerusalem would serve as a protection against their encroachment on the district. The relative serenity that Yehud enjoyed from external raiding during the Persian period may give silent witness to the effective policing the imperial troops did. I am suspicious of the weight placed by Hoglund on the identification of the $q^e hal\ hagg\hat{o}l\hat{a}$ with the ethnic collectives of Yehud. The single occurrence in Ezra 10.8 is a slim base for such a conclusion.

A strength of Smith's paper is in his analysis of the social conflict the exiles experienced upon returning to Yehud. Did the exiles have a 'victim' mentality? Did they see themselves as holier than their Jewish brothers who had not gone to Babylon and known the terror? Is Hag. 2.10-14 reflective of the 'hibakusha' mentality? Are the *'am* and the *gôy* of Haggai the same as that of Nehemiah 5? Smith wavers between a recognition that differences in cult and perhaps faith separate the exiles and the residents, and Mantel's choice that the 'children of the Golah' were socially distinct, both because of the effects of the exile, and because of a class conflict between the 'children of the Golah' and a resident upper class. If the 'children of the Golah' were the minority that maintained social and cultic separation over against a mongrel population of *Yehudim*, then I do not know how to interpret Nehemiah 5. By midpoint in the Achaemenid rule, an economic crisis among the Jews demonstrates in a negative manner their self-consciousness. On my own understanding, Ezra's obsession with intermarriage with foreigners must depend on a factor that emerged within Yehud after Nehemiah. What that is I do not know.

ON MODELS AND TEXTS:
A RESPONSE TO BLENKINSOPP AND PETERSEN

Peter Ross Bedford

As both papers under discussion recognize, the Jerusalem temple of Yahweh was the pre-eminent national shrine of the kingdom of Judah before the dissolution of that state in 586 BCE. It was a monarchical institution which was built and maintained by Judaean kings and which served the ideological and administrative needs of the state. It functioned in a vastly different political and social context in the Persian period. Judah was no longer an independent state, nor did it have an indigenous king. Why then was this temple needed in Achaemenid Judah? Who needed it? What was the function of this temple when there was no longer a state or indigenous king? It is with aspects of such questions that both papers are concerned.

Blenkinsopp's paper, drawing on Weinberg's *Bürger-Tempel-Gemeinde* theory of social organization, focuses on socioeconomic and political aspects of the role of the Jerusalem temple of Yahweh. In common with other major temples in ancient Western Asia in this period, the Jerusalem temple of Yahweh was a political and economic centre, access to which was limited to certain sections of the population. For the community participating in the temple system in Judah, 'the rebuilt temple was as important *socio-politically and economically* as it was in the religious sphere' (my emphasis). This community substantially, though not exclusively, consisted of the Judaeans repatriated from Babylonia. They established their position by taking responsibility for the rebuilding of the temple to the general exclusion of those who had remained in Judah. For Blenkinsopp,

> It is this circumstance of a *limited* participation in temple governance that gives some at least initial plausibility to the thesis of a civic-temple community in Judah during the Achaemenid period.

Because there is so little evidence in the Judaean literary (prophetic and historical) texts of the Persian period for the economic organization of Achaemenid Judah and the possible role of the temple in it, Blenkinsopp, following Weinberg, has to draw on comparative evidence from other temples in the Persian empire. He considers that the Jerusalem temple should conform to their economic and sociopolitical roles. I am compelled to leave to one side the issue of the validity of the *Bürger-Tempel-Gemeinde* hypothesis (hereafter abbreviated to *Gemeinde*) in explaining the examples cited in its support. Since this theory has received little attention from classicists, Assyriologists and ancient historians, it is premature to pronounce judgment on it. More analysis of the parallels is clearly necessary. With regard to the Babylonian temples, for example, much more study needs to be undertaken on their socioeconomic function in society and their role in Achaemenid Babylonia as compared with earlier periods. Blenkinsopp also recognizes this need for further study.

Even if one assumed, for the sake of argument, that the *Gemeinde* structure was valid for other temples in the Persian empire, there is no compulsion to interpret the function and significance of the Jerusalem temple in the light of them. They are not necessarily comparable entities. Further, since it is acknowledged that the Judaean literary texts are not concerned with economic matters one has to be particularly careful of conforming the little information gleaned from the texts to the supposed parallels. Even on matters of social organization, where these texts seemingly offer more information, it would be incorrect to assume that the evidence must be interpreted in the light of other temples, even where certain aspects of social organization appear to be similar. In other words, there is a need to be aware of the problems commonly confronting the use of comparative material.

Consider, as a case in point, one of the important results of the institution of the *Gemeinde* structure. As with the communities Blenkinsopp cites in the parallel examples, the community centred on the Jerusalem temple was supposedly afforded special status and privileges in Judah. What was the nature of this status and its attendant privileges? Blenkinsopp claims that

> By assuming responsibility for the actual rebuilding of the temple, with
> the backing of the imperial authorities and to the exclusion of the native

population (Ezra 4.1-3), they reserved to themselves control of the temple operations, *which translated into a large measure of social control* [my emphasis].

From the evidence of the biblical texts, over whom was 'social control' exercised? Over only those in the community or over the general population of Judah? If the former, then one is simply dealing with a group whose leaders had the authority to discipline its members and to regulate its practices. If the latter is being referred to, then the only 'social control' evidenced is that regulating admission into the community.

The specific examples of areas over which 'social control' was supposedly exercised face similar questions. To what does 'civic status' refer? Certainly not membership in, or rights within, the district of Judah. These would have been available to all inhabitants of the district. Perhaps it denotes citizenship in Jerusalem, where, of course, the temple was built. But if this is the case, one needs to note Neh. 7.4 and 11.1-19, which consider Jerusalem to be woefully under-populated at the arrival of Nehemiah. Since there was therefore no city to speak of, it is questionable that citizenship in Jerusalem is in view. Perhaps 'civic status' refers to membership in the community? If so, then one is again concerned with authority over only a limited group of people.

It can further be asked: over whose land did the community have authority? Over that of the whole population of Judah? Ezek. 11.15-17, the commonly cited text for this contention, simply reflects, as Blenkinsopp notes, the attempts of both the exiles and those who stayed in Judah to interpret their historical experience. In the context of the exile and dissolution of the state each held that it was the locus of the divine plan of restoration. Nothing can be deduced from this outlook regarding the political status of the temple or connections to it. Also, Ezra, whatever the purpose of his mission may have been, could not dispossess people of their real estate. Ezra 10.8 refers to moveable property ($r^e k \hat{u} \check{s}$), not land, so expulsion from the community had no impact on rights to land. How Ezra came to have authority over moveable property is, however, another matter.

Now, there is no evidence to suggest that title to property in Judah was connected to participation in the temple community. Further, the Jerusalem temple itself does not appear to have had any land holdings. This is in contrast to the parallels cited. Blenkinsopp's contention that the temple held land is based on two points. First, that the temple had storerooms. These, however, may simply have stored produce donated to the temple (for example, Neh. 13.12-14), rather than the yield of temple lands. The Levites' abandonment of the temple to return to their own land (Neh. 13.10ff.) may denote that the temple held no land of its own from which it could derive income. That is, as Nehemiah 10 and Neh. 13.10-14 suggest, apart from some beneficence shown by Achaemenid rulers towards the temple, the temple's income was made up of donations (which may later have become taxes). Secondly, Ezekiel 40–48 'emphasize the connection between temple and land'. This utopian vision can hardly be cited as evidence for the role of the temple in Achaemenid Judah. Doubtless it reflects the author's desires for, and expectations regarding, the temple and land, but whether this bears any relationship to the political and social realities is another matter entirely. Weinberg recognized, as Blenkinsopp notes, that the Jerusalem temple held no land, but Weinberg does not realize how serious a challenge this is to his hypothesis. Blenkinsopp recognizes the threat but can muster no evidence to dispel it. Lack of land holdings also raises the issue of how the temple cult and personnel were funded. If it was by donations, then what does this mean for the relationship between the temple and its community?

If the symbiotic relationship between temple and city is a hallmark of the *Gemeinde* structure as portrayed by Blenkinsopp, then it appears that such a relationship may not have developed in Judah before the governorship of Nehemiah, since it is with reference to this period that the first clear evidence for the intensive population of Jerusalem is obtained. It might be supposed on the basis of Ezra 4.12 and Neh. 1.2-3 that Jerusalem had been inhabited for a time after the temple rebuilding and that much of the city's population had been forced to leave when the city walls were torn down sometime later. Nothing is known of Jerusalem in the decades directly after the temple rebuilding, so one must be circumspect in drawing conclusions as to what went on or what role the temple had during that period.

Even if one were to assume that the Jerusalem temple rebuilding was undertaken by the repatriates for the purpose of establishing the *Gemeinde* structure, and that the city was populated at that time, the fact that Nehemiah found the city depopulated means that the *Gemeinde* system had, to some extent at least, broken down. The period of Nehemiah might therefore be seen as the renaissance of the structure. I leave to one side the issue of how this structure would have survived the city's depopulation and instead question that Nehemiah would have been responsible for re-instituting the *Gemeinde* structure. As Kreissig points out in his critical appraisal of Weinberg's hypothesis,[1] Nehemiah was the governor of the whole district of Judah, not just of Jerusalem or the temple community. His responsibilities were over a wider domain. It would be unlikely that he, as governor, would foment division in the district by establishing a community whose members had status and rights beyond other groups. Indeed, the Nehemiah Memoir suggests that his aim was to suppress the power of certain interest groups in favour of the broader population and the unity of the district (Neh. 5–6; 13.28-30). The rebuilding of Jerusalem's walls and the repopulation of the city should be understood as an attempt to establish a focal point for the district as a whole, rather than the resuscitation of the supposed *Gemeinde* structure. The restored city was a symbol of Judah's independence from the authority and meddling of the leaders of neighbouring districts.

Nehemiah 10, which seems to be taken as important evidence for the centrality of the temple and the limited character of the group controlling it, actually suggests to me the opposite. The temple was not of great significance to the Judaean population. If it were, why would there have been a need for an agreement to financially support it as late as the time of Nehemiah? Does not the Levites' abandonment of the temple to return to their own lands (Neh. 13.10ff.) denote lack of funding? Why would the temple have been neglected (Neh. 10.40c)? How strong could the *Gemeinde* structure have been if temple funding had been so low? I understand the agreement in Nehemiah 10 to have been directed to all the inhabitants of Judah. The Jerusalem temple was to become a focus for Judaean identity to counter the influence of those outside the district. Note that those whom Nehemiah prohibits Judaeans to marry and those with whom he strives for political ascendancy over Judah all come from outside the territory of Judah (Neh. 1.19; 4.1; 13.23-28).

Another important issue which can only be touched upon here is the

---

1. H. Kreissig, 'Eine beachtenswerte Theorie zur Organisation altvorder-orientalischer Tempelgemeinden im Achämenidenreich', *Klio* 66 (1984), pp. 35-39 (p. 37).

authority by which the community undertook the establishment of the *Gemeinde* structure. Blenkinsopp understands this form of social organization, unfamiliar in Palestine, to have been introduced by the repatriates. To establish the community's special status and privileges would have demanded the overt support of the Achaemenid Persian authorities. When would such support have been forthcoming? As recent studies have shown, recourse to a supposed policy of administrative reorganization by Darius I to account for this is ill-founded. I would aver that while it is probable that a distinct community of repatriates existed in Judah, its authority did not extend over anyone outside its own membership, and also that membership of the community afforded no status or power in the district of Judah. It is improper to contend that Judah must conform to the supposed parallels cited. Perhaps the *Gemeinde* structure in Achaemenid Judah was different from that evidenced elsewhere, as Weinberg contends. Perhaps the *Gemeinde* hypothesis is not valid for Achaemenid Judah. If the city of Jerusalem remained largely unpopulated until the time of Nehemiah, then the correctness of the *Gemeinde* hypothesis is in any case suspect. As mentioned earlier, even firmer ground for questioning its validity in Judah is that the temple does not appear to have had land holdings.

Petersen speaks of the temple as 'something surely central to Persian period Judaean Yahwism'. Less concerned with its possible wider socioeconomic role in Achaemenid Judah, his paper addresses how the Judaean prophetic texts understood the role of the temple within the community. He draws upon Jonathan Z. Smith's understanding of the temple as 'symbolically expressing hierarchies of power and status'. The 'hierarchy of status' issues identified by Petersen as prominent in the community revolve around the temple, involving claims either over rights to officiate (between priestly houses), or over who could participate in the worshipping community, or over who would have authority in the community. Petersen is doubtless correct to draw attention to the different 'set of hierarchies' in Achaemenid Judah as compared with monarchical Judah.

It is particularly interesting that the issues in need of resolution in the new social and political context of Achaemenid Judah (such as leadership and community self-definition) are related to the temple, given that both the repatriates and those who had remained in Judah had managed their social organization and, presumably, the worship of Yahweh for some 65 years without this temple. Further, assuming that a number of Babylonian exiles were repatriated to Judah at the edict of Cyrus, there was a delay of some 18 years before they commenced rebuilding the temple. Any discussion of the role of the temple in Judaean society must therefore address the purpose of the temple's rebuilding, and how the apparent disregard for the temple, reflected in the delay in rebuilding, was overcome. This thus raises the issue of the nature of the relationship of the temple rebuilding to the important issues perceived by Petersen. I recognize that there can be a difference between the purpose for rebuilding and the social function the temple performed or developed, but the latter cannot entirely be divorced from the former.

Did these 'hierarchy of status' issues play a role in precipitating the rebuilding of the temple or did they arise (or were they exacerbated) by the temple's reconstruction? If the former, then when did these issues become important? The issues Petersen identifies were current in the Babylonian period (as Jeremiah and Ezekiel 40–48 ostensibly claim), but the construction of the temple was apparently not commenced until 520 BCE. If there was a need for the temple, why was it not rebuilt earlier? Perhaps these issues became pressing around the time of rebuilding. If so, then one has to account for the rise of their importance. Also, for whom was this temple significant? If these issues rose to prominence only after the rebuilding of the temple, then one must also account for that and seek other reasons for the rebuilding of the temple. Temple rebuilding itself assumes at least temporary resolution of certain 'hierarchy of status' issues, notably who could participate in the rebuilding. The question of when the temple was to be rebuilt must also have been resolved before construction commenced. Should one assume that these issues were resolved only just before the reconstruction commenced? Should it therefore be concluded that the impetus for the rebuilding came from repatriates who returned not long before the rebuilding?

Finally, I offer some comment on the biblical texts. Both papers under discussion share the commonly stated notion that in Achaemenid Judah there was a distinct social entity or community at whose centre stood the Jerusalem temple and its cult. It is primarily with respect to this community, discussion of whose character I must leave to one side, that the function of the temple is discerned. A corollary of this view is that the Jerusalem temple was a significant institution within the social fabric of Achaemenid Judah, if only because the community centred on the temple was itself an important component of the Judaean population.

It cannot be denied that the Jerusalem temple and the issue of community self-definition figure prominently in the Judaean literary texts of the Persian period. Indeed, interest in these matters is attested in texts from the Babylonian period. Petersen's paper documents the diversity of opinion regarding both the meaning or significance of the temple and the basis for participation in the temple system. Some have interpreted this diversity of opinion as reflecting the existence of 'parties' in Judaean society which were struggling for control of, or at least participation in, the Jerusalem temple community and its cult. Since these literary texts serve as the primary sources for our under-standing of Achaemenid Judah it is not surprising that the issues of temple and community featured therein dominate scholarly percep-tions of the character of the social and political fabric of Achaemenid Judah.

Of what value are these literary texts, however, in reconstructing the social history of Achaemenid Judah, specifically the role of the Jerusalem temple? It is recognized by most commentators that these texts were generated by and reflect the opinions of certain elites and small groups in society whose interest, for whatever reasons, was in the Jerusalem temple and its cult. The emphasis on the need for, and centrality of, this cult thus reflects an inherent bias in these texts. What, if any, elements of these tendentious portrayals should be accepted? Why assume that this temple was important to any others than those who wrote the texts? Why assume that the groups that these texts represent were large and/or influential? The prominence of the Jerusalem cult of Yahweh in these texts should not necessarily lead one to presume that this reflects its important status in Achaemenid Judaean society nor even its general acceptance in the community supposedly defined by its relationship to the temple. The recurrence of the concern for the vindication and centrality of the Jerusalem cult of Yahweh in texts that span the breadth of the Persian period may instead point to a continuing problem with the legitimacy, activities and significance of this cult and its personnel. So, for example, the emphasis in Chronicles and Ezra–Nehemiah on the Judaeans' living in obedience to the Torah with the temple at the centre of their existence prompts one to consider that the historical reality might have been somewhat different. These texts hold out the ideal for the community, stressing their understanding as representing the will of Yahweh and thus the only way to secure divine blessing. Certain prophetic texts (Hag. 1.2ff.; Mal. 2.10-16; 3.6-12; Isa. 65; 66.17) as well as sections of Ezra–Neheniah (Ezra 9–10; Neh. 13) show that the temple and cultic stipulations were not uppermost in the minds of all people. Of course I do not deny that there were segments of the Judaean population for whom the temple was central: the texts show us that there were. I aver only that the perspective of the texts should not be adopted as reflecting the reality regarding the temple's significance in Judah, at least before the governorship of Nehemiah. Both papers recognize that there were those who were against the temple rebuilding for whatever reasons (for example, their eschatological purview; their anti-state stance), but since this position is overshadowed by pro-Temple texts there has been a tendency to assume that the latter view was dominant. All we actually have are texts which inform us that the temple was important. We have no evidence external to the biblical texts by which to verify it.

Are the temple and community, then, literary chimeras? Perhaps not completely. On what basis, however, can one determine where the authors' interpretation of the events recounted begins? If that cannot be determined then how can these texts be used? How can their veracity be judged? Such remarks simply re-emphasize the well-known problems in trying to use these literary texts to write about aspects of the social history of Achaemenid Judah. Both papers under discussion wisely attempt to justify an important social role for the temple by recourse to interpretive paradigms from outside the biblical texts. Such an approach is of course most welcome, but questions can be raised regarding how successfully the paradigms account for the complex issues surrounding the texts.

EMPIRE, TEMPLE AND COMMUNITY—BUT NO BOURGEOISIE!
A RESPONSE TO BLENKINSOPP AND PETERSEN

Richard A. Horsley

Presuppositions, Evidence and Models

In order to carry out even elementary historical-sociological analysis
of the Second Temple, we must face a number of obstacles. Three of
the most serious are the distortive conceptual apparatus of biblical and
religious studies, the paucity and opacity of the evidence, and the
inappropriate social models we tend to project onto historical subjects.
Let me discuss all three briefly.

1. Those of us teaching in state universities sometimes find it necessary to explain to students that courses in study of religion are not
'religious'—we are not propagating or practicing religion. For
entirely different reasons I find myself pleading with colleagues in
biblical studies that our subject matter is not primarily 'religious'.
That is, biblical literature and history are not 'religious' and do not
deal with 'religious' matters in a way separate or separable from other
dimensions of life, such as the 'political' or the 'economic'. 'Religion'
is embedded with kinship and/or local community life and/or 'the
state' in virtually any traditional agrarian society, and hence is insepa-
rable from political and economic matters. Our scholarly habit of
pretending that we are dealing with primarily religious texts or
institutions, which means basically imposing modern presuppositions
and concepts on historical materials that had neither concepts nor
terms for religion, blocks rather than enhances understanding. The
temple in Jerusalem was a political-economic institution. Along with
the high priesthood based there, the temple was the particular form
taken by what we moderns would call 'the state', at least during
Hasmonaean times. Prior to and following the Hasmonaeans, the
temple and its priesthood were part of the Persian, then Hellenistic,

then Roman imperial political-economic apparatus of domination. There was simply no structural or institutional differentiation yet, so we cannot pretend that 'religion' or 'Judaism' is somehow a separable subject of investigation. One of the most important and exciting aspects of Blenkinsopp's paper is that, even though he still seems to think that the relevant biblical texts are informed by 'one-dimensionally religious interests', the material he presents makes it unavoidably clear that the Second Temple in Jerusalem, like other ancient Near Eastern temples, was *the* central social form or institution of political-economic (as well as religious) domination in a temple-community.[1]

2. Evidence for the Second Temple, particularly for the early period, is limited and uncertain. We probably do not have nearly enough data from this tiny area of the world to venture effective social reconstruction. We must reach for comparative material and studies, both from the broader context of the ancient Near East and from other comparable social formations, on the assumption that Second Temple Judah was not all that different from other neighboring societies and that comparisons and contrasts with traditional, class-divided, agrarian societies will be informative. Furthermore—as Carroll has shown elsewhere in this volume—historians can learn more sophisticated ways of assessing how useful information is inscribed in literature, but also how some information given in literature is useless![2]

1.   It might help us to discern the concrete realities of the Second Temple if we avoided the modern concept of 'religion/religious', which does not appear in our ancient sources. The point can be illustrated by imagining that we were staging a play in modern dress about the Second Temple. How would we costume the chief priests? Besides bishops' or cardinals' robes and hats, we would need butchers' aprons, bankers' (and high-level bureaucrats', such as tax-collectors') three-piece suits, Supreme Court judges' robes, and some insignia of executive political office. The set, moreover, would have to indicate that the scene is the capital of a tiny third-world country with the client rulers for an imperial regime in charge.

2.   For example, the population figures which Weinberg presupposes, reconstructs and works with are incredible. These figures seem to be the principal factor leading him to posit a distinction between the *Bürger-Tempel-Gemeinde* and the province of Judah. A critical determination of more realistic estimates for the population of Judah, and the numbers taken into and returning from exile, taken together with known figures for comparable historical circumstances, would lead to a very different reconstruction. As Blenkinsopp points out, a credible estimate of the

3. Any historical reconstruction, however, will depend upon the particular model or scheme that is presupposed or critically assembled. Correspondingly, the model that is projected onto the ancient Near East and onto the biblical history sets up or invites certain hypotheses or conclusions, and inhibits others. Both 'Western' and 'Soviet' or Eastern European scholarship have tended to project a nascent 'capitalism' developing out of disintegrating 'feudalism' in almost any period of change in ancient Near Eastern social structure. This is partly because 'Western' scholars never read Marx (either before or after the discovery of the *Grundrisse*), and because Soviet-influenced scholarship developed for years within a Stalinist straitjacket of four-stage historical development, from primitive commune to slave society, to feudalism, to capitalism, forcing ancient Near Eastern data into either the slave or the feudal model. It was not until the publication of the *Grundrisse*, with its discussion of *various* 'pre-capitalist' economic systems, including the misnamed 'Asiatic mode of production' that historians awoke to the possibility that ancient Near Eastern political-economic forms may have been distinctive, different both from ancient Greek and Roman patterns and from European feudalism. There simply was not sufficient time (from 1964 to the early 1970s when they were publishing) for Eastern European scholars such as Kreissig or Weinberg to assimilate these new elements of Marx's thought.

Thus, Weinberg ascribes the rise of the *Bürger-Tempel-Gemeinde* form to the intensification of trade and an active urbanization process, leading to a fading of social distinctions between the state sector and

population of fifth century Judah must be closer to Albright's estimate of 20,000 than the grossly exaggerated 200,000 of Weinberg. If we take seriously the report in 2 Kgs 24 that craftsmen and smiths as well as high officials and 'mighty men of valor' were deported to the Babylonians, but rely on the more credible estimate of numbers in Jer. 52.28-30 as 4,600 for all three deportations between 598 and 582, then we could reasonably imagine a population of between 50,000 and 100,000—but no more—at the end of the seventh century. The sums of the respective lists of the 'men of the people of Israel' in Ezra 2 and Nehemiah 7 (i.e. not the total declared in the text!), namely 24,141 and 25,406 respectively, provide a highly credible figure for the adult male population in the fifth century, but not for the returned 'Golah-community'. But to assess either these figures or any other data would require a more developed model of such texts as these and detailed checking of family-and place-names against other texts from earlier periods.

the communal-private sector, and the rise of a commodity-money economy. Now, money had indeed been 'invented' or 'discovered' by the sixth century, but a commodity-money economy was an early modern European development. While taxes or tribute payments were measured or accounted by monetary standards under the Achaemenids, they were usually paid in kind, and even the partial monetary economy projected by Kippenberg did not develop.[1]

While trade was important for the lifestyle of imperial courts and provincial urban aristocracies, it is anachronistic to imagine that commercial activity permeated the postexilic Judaean community. Active urbanization had been underway in the ancient Near East since the third millennium, and was later to be modified into 'Western' Hellenistic forms. But it is difficult to discern much difference in social form between a city which was identical with a 'temple-state' and a royal capital that featured temple(s) as central institution(s). Also, with regard to the construction and projection of models, it is worth repeating Jobling's suggestion that we biblical scholars who are trained to focus narrowly on words and pericopes need to develop broader models, including how empires functioned, in order to discern how parts of that system were interrelated. For instance, it is hard to see how a sabbatical release of debts could function in an essentially 'capitalist' economic system.

In sum, we need to shed certain presuppositions, attend to comparative materials, and develop a systemic social model. I assume that priority must be given to the discernment of fundamental patterns of social relations, and secondary attention to particular institutions. Thus, fundamental patterns may persist through changes of empire, or through the development from 'petty-monarchy-with-temple' to 'temple-state'.

*The Fundamental Structure of Political-Economic-Religious
Relations in Judah and the Ancient Near East*

To appreciate what social relations may have been in Second Temple Judah, it may help to have an elementary sense of the fundamental

---

1. See R. Frye, *The History of Ancient Iran* (Munich: Beck, 1984), p. 116; cf. H. Kippenberg, *Religion und Klassenbildung im antiken Judäa* (SUNT, 14; Göttingen: Vandenhoeck & Ruprecht, 1978).

social structure of the ancient Near East in general. If we can assume that Palestine, under the Solomonic monarchy, was typical, then a brief examination of that society may be illustrative.

What is implied by Solomon's 'payment' for timber and gold to Hiram of Tyre, of 'twenty cities in the land of Galilee' (1 Kgs 9.11)? Or what is meant, in concrete political-economic terms, when 'all Israel', gathered at Shechem to acclaim Rehoboam king, instead declared their independence with the words, 'What portion have we in David? We have no inheritance in the son of Jesse. To your tens, O Israel! Look now to your own house, David!' (1 Kgs 12.16)? We shall get nowhere by applying our usual assumptions about property relations or chattel slavery. It would be utterly beside the point to argue, for example, whether the houses in those Galilaean villages were the private property of Solomon, or of the Galilaeans, or whether the Galilaeans were even slaves owned by Solomon. Rehoboam and his advisers assumed that the Israelites were 'under his yoke' and owed him 'service', and the Israelites agreed up to a point, as long as 'hard service' or a 'heavy yoke' were not imposed (1 Kgs 12). Clearly presupposed in narratives like these is that ordinary Israelites were partly 'free' and partly 'unfree'; while not 'owners' in the modern sense, they were nevertheless in possession of lands, and houses, village by village, yet under the power of a monarch and obligated to render him produce for provisioning of the royal table and labor for the construction of the temple and royal palaces. Kings such as Solomon and Hiram had a claim to (a portion of) the produce and labor of villages. The subjects, for their part, understood that they 'had a portion' in the king, in supporting him with their labor and products.[1]

---

1. A better understanding of the ancient Near Eastern and biblical portrayals of claims on land, producers' labor, and produce would help clarify texts such as Neh. 9.36-37 and Lev. 25–27, discussed by Hoglund and Carroll. The Judaeans who lament in the 'prayer' of Neh. 9 are not chattel slaves, and the land is not *owned* by foreign kings; but a portion of the produce of the land that is their inheritance now goes to those foreign kings. Far from the logic of Lev. 25.23-24 being that 'the owner of the land is Yahweh and *not* the people of Israel', the assertion that the land is Yahweh's is the very basis of the inalienability of land as the inheritance of particular families. Far from being a matter of either/or, as with private property in modern capitalist society, land in Israel was *both* an inalienable right possessed by a family over generations *and* (this because) it was the possession of Yahweh. Thus a

Ancient Near Eastern 'societies' or social relations did not consist of independent units of individuals or individual nuclear families, but were apparently built up from communities of 'houses', that is, families or lineages, with some having power over others, and with overlapping claims on the labor and products of subordinate 'houses'. A petty monarchy or aristocratic 'city-state' such as those in second millennium BCE Palestine were comprised of multiple village communities subordinate to the ruling house and to the families of its officials and its military and other 'retainers'. A large empire might thus appear more like a pyramid of subordinate rulers and their respective retainers' families supported by the subordinate village communities of peasant producers in each area. Regardless of the size of the temple-state or monarchy or larger empire, the ratio of producers to rulers-plus-retainers would have remained roughly the same, for in virtually all pre-industrial economies, ninety per cent or more of the population was required to support a central (temple-) city or other ruling apparatus, consisting of perhaps two per cent actual ruling families/houses, plus families who were their servants, artisans and retainers. For most temple-societies and smaller monarchies, what bound the whole together, subordinate houses/lineages and ruling houses—other than the military power of the ruling house—was the belief or understanding that the people were dependent upon the divine powers, and particularly that the land belonged to the local god(s), and that the people were his/her/their servants, with the ruling house(s) being the chief servants or regents of the god(s), and the king or priest perhaps even recognized as the adopted son of the divine overlord.

Evaluation of Blenkinsopp's Contribution

Blenkinsopp has both opened up the discussion to the important international dimension, and established a sound critical conceptual basis. I suggest that he is offering a more appropriate and convincing

hierocracy, acting as regents in a theocracy, could control the use of land in its own interests, as Carroll discerns in Lev. 27. Lev. 27.16-21, for example (if I understand it properly), concerns loans (from the temple treasury?) to needy peasant families at 20% interest on the use-value of their land dedicated to Yahweh as collateral; but if the land is not redeemed by the year of Jubilee, what was family inheritance becomes a priestly possession.

reconstruction of the Second Temple social system than Weinberg, the emergence of whose *Bürger-Tempel-Gemeinde* does not make sense in the context of what we believe we know about social forms in the ancient Near East.[1]

As I understand Weinberg, individual enterprises or economies (*individuellen Wirtschaften*) increasingly separated from the state sector and attached to temples, and hence the *Gemeinde* became an autonomous and privileged organization of the ruling class. Finally, the temple-community and state-community merged into a structural unity. Yet in what I take to be a consensus regarding the development of civilization in the ancient Near East, temple-communities emerged out of villages, and early city-states were often a synoecism or union of two or more temple-communities. A state, consisting initially of an aristocracy or a monarchy, could emerge from a temple-community as well as from a synoecism of temples or tribes (i.e. a 'city'). If a given temple-community or city was conquered from without, the community was usually left more or less intact, with new rulers forming the 'state', whether as 'king' or 'servant(s) of the gods' as patrons/owners of the land, and whether locally resident or acting through an imperial administration, often identical with the local aristocracy. Such arrangements persisted over centuries, from Sargon to the Romans.[2]

The postexilic temple community in Judah did not represent the emergence of a new social form, for such a form had existed for centuries in the ancient Near East, as Blenkinsopp makes abundantly

---

1. Like Blenkinsopp, I am unfamiliar with some of Weinberg's writings at first hand. I have found particularly useful the summary of his position in H. Kreissig, 'Eine beachtenswerte Theorie zur Organisation altvorderorientalischer Tempelgemeinden im Achämenidenreich', *Klio* 66 (1984), pp. 35-39.

2. The various possibilities can be illustrated by the arrangement in Jerusalem as seen at different historical points. What had been a petty Jebusite monarchy was replaced by the Davidic monarchy which became an imperial state under Solomon, but declined to a semi-independent local monarchy (with a temple!), under the Egyptian, Assyrian and Babylonian empires. In Second Temple times, Jerusalem shifted from the centre of a subordinate petty local state which functioned simultaneously as a local centre of the imperial governing apparatus, to an independent temple-state under the Hasmonaeans, then reverted to a client state. Note, however, that the temple-community structure remained essentially intact even when subordinated to an additional layer of Roman client rule, as under Herod the Great.

clear; the shift from petty monarchy with temple to temple-state was not a major one. In the pre-exilic period, the village communities of Judah had been under the rule of a Davidic dynastic house and its supporting apparatus, and the sources often distinguish between the 'people of Jerusalem' and the 'people of Judah', the former probably denoting the non-peasant population, that is, the upper or ruling class (see 2 Kgs 23).

Those deported by the Babylonians were primarily the rulers, officials, priests, military and artisans from Jerusalem. Those who returned later were thus descendants of the Jerusalem elite. They apparently resumed, or attempted to resume, their positions, in this case subordinate to the Persian imperium. In fact, initially there seems to have been a virtual dyarchy in Jerusalem, with a Davidide and a high priest, the former emphasized in Zechariah as the builder of the temple. The Zadokite lineage, however, quickly took the place once occupied by the Davidide house and exercised the same role.

Thus, once we establish more appropriate presuppositions and take due note of ancient Near Eastern social structures generally, the hypothesis of a *Bürger-Tempel-Gemeinde* under Persian sponsorship, constituting a new community with territory and membership separate from the province/area of Judah, appears inappropriate as well as unnecessary, as Kreissig maintains. Rather, if we read our principal biblical sources for the period with the necessary degree of critical scrutiny, we find them reflecting a situation in which the descendants of the exiles are simply re-establishing their traditional position as a 'community' of the powerful—the dominant lineages together with their retainers—for the priestly-temple apparatus which ruled under Persian mandate. The role of the temple as, among other things, symbol of social order is resumed, and authenticates the system. It is thus not surprising that the assistance of the 'Samarians' was rejected (Ezra 4.1-3). Nor is it surprising that some of the 'people of the land' resisted the establishment of the old ruling families in Judah (Ezra 4.3). But one of the oracles in Haggai exhorts the 'people of the land' to take courage over the rebuilding, and the report of the building of the city wall in Nehemiah 3 indicates that work-gangs from Judaean towns (not all of whom could have been returnees), as well as Jerusalemites, participated in the effort. Thus, it appears that ordinary Judaeans as well as Jerusalemites contributed to the work of restoration.

Fundamental social distinctions were maintained, of course, in the restored temple-community. Measures were taken by the nobility, priests, levites and other temple personnel, to maintain their own 'purity' over against the 'peoples of the land' by vowing strict observance of the Mosaic law, and stringent enforcement of prohibition against marriages with such 'peoples' (Ezra 9–10; cf. Neh. 1.1-31). On the other hand, those who 'separated themselves' from the 'pollutions' of the 'peoples of the land' could join in festivals such as the Passover (Ezra 6.20-21)—but such people would not have been 'recruits to the temple community', because social status was already structured by lineage. Such purity restrictions are not in focus, however, when it comes to the glorious enumeration of 'all the people of the nation of Israel', which includes lineages of Judaeans for whom no indication of exile is given (Ezra 2; Neh. 7). Temple personnel appear to comprise more than one sixth of the total of the list in Ezra 2, and this would leave the remainder of those mentioned with a huge economic burden if such personnel were not engaged in productive labor. But only 'the priests, the levites and some of the people' lived in and around Jerusalem, while 'the singers, the gatekeepers and the temple servants' lived in their towns, presumably engaged in agricultural work. Only gradually would the returnees have been able to consolidate their power. Just as it took a generation for the priesthood, rather than the royal house, to gain sole power, so too there were probably struggles among priestly lineages, with the levites slipping in status. By the time of Nehemiah's mission, however, some ruling families had so successfully established their dominance that reforms introduced by the imperial governor himself were necessary to mitigate the most severe effects of debt and even debt-slavery (Neh. 5.1-10). But such mitigation was only part of Nehemiah's agenda of strengthening the centralized power and authority of the priestly aristocracy in a well-fortified and well-regulated ruling apparatus in Jerusalem. As Carroll has pointed out, texts such as Leviticus 27 indicate explicitly the way in which the priests were able to consolidate effective control over political and economic affairs.

It was, of course, in the interests of the imperial regime as well as the temple-centered Judaean ruling class not to allow a few exploitative officials and nobles to weaken the productive base of the economy. Far from wanting to break down traditional patterns of economic self-sufficiency in favor of interdependent economic systems, as

Hoglund argues, the Achaemenid regime sought to restore and strengthen traditional patterns. Here Blenkinsopp's opening remarks need to be broadened and sharpened at the same time. It is inadequate to say merely that temples (supposedly 'religious' institutions), as 'storage and redistribution centers', provided 'stimulation of the regional economies'. Rather, temples as the religiously legitimated political-economic base of provincial ruling classes provided *the social form* of domination and exploitation in certain areas—'to the evident advantage of the imperial exchequer' indeed! Accordingly, since (as in Judah) the priesthoods also 'served as custodians of the legal traditions in the various regions; and...the central government promoted the codification and implementation of local traditional law as an instrument of the *pax Persica* throughout the empire', it is clear that the Persians underwrote the service of local deities as a traditional form of domination and exploitation.

Petersen and Prophets

Historians should certainly be aware that 'forms of social interaction' change over time; but given the relative stability of ancient Near Eastern structures, one ought not to expect that the role of the temple will necessarily change as well. It seems doubtful that 'a set of hierarchies obtains during the Second Temple period which is different from the set of the First Temple period'. That must depend on the standard of comparison. To be sure, the attempt to re-establish a Davidic dynasty failed, with the result that in the ensuing hierocracy God became more exclusively a symbol of community loyalty. But did social interaction change from the sixth century to the fourth? The 'new' ruling families were descended from the old ones, and the pattern of domination and exploitation remained essentially the same. The major difference was the degree of subordination to the imperial regime. But perhaps even because of this, the temple may have become more of a 'royal' symbol. According to Ezra 6.9-10, the Jerusalem priests offered daily prayers and burnt offerings to the God of Heaven for the well-being of the Persian king and his sons.

With regard to Persian period prophetic texts, the posing of more concrete social questions may require some different approaches. As biblical scholars we have been trained to look for textual references to particular subjects and to analyse and comment on those, as if that would provide us with an individual author's or document's view on those subjects. This approach is surely inadequate for socioliterary analysis, and it is probably unwarranted to begin with unless some attempt is made to place a particular reference in broader literary (and historical) context. For example, we need to know much more about the literary history of the book of Jeremiah before we are able to appreciate the context and the thrust of particular statements regarding the reconstruction of Jerusalem and the royal palace in the 'Book of Consolation' (Jer. 20.18; 31.38-40).[1] Hopes for a restoration of the *levitical* priesthood (Jer. 33.17-18), if examined in historical context, may have been directed effectively at the Zadokite house, whether in prospect or retrospect, and thus been *anti*-hierocratic, in opposition, say, to the situation envisaged in Ezekiel 40–48. The most striking thing about Jeremiah in regard to the temple is the outright condemnation of the First Temple as in violation of the Mosaic covenant (Jer. 7 and 26; cf. the confrontation with Hananiah in chs. 27–28). Are we to assume that, given these oracles to be genuinely pre-exilic and thus borne out by subsequent events, they had no influence either on the ruling class in exile or those left behind in Judah? Is it not at least possible that collections of Jeremianic material, and reports of events such as Ezra 4.4 are windows onto a virtually undocumented but nevertheless important stream of anti-temple feeling among Judaeans?[2]

Establishing a clearer sense of the fundamental social structure of Second Temple Judah should make possible much more precision over conflicts and struggles expressed or reflected in prophetic literature such as Malachi or Trito-Isaiah. It seems evident that the levites lost status and influence early in this period. Isaiah 56 and 66 express strong criticism not only of those who control the temple, but of the temple itself. *Pace* Blenkinsopp (who finds parallels with Ezra 9), Isaiah 66 can easily be read as anti-temple. Isaiah 56 more clearly

---

1. Carroll's probing into Jer. 32 suggests that for this book we need a critical literary and social analysis on the lines of that undertaken by R.B. Coote for the book of Amos (*Amos Among the Prophets: Composition and Theology* [Philadelphia: Fortress Press, 1981]).

2. On Ezek. 40–48, Petersen refers appreciatively to J.Z. Smith's *To Take Place*. But, if I read Smith rightly, he is explaining how Ezekiel should be read as a charter of social relations rather than a plan for a reconstructed temple building.

stands in opposition to the kind of social distinctions reported and advocated in Ezra 9.

There appears to be little evidence for the importance of the temple as an 'eschatological symbol'. Petersen in fact seems to have set the record straight on this, suggesting in effect that Haran and Clements (among others) are imposing a modern scholarly concept onto Second Temple literature and history. An important conclusion can be drawn far more sharply in this regard: reference to an 'eschatological temple' is rare in Jewish literature of the entire Second Temple period, indeed so rare that its near-absence requires explanation. Extant literature of the period, much of which was written by dissident groups, tends to be critical of the temple as well as of the rulers based in it, and looks for alternative images of renewal, or, like the Qumran literature, holds that the true 'house of God' is a community.[1]

---

1. Cf. the perpetuation of the older theologically determined misconceptions about the 'eschatological' or 'rebuilt' temple in E.P. Sanders, *Jesus and Judaism* (London: SCM Press, 1985).

TEXT AND THE WORLD—AN UNBRIDGEABLE GAP?
A RESPONSE TO CARROLL, HOGLUND AND SMITH

David Jobling

Introduction

I respond with enthusiasm to the idea of a sociology of the Second
Temple period, since it seems to me on much firmer ground than a
sociology of Israel in earlier periods. I also hoped that the project
would include in its scope, from the very outset, the issue of the use of
the Bible as a source for sociology and historiography, as this issue
has been pressed from the side of the newer literary criticism. Robert
Carroll's paper takes up that concern, and it is here that I shall
concentrate. I shall make some reference to the other two papers, and
offer at an appropriate point a somewhat practical and programmatic
critique of all three papers from a position of my own. But my main
intention is a theoretical one—to do a symptomatic reading of
Carroll's paper in relation to what I perceive to be going on in
biblical studies. In Carroll's own words, 'to do injustice to these
texts'—I hope a strong and usable injustice.

Carroll and the Unbridgeable Gap between Texts
and the Real World

I shall hang what I have to say on three quotations from Carroll's
paper. The first is from his very last sentence: 'But the gap between
texts and the real world remains as unbridgeable as ever'. For present
purposes, 'texts' means the biblical text and its parts, and 'the real
world' means the project of a sociology of the Second Temple. Can
such a project use the Bible as evidence, and, if so, under what
conditions?

The gap Carroll perceives is the one which, writ large, Norman
Gottwald sees between the two emergent paradigms in biblical studies,

the 'new literary' and the 'social science' paradigms.[1] But the bridge-ability, and even the existence, of such a gap is a matter of perspective. From the side of sociology, or sociohistory, the gap does not seem unbridgeable. Indeed one would not be aware, from reading the papers by Smith and Hoglund, that the gap existed. Where they think it appropriate, they straightforwardly draw on the Bible to help build the sociological picture. Gottwald recognizes the existence and the importance of the gap, but, viewing it as he still does from the sociohistoric side, believes it bridgeable. The specificity of the textual object must be taken seriously; sociologists and historians must learn from literary scholars (among whom he finds the structuralists especially promising) about the specific ways in which meaning or truth is inscribed in literature. Given such sophistication, the Bible may be used in evidence.

Until the end of his paper, Carroll seems willing to participate in this game. Certainly his reading of texts is very sophisticated, but he is not loath, through his brilliant readings, to discover nuggets of what may prove to be sociological evidence. And the epigraph to his paper from Vargas Llosa seems to carry the same message: 'literature presents us with a side of history which cannot be found in history books'—these words are still written from the side of historiography, and insist only on *the right kind* of use of literature as evidence. Is there any reason why 'history books' might not learn how to include this other 'side of history'?

It is, however, with increasing reluctance that Carroll gives up his nuggets of evidence, and his concluding gesture is to take them all back again, by insisting on the unbridgeability of the gap. How are we to read this gesture? I would like to read it in the light of a second quotation:

> While I refuse to privilege theory or ideology in its application to biblical texts—Fredric Jameson notwithstanding!—this paper is not the place to produce a critique of ideological analysis of the Second Temple period. I wish only to consider a few texts. . .

For the purposes of this paper, Carroll intends to defer 'theory' and adopt an empirical approach. One is tempted to hear in this a characteristically British attitude. I do not believe that Carroll really

<hr>

1. N.K. Gottwald, *The Hebrew Bible: A Socio-Literary Introduction* (Philadelphia: Fortress Press, 1985), pp. 20-31.

shares the general anti-theoretical stance of British biblical scholarship (indeed he has given us one of the best examples of the application of a sociological model to biblical studies)[1] but he prefers to defer theoretical discussion. He does not, in this paper, theorize the unbridgeability of the gap. He clearly wants to associate himself at some level with the defence of the biblical text, from the side of a literary sensibility, against the long dominance of historicism, and he no doubt shares with other literary critics the sense that most of the recent sociohistorical use of the Bible is no more than a continuation of the same dominance. But it is not out of any theoretical position that he defends the text. He does not espouse the New Criticism (or, what is essentially the same thing, 'deconstruction', as misrepresented by many literary critics). He does not echo such extreme defences of the autonomy of the biblical text as, for instance, that of David Robertson. No: the unbridgeability of the gap is an empirical discovery, not a theoretical position. When one tries to read sociology from the Bible, one discovers 'too many complicated strands' so that 'meanings are too many and contentious'. But the empirical result of this empirical approach is to leave us with a contradictory sense, at the end of Carroll's paper, as to what he really thinks on the main issue of the usability of the Bible in the sociological project. After playing the game rather persuasively, he peremptorily denies the possibility of playing it at all!

I do not blame Carroll for declining to associate himself with extreme views of the autonomy of the biblical text. Now that a breakthrough has been made in establishing the necessity of literary study of the Bible, this sort of 'defence' seems shrill and ineffectual, unconvincing in itself, and failing to prevent historians and sociologists from doing whatever they want to with the Bible. The defence needs to be conducted on other grounds and as we move onto this ground, we may, I believe, discover that what we are engaged in is no longer a defence of the text, but a collaborative development of entirely new ways of thinking about reality, textuality, and their connectedness.

But Carroll forbids himself, and us, access to this new ground by his deferral of theory. The particular target at which he defers firing

1.   *When Prophecy Failed: Cognitive Dissonance in the Prophetic Tradition of the Old Testament* (London: SCM Press, 1979).

is Marxist biblical criticism. My present remarks would be unthinkable without the Marxist impulse, and I would ask Carroll to let there at least *be* a significant amount of Marxist analysis of the Bible before we start to reject it! What Carroll is rejecting is one kind of imposition on the text from the Marxist side, the importation of sociopolitical models not appropriate to the material. He may be right about this; but he does not avoid (and perhaps wants to convey) the impression of a wholesale rejection of Marxist and related theorizing. In my view, it is from that direction, from positions confessedly Marxist or in positive interaction with Marxism, that some of the most creative recent theorizing has been coming.

For example, why not turn Vargas Llosa around, and say that 'historiography presents us with a side of literature which cannot be found in literature books'? This, of course, is precisely the project of Hayden White's *Metahistory*, but it still feels very unnatural to us in biblical studies. Literary critics might be more willing to accept that social location is something which inevitably, and significantly, befalls texts, if there were a corresponding acceptance that 'textuality' is something that inevitably, and significantly, befalls sociological data. We scarcely know what this means, but it seems to suggest that we need literary analysis not only of the biblical text, but of *all* the written works, ancient or modern, of which sociologists make use. Or take the project of Fredric Jameson, in *The Political Unconscious*, to explore the possibility of correlating, without privileging one side or the other, the failure of texts to complete their semiotic systems and the failure of social formations, and eventually of historical 'modes of production', to complete their systems of exchange.[1] Or again, take the project of Mieke Bal, in *Murder and Difference*, to account for a human production (such as a text) through analysis of the multiple and conflictual coding which it inscribes (a code being any human subsystem which becomes sufficiently objectified to begin to shape our perceptions of reality); she examines Judges 4 and 5, and their interpretation, under the historical, theological, anthropological and literary codes.

---

1.   I am currently planning a *Semeia* volume on Jameson and the Bible. Why is Carroll's deferral of theoretical debate 'notwithstanding' Jameson? Maybe I should ask him to explain, through a contribution to the volume!

A Brief Critique of the Three Papers

At the end of my remarks, I shall return to the point I have now reached, and develop it in another direction. But first I shall sketch in a very general way a methodological position from which to respond to our current situation in sociohistorical reading of the Bible, and use it to critique the three papers before us, and if my criteria seem rather grandiose in relation to the limited aims of these papers, I do not believe there is any harm in that: what I want to do is to spur methodological debate. I have two points. First, in order to deal with the gap as bridgeable, I think, paradoxically, that we should begin by maximizing it. I believe we can use a period of extreme reticence in trying to relate models of societies to models of texts. We cannot defer the correlation endlessly, but we should take care that our models have reached some adequate stage of autonomous development before attempting promiscuous correlations, before even deciding what might count as a correlation. Secondly, I believe that, on each side of the gap, modelling needs to occur more at the macro-level, that is, on the largest possible scale. This does not preclude—indeed, it can only happen in critical relation to—smaller-scale modelling. But our bias for various reasons is an anti-totalizing one, and we need to remember that parts can exist only in relation to wholes. Thus, on the biblical side, while we analyse pericopes, chapters, books, etc., as semiotic systems, we ought not to stop short of such an analysis of the 'canon' as a whole, while on the sociopolitical side, as we analyse a variety of sectors, we need to pay attention to the total system (which in our case basically means how the ancient empires worked). In relation to these criteria, I see Carroll and Hoglund to be working in valuable ways on the opposite sides of the gap, while Smith is trying to work on both sides at once in a way which is of less value because methodologically dubious.

Carroll's paper is valuable at two levels: first, in his clear awareness of the gap, which should, but does not seem to, trouble the other contributors; secondly, in his work with texts, which is extremely sensitive to, and skilled at eliciting, their agenda or subtexts, and the intricacy of the play of many sub-texts in a given sub-text (he is excited and awed by the immense scope of what Greimas calls the 'readability' of texts). I would prefer a more self-conscious methodological account, and a bolder presentation of the 'system' of meaning in the texts (both of which would be not difficult to provide), but this is partly a matter of style. As regards my concern for analysis on the macro-scale, Carroll keeps in mind the larger literary contexts of his brief passages, and is notably strong on 'intertextuality', identifying the same sub-text (e.g. 'the myth of the empty land') in texts which in no way superficially resemble each other.

Hoglund perceives the need for analysis of the Persian imperial system, and provides valuable insight into the systems of land-disposal, trade and economics, transportation, and military defence. He also takes note of the *ideological* machinery—how imperial propaganda functioned in the economic sphere. As I have indicated, I favour this macro-scale line of approach, and there is no mistaking how immediate is its potential impact. If the Judaeans were in a system where 'land claims' (howsoever based) did not exist, then major aspects of the other two papers must be rethought. Towards the end of the paper Hoglund jumps too quickly, in my view, into comparison with the biblical text. I find him fairly convincing when he reads Nehemiah in the context of Persian military preparations, though the necessary textual work has not been done. But in his last section, on ethnic collectivization, he seems to me to rely on the Bible at the expense of sharp sociological analysis. We need a clearer account of how population relocation functioned in the imperial system. Was its purpose to maintain social cohesion, or to break morale? Is there anything special to say about *restoring* to its land a previously dislocated population?

Smith seems to me to fall methodologically *into* the gap. At the level of sociological modelling, he offers valuable analysis of mass deportation in ancient times, including its psychological dimension, and of the formation of resisting communities. I would like this analysis to be more in touch with the global view of Persian imperialism that Hoglund aims at. But my much greater problem is that Smith does his sociology too near the text, and in an unpredictable relationship to it. In dealing with mass deportation he uses biblical odds and ends to fill out the sociological picture, and simply accepts the Bible as evidential bedrock (for example, the Bible *proves* that the exilic community was big enough for certain comparative data to be usable). In dealing with the formation of a resisting community, he works in the opposite direction, beginning with biblical categories and moving to possible analogues (such as the 'hibakusha' communities). Finally, he deals with conflict between such a community and those outside it by means of exegesis of a biblical passage. I do not want to deny the poten tial value of the links Smith makes, but methodological clarification, and the following of some sort of procedure, would increase the value.

This Discussion and the Question of Ideology

So much, and all too briefly, for the three papers. Let me introduce some closing remarks with a third quotation from Carroll:

> At this stage of the argument there are too many complicated strands of narrative and ideology for a simple picture of things to emerge. Whenever a woman or women appear in a biblical text the reader must sit up and take notice.

Someone said, I believe of the practice of psychiatry, that it is not merely impossible, but also very difficult. Carroll raises the spectre, at the end of his paper, of such an extreme difficulty in our enterprise as to amount to impossibility; there is too much going on in texts for us to control. The models I have pointed to (White, Jameson, Bal, and others could be named) do not tend to simplify the task; they accept its complexity, and indeed affirm methodologically the impossibility of achieving any 'closure' (though they insist on the possibility of usable results). It seems to me that the question cannot be avoided, cannot be avoided precisely as a *methodological* question, why we choose to pursue a task so difficult, so unending, so set about with impossi-bilities, as a sociology of the Second Temple. To what ends, out of what allegiances, do we take up this work? What are our guiding metaphors? I would like to look at two, from the papers before us.

1. Smith wants to 'remove some of the mystery surrounding the Persian period'. This sounds like a model of truth-seeking, within a code (to use Bal's term) of objectivity or enlightenment. It sounds like the founding metaphor of historical criticism (but definitely not of literary criticism!). Is this our commitment? Or does work on biblical sociology stem from commitments, ground itself in metaphors, which are unlike the ones that fire historical (or, for that matter, literary) criticism? Are there alternatives to 'truth-seeking'? What has all this to do with the currently hot issue of 'ethics of interpretation'? What sort of a move is it ethically to commit oneself to an impossible search for truth, to the bridging of an unbridgeable gap?

2. Carroll uses another metaphor. His paper is 'an attempt to do injustice' to texts and ideologies—a variant of Harold Bloom's 'misreading'. I prefer Carroll to Bloom here; misreading sounds like an intellectual peccadillo, but doing injustice has wide connotations. Is ours an anti-social, even criminal, endeavour? Interpretation is a crime, of course, and crime as metaphor for intellectual practice is pervasive in French theory. For example, Roland Barthes: 'Ideological criticism is today precisely condemned to operations of theft'.[1] To broach the issue of the sociology of the Second Temple is to attempt to burgle a house equipped with an efficient security system. The biblical text does not want us to know about the sociology of the Second Temple. And there are also in our own scene considerable interests which do not want us to probe such things!

We might, at any rate, ponder the connectedness of our discourse to what in our own scene we think of as 'committed' discourses. Ponder how decisive the committed discourse of a Norman Gottwald has been in creating the possibility and the necessity of this group. Or how it is 'committed' critics like Bal and Jameson who enable and demand the shift from impossibility to difficulty. At the end of *Murder and Difference*, Bal looks again at what has been done with her texts under the various scholarly codes mentioned above, but from the perspective of the 'gender code'. The scholarly codes embody an interest in the *division* of specialist knowledge, but the gender code has inevitably developed as transdisciplinary, since those whose interest lies in discerning its workings find it operative in every other code. Perhaps our gap is indeed unbridgeable under the codes of objectivity, but that is not going to deter readers with a certain commitment from bridging this and all gaps between texts, ancient and modern, and 'real worlds', ancient and modern!

Near the end of Carroll's paper, there drifts unexpectedly into view a fragment of what we recognize as feminist discourse. One could think of it as an excellent example chosen by Carroll to establish how biblical sub-texts complicate each other—to the point of rendering unbridgeable the gap between text and world. Or one could think that it drifts into view by some volition of its own, to announce a perspective from which such an admission of unbridgeability is an unacceptable ideologeme!

1. *Image, Music, Text*, p. 208.

INDEXES

INDEX OF REFERENCES

OLD TESTAMENT

2.15-17	140	2.10-14	86-90, 93, 153	11.13	141
4.18	140	2.15	35	13.2	91
		2.18-19	135	14.20-21	141, 142
Amos		2.19	93		
5	87	2.20-23	137	*Malachi*	
5.10	87			1.6-14	141
5.11	93	*Zechariah*		1.18	36
7.13	39	1–8	130, 136, 137	2.1-9	141
				2.4-9	141
Micah		1.16	35, 136	2.10-17	141
2.1-5	114	2.9	142	2.10-16	162
6.15	93	2.10-16	35	3.1	141, 142
		3	136	3.6-12	162
Nahum		3.7	136	3.10	141
3.10	77	4.1-5	93	3.23	141
		4.6-10	137	*1 Esdras*	
Jonah		4.9	38	5	80
2.2	128	5.5-11	53	5.68	46
		5.11	23, 93	9.4	50
Haggai		6.9-14	38		
1.1	36	6.9-13	136	*1 Maccabees*	
1.2ff.	162	6.12-13	38, 137	5.65	44
1.2	88	6.12	35	11.34	44
1.4	35	6.15	35, 136		
1.9	35	7.3	136	*2 Maccabees*	
2.3	39	8.9	35, 137	3.5-6	49
2.7-9	135	9.8	141, 142	3.10-12	49
2.7-8	136	10.2	91		
2.10-19	91				

NEW TESTAMENT

Revelation
21.22   127

JOSEPHUS

Antiquities		14.110-13	49	*Against Apion*	
10.100-103	78	19.5.2.280-285	101	1.128-42	83
11.148	50			*War*	
				6.282	49

OTHER ANCIENT REFERENCES

AP		8.2	47	*Diodorus*	
6.3-10	47	10.3	47	1.95-4-5	25

INDEX OF AUTHORS

Weinberg, J., 15, 26-29, 40-44, 46-49, 53, 54, 80, 84, 85, 94, 128, 154, 155, 157-59, 164, 165, 169
Weinberg, S.S., 75
Weippert, H., 104
Weisberg, D.B., 30, 31, 48
Weisberg, D.L., 77
Weissbach, F.H., 79
Welch, A.C., 88
White, H., 178, 181
Whitelam, K.W., 13
Widengren, G., 100
Wiesehöfer, J., 100
Wilkie, J.M., 78

Williamson, H.G.M., 98, 101, 102, 109, 115
Wilson, R., 82
Wiseman, D.J., 32
Woolley, L., 24
Wurz, H., 75, 76

Yamauchi, E.M., 25, 51, 94, 95
Yardeni, A., 100

Zadok, R., 51, 74
Zawadski, T., 28
Zeitlin, I., 79
Zimmerli, W., 50, 133

DATE DUE

NOV 28 1994			
JUL 3 0 2001			
APR 1 5 2005			
JUN 0 2 2005			